364800000065 79   P9-DGK-565

The Labor Almanac

The
LABOR ALMANAC

ADRIAN A. PARADIS
GRACE D. PARADIS

LIBRARIES UNLIMITED, INC.   **1983**

Littleton, Colorado

Copyright © 1983 Adrian A. Paradis
All Rights Reserved
Printed in the United States of America

No part of this publication may be reproduced, stored in a
retrieval system, or transmitted, in any form or by any means,
electronic, mechanical, photocopying, recording, or otherwise,
without the prior written permission of the publisher.

LIBRARIES UNLIMITED, INC.
P.O. Box 263
Littleton, Colorado 80160-0263

Library of Congress Cataloging in Publication Data

Paradis, Adrian A.
    The labor almanac.

    Includes index.
    1. Labor and laboring classes--United States--Hand-
books, manuals, etc. 2. Trade-unions--United States--
Handbooks, manuals, etc. 3. Labor policy--United
States--Handbooks, manuals, etc. I. Paradis, Grace D.
II. Title.
HD8072.5.P37   1983   331'.0973   83-915
ISBN 0-87287-386-2

Libraries Unlimited books are bound with Type II nonwoven material that meets
and exceeds National Association of State Textbook Administrators' Type II
nonwoven material specifications Class A through E.

RECEIVED

MAY 22 1987

DEPARTMENT OF LABOR
LIBRARY
TRENTON, N.J. 08625

PREFACE

After researching and writing two books on labor subjects (*Labor in Action*, Messner, 1963, and *Labor Reference Book*, Chilton, 1972), it became apparent to us that the labor movement was so important to the nation's social and economic well-being that it, like many businesses and professions, should have its own reference volume. Subsequent consultation with librarians, labor leaders, and others convinced us that there was a need for an authoritative almanac. It seemed that such a book should detail the historical milestones of workers' struggles, as well as present information about labor, its leaders and unions, legislation, federal and state regulatory agencies, statistics and data, and terminology. Much of the information presented here has not been compiled previously, nor has it been readily available.

ORGANIZATION OF THE ALMANAC

This almanac is organized into eight sections, plus a comprehensive index designed to make every proper name and fact easily accessible to the user. A section entitled Labor History Highlights begins the book, presenting a year-by-year chronology of historical facts and data about labor since 1636. Section II, National Labor Organizations, follows with a listing of almost 300 unions and other labor-related organizations constituting the current labor establishment. Prominent people in today's labor movement, based for the most part on the previous section, compose the next section, Prominent Labor Leaders.

As the labor movement developed so did a body of legislation, most of which was designed to protect workers' rights and to curb union monopoly and abuses. With the laws came regulatory agencies, and these subjects constitute the next two sections: section IV, Principal Federal Labor Laws and Executive Orders Affecting Labor, and section V, Federal Government Agencies Concerned with Labor Relations.

Addressing the widespread concern about employment security, the next section, State Agencies Concerned with Labor and Labor Relations, lists all of the state labor departments, employment security offices, and occupational information committees.

The last two sections provide sources of statistical and other information about labor, along with a glossary of labor terms.

SOURCES

For the most part, information about labor unions contained in this almanac was supplied by the unions in response to questionnaires. In those cases where repeated follow-up mailings failed to bring response, telephone numbers and addresses were checked by contacting the unions, consulting current telephone directories, or using the various telephone companies' directory services. It seems that unions with small staffs found it difficult to respond.

Much of the other information came from federal government publications and U.S. Department of Labor files. One of the best sources of information about the labor movement has been the Bureau of Labor Statistics. However, in common with all government agencies, the bureau has regrettably had to retrench and at least temporarily cancel publication of certain data.

Sources drawn on for compiling the chronology included books on the history of the labor movement, encyclopedias, almanacs, government publications, files of the *New York Times* and the *Wall Street Journal*, and *Facts on File*.

ACCURACY AND COMPLETENESS OF INFORMATION

Every effort has been made to ensure accuracy and completeness of information. Since this was the first time some unions had received a request to make public the names of officials and their membership size, many were understandably reluctant to comply, especially for a new publication which has not yet found public acceptance.

It should be emphasized that the absence of an individual's name from this reference work does not necessarily mean he or she does not qualify for inclusion. Every reasonable effort has been made to include all major national labor unions and the names of prominent labor leaders. We apologize for any unintentional omissions. However, the shifts among union and government officials are continuous, and there are inevitable mergers and other organizational changes which foredoom any attempt to provide a truly accurate and current roster of leaders at a given date. It is hoped that any discrepancies may be corrected in future editions.

It had been our hope to include other important data and certain basic statistics, as well as information on various aspects of employment security, such as unemployment insurance and workmen's compensation eligibility requirements and payments for each of the states. Reductions in government spending have cut back the compilation and publication of many statistics. Furthermore, due to the current economic malaise and the adjustments authorized by the various states from time to time to provide for the unemployed, it seemed best to omit from this edition what would be incomplete or obsolete data at best, and instead to indicate the sources where this type of information can be found (section VII, Sources of Labor Information and Statistics).

It has been our aim to present all information in a logical manner for ease of use and reference. The nature of the data included made it impossible to follow a standard format throughout, thus the form of presentation varies greatly from section to section.

ACKNOWLEDGMENTS

During the two years of editorial preparation of this volume we encountered unfailing courtesy and cooperation on the part of all whom we contacted. Those who helped are too numerous to mention here, but we do want to thank the officials of unions and their office personnel who took the time and trouble to complete the questionnaires; staff members of the U.S. Department of Labor in Washington, and especially personnel of the Boston office of the Bureau of Labor Statistics; Elizabeth Shenton of The Arthur and Elizabeth Schlesinger Library on the History of Women in America; Mrs. Constance Rinden, Law Librarian, Law Division, New Hampshire State Library; Virginia Close, Reference Librarian, Baker Library, Dartmouth College; Robert Lazar, Archivist, ILGWU Archives; Robert H. Wood, Management Consultant; and Heather Cameron, Head, Editorial Department of Libraries Unlimited.

Finally, we should like to thank those librarians and government and labor officials who encouraged us to undertake this task. Without their backing and conviction that this reference source was needed, we might have stopped many times when the mails failed to carry or the progress seemed slow and uncertain.

If information contained in this volume assists in any way toward bridging certain gaps, or helps improve working relationships between those representing labor and their counterparts in management, then the efforts made in gathering, editing, and publishing such data will assuredly be rewarded. Suggestions for broadening and improving the almanac's scope in future editions, and thereby increasing its usefulness, will be greatly appreciated.

Adrian A. Paradis
Grace D. Paradis

TABLE OF CONTENTS

I

LABOR HISTORY HIGHLIGHTS

This chronological listing of events important to the labor movement includes the following: organization dates of trade unions; important court decisions and legislation affecting the labor movement; noteworthy strikes; labor-related riots and public disturbances; and unusual events related to the movement.

Where known, the disbanded dates of labor organizations are included. It should be noted, however, that many unions never officially disbanded, while several have merged with other groups. Current information about unions will be found in section II, National Labor Organizations.

Note: An asterisk (*) following the title of a federal law indicates that a description and its statutory citation will be found in section IV, Principal Federal Labor Laws and Executive Orders Affecting Labor.

1636

First recorded labor disturbance occurred on Richmond Island, Maine, when Robert Trelauney refused to pay his employee-fishermen for their catch.

1642

On March 2 the Grand Assemblie at James City, Virginia, passed a law: "beit also enacted that no person or persons whatsoever for any offence already committed or to be committed shall be hereafter adjudged to serve the collony."

1648

On October 18 permission was granted to "shoomakers of Boston ... to assemble and meete together in Boston, at such time and times as they shall appoynt, who being so assembled, they, or the greatest number of them, shall have powre to chuse a master and two wardens, with fowre or six associats, a clarke, a sealer, a searcher, and a beadle.... "

1776

New York City Journey Printers struck; first recorded strike.

1786

First authenticated strike of workers occurred in the United States; Philadelphia printers won a minimum weekly wage of $6.

1794

Federal Society of Journeymen Cordwainers organized in Philadelphia, called first "continuous organization" of workingmen, and possibly the original trade union; other groups of skilled workers organized trade societies in many cities.

1806

Six law suits involved cordwainer conspiracy cases: Philadelphia in 1806, New York in 1809, and Pittsburgh in 1815 (records lost on other three). When journeymen shoemakers demanded a minimum wage, employers charged the cordwainer societies of being guilty of restraint of trade. The courts ruled against the unions — decisions which proved harmful to all new labor societies.

1824

First strike by women called by the weavers in Pawtucket, Rhode Island, objecting to increased hours with reduced wages.

1825

United Tailoresses Society of New York organized as a protective organization.

1828

Philadelphia's Mechanics' Union of Trade Associations established as first city federation of labor.

Twenty-four New York workmen fined for criminal conspiracy when participating in a strike.

New York trade associations won a 10-hour day.

Some 300-400 mill workers in Dover, New Hampshire, struck to protest low wages, a 13½-hour day, and expensive rooming charges.

Workingmen's Party formed in Philadelphia.

1829

Ebenezer Ford of New York's Working Men's Party elected to the New York State Assembly; first labor union political candidate elected.

1831

Establishment of New England Association of Farmers, Mechanics and Other Workingmen, a union which welcomed all workers (dissolved in 1834).

1834

Women workers in Lowell, Massachusetts, textile factories struck for higher wages; ringleaders were fired and a pay increase refused.

National Trades Union formed in New York City; first attempt at a national labor federation.

1835

In Philadelphia, 16 trade associations struck, paralyzing the city and winning a 10-hour day; strikes followed in other cities and by year-end labor enjoyed a 10-hour day throughout the Middle Atlantic States.

The New York Supreme Court decided in *People* v. *Fisher* that it was illegal for a society of cordwainers to conspire to raise wages. The decision encouraged other employers to forbid trade societies, whether or not they engaged in strikes.

1840
President Van Buren established a 10-hour day for federal employees.

1842
In *Commonwealth* v. *Hunt*, Massachusetts Judge Lemuel Shaw decided that the doctrine of conspiracy did not apply to labor unions, thereby recognizing the legality of unions and their right to engage in economic, legal, and political activities.

First sit-down strike by Pittsburgh puddlers and boilermakers who seized a mill.

Connecticut and Massachusetts adopted laws prohibiting children from working more than a 10-hour day.

Glass Bottle Blowers Association of U.S. and Canada established.

1844
Sarah G. Bagley worked in Lowell and founded the Lowell Female Labor Reform Association, an auxiliary of the New England Workingmen's Association. She tried to organize women on the East Coast but poor health forced her to give up her organizing.

1847
New Hampshire passed the first state law setting 10 hours as the legal workday.

1850
American League of Colored Laborers formed in New York City.

1850s
Formation of several national trade unions, loose organizations with no power over local affiliates; many disappeared by the time of the Civil War.

1852
International Typographical Union formed, first national union to continue until the present.

1859
International Molders' and Allied Workers' Union organized.

1860
Some 20,000 New England shoemakers struck in Maine, Massachusetts, and New Hampshire; won increase over their $3 weekly wage.

1863
Brotherhood of Locomotive Engineers organized.

1864
Décorative Plasterers and Cement Masons International Association of U.S. and Canada formed.

Contract Labor Act of 1864* adopted.

1865
Ira Steward of Boston created the Grand Eight-Hour League of Massachusetts; other leagues were forming throughout the country.

1866
William H. Sylvis formed the National Labor Union at a meeting of 77 union delegates from 13 states, creating the first "permanent labor union" (collapsed in 1872).

1867
Knights of St. Crispin organized to protect shoemakers against competition of "green hands" and apprentices operating new shoemaking machinery.

1868
First federal eight-hour-day law adopted.

Daughters of St. Crispin, national organization of women shoe operators, held first convention in Lynn, Massachusetts.

Augusta Lewis Troup formed the Working Women's Association and the Women's Typographical Union.

Window Glass Cutters League of America established.

1869
Noble and Holy Order of the Knights of Labor formed in Philadelphia by Uriah S. Stephens; at first a secret society; peak membership grew to 700,000 but faded from labor scene by mid-1890s.

Colorado National Labor Union formed.

1873
Brotherhood of Locomotive Firemen and Enginemen organized.

1874
First union label adopted by the Cigar Makers' International Union.

1875
National Marine Engineers' Beneficial Association formed.

The "Long Strike of 1875" lasted from January to June, when members of the Miners' and Mine Laborers' Benevolent Association lost their strike and were forced to accept a 20% wage cut. This was followed by the "Molly Maguire Riots," the arrest of 24 miners charged with criminal offenses, and the execution of 10 workers. The trial and executions ended labor unionism in the anthracite area of eastern Pennsylvania and created serious antilabor feelings throughout the nation.

1877
The "Railway Strike of 1877" was called the most violent and important strike of the nineteenth century. It was long coming. Railroad wages had been cut over a

three-year period, union members were fired and blacklisted, and there were other grievances. After further 10% wage cuts were announced in June, a strike began on the Baltimore and Ohio on July 16 and quickly spread to other roads. Mobs of workers destroyed railroad property, hundreds were killed, countless numbers injured, and property damage was estimated at $10 million. Thereafter union members felt they must be more aggressive in dealing with management, and decided to enter politics to win reforms, having gained nothing from the strike.

Granite Cutters' International Association of America formed.

1878
American Flint Glass Workers Union of North America organized.

Lakes Seamen's Union founded; first important seamen's labor organization.

1879
Massachusetts adopted the first law requiring factory inspection.

1880
International Brotherhood of Boilermakers, Iron Shipbuilders, Blacksmiths, Forgers and Helpers formed.

1881
Federation of Organized Trade and Labor Unions of the U.S. and Canada, predecessor of the American Federation of Labor, formed in Pittsburgh.

United Brotherhood of Carpenters and Joiners of America organized.

1882
Stove, Furnace and Allied Appliance Workers International Union of North America and the Upholsterers International Union of North America formed.

First Labor Day celebration held in New York City.

1883
Brotherhood of Railroad Trainmen formed.

1884
Labor unions started the use of the boycott; 30 cases in 1884 and almost 200 in 1885.

Bureau of Labor created in the Department of Labor.

1885
Knights of Labor, under Terrence V. Powderly, forced Gould-controlled railroads to negotiate; first time labor had compelled management of a large company to bargain.

1886
Haymarket Riot on May 4 in Chicago; climaxed 10 years of labor violence as 10 were killed and 30 injured. It led to a rash of laws curbing activities of labor unions.

Formation of the American Federation of Labor with Samuel Gompers as the first president; successor to the Federation of Organized Trades and Labor Unions.

First national general strike held on May Day as 340,000 workers rallied in several cities to demand an eight-hour workday.

Bakery and Confectionery Workers' International Union of America and the International Union of United Brewery, Flour, Cereal, Soft Drink and Distillery Workers of America founded.

1887
Brotherhood of Maintenance of Way Employes; International Organization of Masters, Mates and Pilots; International Brotherhood of Painters and Allied Trades; and the Journeymen Barbers, Hairdressers, Cosmetologists and Proprietors' International Union of America established.

1888
Congress created a Department of Labor under direction of a commissioner.

Brotherhood of Railway Carmen of the U.S. and Canada, the International Association of Machinists and Aerospace Workers, the Retail Clerks International Association, and the United Hebrew Trades of the State of New York organized.

1889
National Association of Letter Carriers of the U.S.A. and the United Association of Journeymen and Apprentices of the Plumbing and Pipe Fitting Industry of the U.S. and Canada formed.

1890
International Brotherhood of Pottery and Allied Workers and the International Union, United Mine Workers of America, organized.

1891
Hotel and Restaurant Employees and Bartenders International Union established.

1892
"Homestead Strike" occurred after the Amalgamated Association of Iron and Steel Workers refused to accept a wage cut in July at the Carnegie Steel Company. Workers were locked out and a battle ensued between steel workers and hired Pinkerton guards, a dozen men being killed on each side and the so-called strike then spread. On November 20 the union conceded defeat, the men returned to work, and steel unionism received a serious setback in the Pittsburgh area for years to come.

Amalgamated Transit Union and the International Longshoremen's Association formed.

1893
Eugene Debs established the American Railway Union.

International Alliance of Theatrical Stage Employees and Moving Picture Operators of the U.S. and Canada and the International Plate Printers, Die Stampers, and Engravers' Union of North America formed.

1894
"Pullman Strike" occurred when wages were reduced; to support the Pullman workers, Eugene Debs called for a general strike of rail workers belonging to the American Railway Union. In the Chicago area, especially, there were rioting, property damage, and 12 deaths in July. A blanket court injunction forbidding any person from interfering with the mails resulted in the arrest of many strikers and their leaders. Debs was imprisoned for contempt of court, the strike was broken, the men returned to work, and the union's effectiveness was destroyed.

Some 500 unemployed men marched from the Midwest to Washington, DC, led by Jacob S. Coxey, who was arrested for trespassing on the grounds of the Capitol.

Congress adopted legislation designating Labor Day as a national holiday.

1895
Boot and Shoe Workers Union and the Tobacco Workers International Union formed.

1896
American Federation of Musicians of the U.S. and Canada, the International Association of Bridge, Structural and Ornamental Iron Workers, and the International Union of Operating Engineers organized.

1897
Amalgamated Meat Cutters and Butcher Workmen of North America and the International Seamen's Union founded.

1898
Congress enacted the Erdman Act.*

United Brick and Clay Workers of America established.

1899
International Association of Siderographers and the Wood, Wire and Metal Lathers' International Union organized.

1900
International Ladies' Garment Workers Union formed.

1901
Amalgamated Association of Iron, Steel and Tin Workers conducted a three-month strike against the U.S. Steel Corp. and lost 14 union contracts on returning to work.

Brotherhood of Railroad Signalmen, the International Federation of Trade Unions, the International Union of Elevator Constructors, and the United Textile Workers of America organized.

1902

The "Anthracite Coal Strike of 1902" was called May 9 by the United Mine Workers after the mine operators refused to negotiate benefits the union wanted. Six months later, after pressure was brought by President Theodore Roosevelt, the men returned to work on October 23 when the union agreed to arbitrate, and an Anthracite Strike Commission was appointed. In March 1903 the Commission awarded a 10% pay raise and a nine-hour workday but failed to recognize the union.

United Telegraph Workers established.

1903

Department of Commerce and Labor established, absorbing the Bureau of Labor.

International Brotherhood of Teamsters, Chauffeurs, Warehousemen and Helpers of America and the National Rural Letter Carrier's Association formed.

Women's Trade Union League established in Boston (disbanded in 1947).

1904

National League of Postmasters of the U.S. established.

1905

In *Lochner* v. *New York*, the U.S. Supreme Court decided that a maximum hour law for bakery workers was unconstitutional.

Industrial Workers of the World, better known as IWW or "The Wobblies," organized.

1906

Upton Sinclair published *The Jungle*, revealing shocking conditions in the meat-packing industry, one of several muckraking books or "literature of exposure" which led to corrective action in some industries as well as to corrective legislation.

1908

In *Muller* v. *Oregon*, the U.S. Supreme Court upheld the right of a state to enact a 10-hour workday law for women to protect their health.

In *Adair* v. *United States*, the U.S. Supreme Court invalidated that part of the Erdman Act of 1898 which outlawed the use of yellow-dog contracts.

In *Loewe* v. *Lawlor*, better known as the Danbury Hatters case, the U.S. Supreme Court outlawed secondary union boycotts when the United Hatters of North America struck a hat-making firm and conducted a boycott against it. The homes of 140 union members were ordered sold by the district court to satisfy the judgment against the union.

National Association of Postal Supervisors organized.

1909

First large all-women's strike called in New York City by shirtwaist workers.

1910
Civil Service Employees Association formed.

1911
New York City Triangle Shirt Waist factory fire killed 146 young women who were locked into their working quarters on a top floor of the building, and thus unable to escape. The tragedy brought new laws that improved working conditions.

International Allied Printing Trades Association formed.

1912
The "American Woolen Company Strike" in Lawrence, Massachusetts, began January 12 under a call by the Industrial Workers of the World to some 20,000 workers facing a drastic wage cut. Police brutality brought protests from all parts of the nation, and on March 12 when the company capitulated and granted wage increases, the victory brought considerable prestige to the IWW.

Massachusetts adopted the first minimum wage law for women and minors.

Children's Bureau established in the Department of Commerce and Labor.

1913
Congress created the independent Department of Labor.

Newlands Act of 1913* adopted.

The "Patterson Silk Workers' Strike" (Patterson, NJ) attracted the IWW to help the strikers, but five months of police opposition to the union and strikers, plus hunger, forced the strikers to return to work without winning any benefits. This defeat was a blow to the IWW's reputation as an effective organizing group.

Actors' Equity Association and the National Alliance of Postal and Federal Employees organized.

1914
Clayton Act of 1914* adopted.

Amalgamated Clothing Workers of America formed.

1915
LaFollette Seamen's Act of 1915* adopted.

Yiddish Writers Union organized.

1916
Adamson* and Child Labor* Acts of 1916 adopted.

American Federation of Teachers and the International Jewelry Workers Union established.

1917
Many states began to outlaw the IWW because of its antiwar stand and record of violence by passing criminal syndicalism laws. Numerous arrests were made;

William Haywood, its leader, jumped bail and fled to Russia, and the organization lost much of its effectiveness and membership thereafter.

In *Hitchman Coal and Coke Co.* v. *Mitchell*, the U.S. Supreme Court ruled that an employer "had a legal and constitutional right to exclude union men from its employ," thus upholding the "Yellow Dog" contract.

National Federation of Federal Employees established.

1918
National War Labor Board appointed by the president to mediate industrial disputes.

Twenty-four international unions formed the National Committee for the Organizing of the Iron and Steel Industry and successfully signed up some 400,000 workers. A strike in 1919, broken by the industry, put an end to the committee.

United States Employment Service established in the Department of Labor.

In *Hammer* v. *Dagenhart*, the U.S. Supreme Court invalidated the Owen-Keating Child Labor Act.

American Train Dispatchers Association; International Association of Fire Fighters; International Federation of Professional and Technical Engineers; the Oil, Chemical and Atomic Workers International Union; and the United Scenic Artists formed.

1919
The "Boston Police Strike" started 5:45 p.m. September 9 when 75% of the police force left their beats after two dozen policemen had been suspended for joining the new AFL union. After the suspended policemen were fired, Samuel Gompers, president of the AFL, telegraphed Governor Calvin Coolidge, complaining that the action was unwarranted. Coolidge replied that there was "no right to strike against the public safety by anybody, anywhere, anytime." The men were not reinstated, the strike was broken, and Coolidge became a national hero.

On September 22 some 343,000 members of the National Committee for the Organizing of the Iron and Steel Industry struck for higher pay and better working conditions. Using strikebreakers, the steel companies gradually restored normal operations, and by January 1920 so many workers had returned to their jobs that the strike was cancelled.

A general strike in February crippled the city of Seattle for four days when 60,000 workers supported the striking metal trades workers who sought a wage increase.

A strike called for the United Mine Workers for November 1 involving 425,000 workers was prohibited by a court order, thus establishing the precedent of applying injunction law to halt a strike.

AFL proclaimed a new "Labor's Bill of Rights" calling for a living wage and limitations on the use of injunctions.

Women's Bureau established in the Department of Labor, with Mary Anderson its first director.

Associated Actors and Artists of America and the International Labor Organization formed.

1921

In *Truax* v. *Corrigan*, the U.S. Supreme Court declared an Arizona law unconstitutional which prohibited the use of injunctions in law disputes. In *Duplex Printing Press* v. *Deering*, the court said that the Clayton Act did not legalize secondary boycotts or protect unions from injunctions brought against them for restraint of trade.

Representatives of numerous business and industrial organizations which favored the open shop met in Chicago and adopted the patriotic term "American Plan" as the name for the open shop.

Service Employees International Union formed.

1922

The "Herrin Massacre" took place during a coal strike John L. Lewis had called in April, when some 650,000 members of the United Mine Workers struck. On June 21 the Southern Illinois Coal Company at Herrin, Illinois, hired strikebreakers from another union. Violence flared, a truce was arranged, and it was agreed that the strikebreakers and guards were to leave the mine property safely and go home. As they departed, the strikers attacked and killed 19 men and injured others. Some concessions were obtained from the operators before all the miners returned to work, but the massacre damaged the union's reputation as well as the labor cause.

In *Bailey* v. *Drexel Furniture Company*, the U.S. Supreme Court invalidated provisions of the Revenue Act of 1919 which approved a tax on companies employing children; and in *Coronado Coal Co.* v. *United Mine Workers*, strike action was held to not be a conspiracy to restrain commerce within the Sherman Antitrust Act, but unions were held suable for their acts.

American Society of Arbitration formed in New York City.

1923

In *Adkins* v. *Children's Hospital*, the U.S. Supreme Court found that a law setting minimum wages for women in the District of Columbia was unconstitutional. This decision put all minimum wage laws in doubt.

1926

Railway Labor Executives Association established.

Railway Labor Act of 1926* adopted.

1927

Labor Research Association organized.

1928

New Bedford (Massachusetts) textile strike idled 28,000 workers for six months because of their refusal to accept a 10% reduction in wages. The strike was settled with a 5% reduction and an agreement that the employers would give 30 days' notice of future intentions to cut wages.

1929

On October 24 the stock market in New York crashed, ushering in the Depression of the 1930s which, although it brought high unemployment and widespread misery, was responsible for vast social and economic reforms, including far-reaching labor legislation.

1930

Unemployment in the United States was estimated between three and six million men and women.

1931

Davis-Bacon Act of 1931* enacted.

1932

Norris-LaGuardia Act of 1932* adopted.

First unemployment insurance act adopted in Wisconsin.

1933

President Franklin Delano Roosevelt inaugurated on March 4. He subsequently introduced his New Deal program of economic and social reforms.

Emergency Railroad Transportation Act of 1933,* National Industrial Recovery Act of 1933,* and Wagner-Peyser Act of 1933* adopted.

Mrs. Frances Perkins became Secretary of Labor; first woman named to the cabinet.

1934

United Textile Workers called one million workers out on strike to demand recognition of the union, abolition of the stretch-out and speed-up, and a 30-hour week, with no reduction in the minimum $14 a week wage. After three weeks, the textile workers returned to their jobs under the same conditions as before they struck, but some 80,000 workers in the South lost their jobs.

Creation of the National Industrial Recovery Board which consisted of representatives from management, labor, and the public. The board was superseded by a new board created under the National Labor Relations Act of 1935.*

Railway Labor Act of 1934* adopted; established the National Mediation Board.

A law passed in 1934 granted retirement payments to certain railroad employees but was declared unconstitutional by the U.S. Supreme Court the following March. In May 1937 a new Railroad Retirement Act was passed and amended in 1951. The amendment increased the benefits and guaranteed that no beneficiary would receive less than what was provided by the Social Security System. A three-man Railroad Retirement Board administers the Railroad Retirement and Railroad Unemployment Insurance Acts and the Health Insurance for the Aged Act insofar as it affects railroad retirement beneficiaries.

1935

John L. Lewis organized nine labor unions into the Committee for Industrial Organization, within the AFL.

In *Schechter Poultry Corporation* v. *United States*, the U.S. Supreme Court declared the National Industrial Recovery Act unconstitutional.

Bituminous Coal Conservation Act of 1935 (Guffey Act),* the Social Security Act of 1935,* and the National Labor Relations Act of 1935* adopted.

United Automobile Workers organized.

1936
Steel Workers' Organizing Committee established.

Non-Partisan League established by CIO leadership to help reelect Franklin D. Roosevelt to a second term; the CIO also supported the formation of the American Labor Party.

Walsh-Healey Act of 1936* adopted.

Sitdown strike at General Motors' Cleveland Fisher Body plant.

1937
Flint Fisher Body No. 2 plant sitdown strike settled with recognition of the United Automobile Workers as bargaining agent for its members.

Steel Workers' Organizing Committee recognized by United States Steel Corporation; many important concessions were granted to the union.

In *N.L.R.B.* v. *Jones and Laughlin*, the U.S. Supreme Court upheld the constitutionality of the Wagner Act, a victory for the New Deal and organized labor.

Walter Reuther, organizer for the UAW, beaten in the famous "Battle of the Overpass" at the Ford Motor company plant.

During the May 30 "Memorial Day Massacre," seven were killed and scores injured in a strike at the Republic Steel Corporation.

John L. Lewis' Committee for Industrial Organization stricken from membership in the AFL.

Apprentice Training Service Act of 1937* adopted.

Report of the La Follette Civil Liberties Committee revealed wide disregard of constitutional rights of workers. Some 2,500 companies were said to have hired labor spies and many had employed strikebreakers.

National Maritime Union of America founded.

1938
John L. Lewis reorganized the Committee for Industrial Organization into the Congress of Industrial Organizations (CIO).

Fair Labor Standards Act of 1938* adopted.

Seafarer's International Union formed to replace the defunct International Seamen's Union.

1939
In the Fansteel Metallurgical Corporation case, the U.S. Supreme Court outlawed sit-down strikes as trespassing on private property.

1940
John L. Lewis broke with President Roosevelt and refused to support his bid for a third term.

1941
The National Labor Relations Board ordered the four "Little Steel" corporations (Bethlehem Steel Corp., Inland Steel Co., Republic Steel Corp., and Youngstown Sheet and Tube Co.) to recognize the United Steelworkers of America (the new name for the former Steel Workers' Organizing Committee).

Ford Motor Company was ordered to rehire 2,566 workers discharged for union membership and pay $2 million in back wages; union was finally recognized by Ford.

Strikes were called in the "captive coal mines" operated by the steel industry over the issue of union shop. Dispute was settled by an arbitration board which ruled in favor of union shop.

In *United States* v. *Derby Lumber Company*, the U.S. Supreme Court upheld the legality of the Fair Labor Standards Act.

1942
War Labor Board established by executive order with authority to settle industrial disputes.

"Little Steel formula" adopted by War Labor Board; provided for 15% wage increase for Little Steel workers and set a pattern for other wage increases.

United Mine Workers seceded from the CIO.

Economic Stabilization Act of 1942* adopted.

1943
After numerous United Mine Workers struck, the government seized the mines on May 1. The men returned to work, but there were three more work stoppages before a formula was worked out in October within the Little Steel formula.

United Mine Workers admitted to the AFL.

Political Action Committee organized by the CIO, with Sidney Hillman its chairman; purpose was to support President Roosevelt's bid for a fourth term.

Smith-Connally Act of 1943* adopted.

1945
Wage Stabilization Board appointed.

Wave of strikes lasted from fall of 1945 into the spring of 1946, over the question of industry's ability to pay higher wages.

General Motors' strike for a wage increase of 30%; which began during October and lasted 113 days into March 1946.

1946
Full Employment Act of 1946* adopted.

Lea Act* became law to curb featherbedding practices of James C. Petrillo's American Federation of Musicians.

Hobbs Anti-Racketeering Act* adopted to restrain illegal activities of the Teamsters Union.

During the spring, a coal strike was called by John L. Lewis to obtain an employee welfare fund. Lack of coal created national brown-outs, whereupon the government seized the mines under the Smith-Connally Act and an agreement was finally concluded. In the fall the United Mine Workers struck again; the government obtained an injunction against the strike, but the union maintained this move was contrary to the Norris-LaGuardia Act, which prohibited the use of injunctions in labor disputes. In 1947 the U.S. Supreme Court in *U.S.* v. *John L. Lewis* upheld the principle that the act did not apply in the case of a strike which threatened national security and welfare. The union was fined $700,000 but eventually gained its objectives, a new contract being ratified in 1947.

After a one-month strike, the United Steelworkers accepted a raise of 18½¢ an hour, which became a recognized "first round increase." Later the United Automobile Workers accepted the same hourly increase to end a 3½-month strike.

Railroad trainmen and locomotive engineers threatened to strike in the spring over the issue of work rules, and the government seized the railroads. The men then walked out but returned to work after the President issued an ultimatum.

1947
The Portal-to-Portal Act,* and the Taft-Hartley Act* were voted by the Congress, and the Condon-Wadlin Act of 1947* was adopted by the New York State Legislature.

1948
General Motors Corporation and the United Automobile Workers signed the first major contract with an "escalator clause" which provided for increases based on the Consumer Price Index.

1949
As unemployment rose from two to four million, two-thirds of the states increased the amount and duration of unemployment benefits.

A lengthy coal strike was followed by a shorter steel walkout which ended with a plan providing for a $100 a month pension, including Social Security for retired workers. By year-end, 8.5 million workers had similar pension agreements.

The President's Conference on Industrial Safety was held in Washington, DC, and attended by a thousand leaders of business, labor, government, and safety organizations. The President challenged the participants to reduce job accidents by 50% by the end of 1952. (Similar conferences were held in 1950 and 1952.)

An amendment to the Fair Labor Standards Act of 1938 directly prohibited child labor for the first time.

The International Confederation of Free Trade Unions, a worldwide labor organization, was formed during December in London. The AFL, CIO, and United Mine Workers participated.

1950

Social Security benefits were extended to more than 10 million additional workers.

General Motors Corporation agreed on a five-year contract with annual "improvement factor" increases in wages, cost of living adjustments, pensions, insurance benefits, and a modified union shop.

The AFL and CIO formed the United Labor Policy Committee to watch and report on governmental policy, but the AFL withdrew in August 1951.

The CIO expelled seven affiliates which were still Communist-dominated.

About five million workers were involved in numerous wildcat strikes, most of which were settled with a 10¢ an hour wage increase.

1951

The first amendment to the Taft-Hartley Act permitted negotiating union-shop agreements without previous employee polls.

1952

Railroads which had been under army control since August 27, 1950, when seized by the government, were returned to their owners May 23 after contracts were signed between management and nonoperating railroad unions.

The longest and most costly steel dispute in the industry history lasted 53 days, during which the President seized the mills, but the U.S. Supreme Court ruled he lacked such power. The settlement included a 16¢ an hour wage increase.

1953

AFL and CIO signed a no-raiding agreement.

A complicated dispute between the International Longshoremen's Association and the New York Shipping Association over wages and hiring practices was highlighted by violence and gangsterism.

1954

In July the AFL and the CIO agreed to merge into the AFL-CIO.

In *Garner* v. *Teamsters Union*, the U.S. Supreme Court ruled that states could not regulate labor conduct in interstate commerce if the activity were already subject to federal law.

1955

General prosperity brought improved unemployment benefits to workers at Chrysler, Ford, and General Motors corporations.

Guaranteed semiannual wage contracts signed by automobile and other industries provided unemployed workers 60-65% of normal earnings, the companies paying the difference between unemployment compensation and the guaranteed wage, for six months.

Committee on Political Education organized by AFL-CIO.

Establishment of the American Federation of Labor and Congress of Industrial Organizations (AFL-CIO) on December 5, 1955, brought unions together, representing approximately 16 million workers or more than 85% of the membership claimed by all unions in the United States.

1956
After a five-week strike, workers in the steel industry returned to work with a three-year contract without the usual wage reopening provisions and with generous benefits.

1957
The Senate appointed the McClellan Committee (Select Committee on Improper Activities in the Labor or Management Field) to investigate racketeering in labor-management relations.

AFL-CIO Executive Council suspended the United Textile Workers, the Teamsters Union, the Laundry Workers, and the Bakery and Confectionery Workers in its effort to clean up unionism.

The NLRB ruled an employer may withhold production and sales data from a union if the company did not plead inability to raise wages.

1958
First drop in union membership in two decades was recorded.

A U.S. district judge set up a board of three monitors to oversee officers of the Teamsters Union. The first semiannual report of the monitors urged various reforms and accused officers of some locals of misconduct.

Welfare and Pension Plans Disclosure Act* adopted.

1959
Landrum-Griffin Act* adopted.

ILGWU set aside an annual budget of $1 million to promote its union label among customers.

Four-month steel strike which began July 15 ended with the industry agreeing to the steel union's demands for increased pension and insurance payments, a wage rise, and maintenance of existing work rules. The new contracts were not signed until January 1960 after the national emergency provisions of the Taft-Hartley Act had been invoked. A back-to-work injunction was issued October 21, but the men did not return to work until the U.S. Supreme Court had upheld the injunction on November 7, the 116th day of the strike.

1960
Three-year successful boycott by blacks begun of Philadelphia stores and companies which did not hire blacks or denied them advancement and job equality.

1961

Restrictive work rules were eased and increased use of labor-saving equipment was sanctioned by an agreement signed by the Pacific Maritime Association and the International Longshoremen's and Warehousemen's Union. In return for union concessions, the association agreed to establish a pension fund and guarantee union members certain minimum weekly earnings and no layoffs under certain conditions.

The AFL-CIO refused to readmit the 1.2 million-member Teamsters Union.

American Motors Corporation signed a three-year settlement establishing a "progress sharing" or profit-sharing plan.

Coverage under the Fair Labor Standards Act was extended to an additional 3.6 million workers, mostly in construction and retail trade.

Telegraphers on the Southern Pacific Railroad were guaranteed their jobs or equivalent wages during their lifetimes.

1962

One hundred of the largest unions signed agreements with the President's Committee on Equal Opportunities to end discrimination within their ranks.

The Manpower Development and Training Act of 1962* was adopted.

Electrical workers in New York City obtained a five-hour workday.

Under an Executive Order signed January 17, federal employees' unions were granted the right to bargain collectively with government agencies.

International Longshoremen's Association shut down East and Gulf ports from December 23 until January 25, 1963, after it refused to eliminate featherbedding and to reduce work crews; the strike cost the nation an estimated billion dollars.

1963

The Equal Pay Act of 1963* was adopted, prohibiting wage differentials based on sex for workers covered by the Fair Labor Standards Act.

By this year, 20 states had enacted right-to-work laws and 23 had adopted equal pay laws.

Kaiser Steel Corporation and United Steel Workers signed a productivity-sharing plan, giving workers a third share in all cost savings, and guaranteeing workers against loss of employment or income due to automation.

President John F. Kennedy put into effect various programs aimed at eliminating discrimination in hiring of workers on jobs financed wholly or partly by federal funds.

Congress passed the Railroad Arbitration Act which called for arbitration of two long-standing issues in the railroad dispute: the use of firemen on diesel locomotives and the makeup of train crews. The arbitrators ruled for the gradual elimination of firemen in 90% of freight and yard service and sent the "consist issue" back to the unions and railroads for further negotiation and arbitration if necessary.

Railroad Arbitration Act of 1963* adopted.

1964
The 4½-year dispute between the railroads and the unions was resolved with a final agreement signed by five operating unions.

The Civil Rights Act of 1964* and the Economic Opportunity Act of 1964* were adopted.

1965
The Service Contract Act of 1965* provided wage standards for employees performing work on federal service contracts, the standards to be comparable to those applicable to employees on federal construction and supply contracts.

Amendment to the Social Security Act provided the "Medicare" plan, or health insurance for those over 65.

1966
National Farm Association Workers merged with other farm worker groups to form AFL-CIO United Farm Workers Organizing Committee.

Three newspapers in New York City merged to form the *World-Journal Tribune* but were unable to negotiate new contracts and a 140-day strike followed, the longest in a major American city.

The Fair Labor Standards Act was amended to extend minimum wage protection to some 10 million workers previously excluded from the benefits of the act.

1967
The Age Discrimination in Employment Act of 1967* was adopted.

New York State adopted the Taylor Act to replace the Condon-Wadlin Act. It provided collective bargaining rights for government workers in the state and prohibited strikes; penalties for striking were switched from employees to unions and their officials.

The Mine, Mill and Smelter Workers merged with the United Steelworkers. In mid-July the merged unions and 25 others struck major copper producers and remained on strike during the rest of the year.

James R. Hoffa, president of the Teamsters Union, began serving an eight-year jail sentence for jury tampering.

After a two-day railroad stoppage, Congress established a five-man arbitration board which imposed a two-year settlement.

1968
The United Automobile Workers formed the Alliance for Labor Action (disbanded in 1971) with the Teamsters Union after George Meany suspended the UAW for non-payment of dues. Walter Reuther, president of the UAW, had charged the AFL-CIO had become complacent and out of touch with the times.

JOBS (Job Opportunities in the Business Sector) initiated by the National Alliance of Businessmen, a government agency. Its purpose was to provide federal funds to cover the cost of training workers who did not come up to company standards.

Florida teachers conducted the first statewide strike by teachers, many of whom realized salary increases and improved working conditions.

The Consumer Credit Protection Act of 1968 contained provisions restricting wage garnishment.

The Amalgamated Meat Cutters and Butcher Workmen of America absorbed the United Packinghouse, Food and Allied Workers, combined membership of approximately 500,000.

The United Automobile Workers disaffiliated from the AFL-CIO.

1969

The U.S. Department of Labor issued an "affirmative action" order to end discrimination in federally funded contracts in Philadelphia, with builders being asked to submit specific minority hiring goals. Called the "Philadelphia Plan," its legality was upheld by the Attorney General.

The Chrysler Corporation received a $13.8 million contract under the JOBS program to train 4,450 hard-core unemployed workers.

The Federal Coal Mine Health and Safety Act of 1969 provided payments to miners who had contracted black lung disease, and stipulated that periodic chest X-rays be given all miners; it also required that miners be equipped with nonspark equipment and that there be strict safety controls. The eligibility process of the legislation to aid miners with black lung disease was broadened by the Black Lung Benefits Act of 1972.

1970

The first strike in U.S. Post Office history lasted a week, gaining the workers a wage increase and full collective bargaining privileges for the future, except that arbitration, not strikes, would be used to settle disputes.

Hawaii and Pennsylvania became the first states to pass laws giving most public workers the right to strike, subject to following certain procedures.

Occupational Safety and Health Act of 1970* adopted.

Joseph A. Yablonski, United Mine Workers' official, his wife, and daughter were found shot in their Clarksville, Pennsylvania, home. UAW chief, W. A. (Tony) Boyle was convicted of the killing.

The United Farm Workers Organizing Committee reached an agreement with most of the California table grape producers after a 4½-year boycott.

After an emergency strike ban expired, four rail unions called a nationwide rail strike. The strike was halted after one day by a federal injunction, and Congress voted to extend the ban until March 1, 1971, and to increase retroactive pay.

1971

President Richard Nixon instituted a 90-day wage-price-rent freeze with a pay board to stop "inflationary wage and salary increases." The President also suspended provisions of the Davis-Bacon Act in order to curb wage and price increases in the construction industry. Later he revoked the suspension and issued an executive order calling for a "cooperative" system of "constraints."

The American Postal Workers Union with 300,000 members was formed by the merger of the United Federation of Postal Clerks, the National Association of Post Office and General Services Maintenance Employees, the National Federation of Post Office Motor Vehicle Employees, the National Association of Special Delivery Messengers, and the National Postal Union.

1972

The longest dock walkout in the nation's history—139 days—took place on the West Coast and was settled with a wage increase.

The AFL-CIO issued a national charter to the United Farm Workers Organizing Committee.

The Equal Employment Opportunity Act of 1972* was adopted.

District 50, Allied and Technical Workers (once a division of the United Mine Workers) merged with United Steelworkers, making a total membership of 1,250,000.

United Papermakers and Paperworkers Union merged with the International Brotherhood of Pulp, Sulphite, and Paper Mill Workers to form United Paper Workers International Union with 345,000 members.

The International Brotherhood of Bookbinders and the Lithographers and Photoengravers International Union merged to form the Graphic Arts International Union with 120,000 members.

1973

After a three-day strike, Chrysler Corporation signed a three-year agreement with the United Automobile Workers which emphasized nonwage rather than pay items.

American Telephone and Telegraph Company agreed to pay $15 million to victims of sex and racial discrimination, and also introduced new wage and promotion policies for minorities and women, at a cost of $23 million for the first year.

The Rehabilitation Act of 1973* and the Comprehensive Employment and Training Act of 1973* were adopted.

Washington was the first state to permit a union shop for its civil servants.

The 135,000 member International Printing and Graphic Communications Union was formed by a merger of the International Printing Pressmen and Assistants Union of North America and the International Sterotypers', Electrotypers', and Platemakers' Union of North America.

The International Union of United Brewery, Flour, Cereal, Soft Drink and Distillery Workers merged with the International Brotherhood of Teamsters.

1974

The Coalition of Labor Union Women was founded by some 3,000 women unionists from 58 labor organizations meeting in Chicago. The coalition was formed to promote equal rights and better wages and working conditions for women workers.

The Trade Act of 1974* and the Employee Retirement Income Security Act of 1974* were adopted.

Nine steel companies agreed to the largest back-pay award on record with a payment of $30.9 million to women and minorities.

The Council on Wage and Price Stability was created to use persuasion instead of force to limit price and wage increases.

The Amalgamated Clothing Workers of America struck on June 1 for the first time since 1921 with 110,000 workers in 30 states supporting the walkouts. Seven days later the union settled with the Clothing Manufacturers Association.

1975
The nation experienced its highest unemployment rates since 1941, 9.2% in May.

In July more than 80,000 employees of the State of Pennsylvania struck but within a week reached an agreement and returned to work.

A walkout by interns and resident physicians in 22 New York City hospitals lasted for three days and was the first in the nation's history.

California became the first state to pass legislation covering farm labor relations.

1976
A settlement with General Motors Corporation following a strike was called "a step toward the four-day work week," by United Automobile Workers' President Leonard Woodcock as the negotiators endeavored to cut working time in order to preserve jobs and create new ones.

1977
The problem of illegal aliens working for subsistence wages and allegedly taking jobs from Americans was recognized by labor leaders as becoming serious.

The United States withdrew from the International Labour Organization because of dissatisfaction with the political involvement of the United Nations agency.

Federal Mine Safety and Health Act of 1977* adopted.

1978
United Mine Workers ratified a settlement providing for wage and other benefits after a 110-day strike, during which the terms agreed upon by the UMW president, Arnold Miller, were rejected twice. After the second turndown President Carter invoked the emergency dispute procedures of the Taft-Hartley Act, but many miners refused to return to work. A three-year agreement was finally ratified.

The Full Employment and Balanced Growth Act of 1978* and the Civil Service Reform Act of 1978* were adopted.

The Civil Service Employees Association joined with the American Federation of State, County and Municipal Employees, creating a membership of over one million. The Bakery and Confectionery Workers merged with the Tobacco

Workers Union to form the Bakery, Confectionery and Tobacco Workers International Union with approximately 175,000 members. The Sleeping Car Porters became a division of the Brotherhood of Railway, Airline and Steamship Clerks, its membership reduced to about 1,000 from a World War II high of 12,000.

President Carter asked labor and management to restrain compensation increases to 7% and suggested the same for prices.

The Age Discrimination in Employment Act of 1967 was amended to raise the compulsory retirement age for most workers from 65 to 70 and eliminate the mandatory age 70 retirement for federal workers.

Pilots of Northwest Orient Airlines conducted a 109-day strike, and a strike against New York City newspapers lasted 89 days; from July 10 until late September the Railway Clerks of the Norfolk and Western Railroad struck, the walkout spreading to almost all other roads, it being ended by a court order which submitted the job security issue to a Presidential Emergency Board.

The Labor-Management Cooperation Act of 1978 encouraged establishment of local labor-management committees to foster economic development.

1979
Alice Peurala was the first woman elected to head a local steel union.

COLA (cost of living adjustment) clauses became widespread in most union contracts.

The United Automobile Workers and Chrysler Corporation agreed on a three-year contract which would save the company $203 million in two years; in addition, Douglas Fraser, union president, was to become a member of the Chrysler Board of Directors.

The Amalgamated Meat Cutters and Butcher Workmen of North America and the Retail Clerks International merged to form the United Food and Commercial Workers International Union.

The first bargaining unit of lawyers working for a private law firm was formed in the District of Columbia when 19 attorneys organized the Federation of Legal Staff and Attorneys.

The U.S. Steel Corporation closed 15 plants in eight states, eliminating 13,000 jobs.

Lane Kirkland succeeded George Meany as president of the AFL-CIO.

In *Kaiser Aluminum & Chemical Corp.* v. *Weber, Weber* v. *U.S.*, and *United Steelworkers of America* v. *Weber*, the U.S. Supreme Court ruled that unions and employers may adopt quotas when hiring employees in order to overcome racial imbalance in "traditionally segregated job categories."

The AFL-CIO as well as the Auto Workers and the Teamsters agreed to participate with the government in a new wage and price restraint program, wage restraints to be handled by an 18-member Pay Advisory Committee with equal representation from labor, management, and the public. The committee was to become an advisory panel to the Council on Wage and Price Stability, and John T. Dunlop was appointed chairman.

1980

After trying for 17 years to unionize J. P. Stevens and Company, the Amalgamated Clothing and Textile Workers Union signed its first collective bargaining agreement with the company.

Ronald Reagan who became president-elect, had served as president of the Screen Actors Guild from 1947-1952 and 1959-1960. Despite organized labor's opposition, more union members were thought to have voted for Reagan than any Republican nominee since Dwight Eisenhower.

MultiEmployer Pension Plan Amendments Act of 1980* adopted.

Joyce Miller became the first woman elected to the AFL-CIO executive council. Dorothy Shields became the first woman elected as an AFL-CIO staff department head, in the Education Department.

1981

The American Radio Association merged into the Masters, Mates and Pilots Union, an affiliate of the International Longshoremen's Association.

In labor negotiating sessions, "Give-backs" of former union-negotiated and previously won pay increases became more common.

In *First National Maintenance Corp.* v. *NLRB*, the U.S. Supreme Court ruled that management does not have to negotiate in advance with a union over closing individual plants or dropping production lines. In *County of Washington* v. *Gunther*, the court ruled that employers may be sued by women for sex discrimination, even though the jobs performed are not the same as those of male employees.

When 8,590 members of the Professional Air Traffic Controllers' Organization (PATCO) who were on strike refused to obey a presidential ultimatum to return to their jobs, President Reagan ordered them dismissed without right to be hired by other government agencies, including military services.

1982

In *United Transportation Union* v. *Long Island Railroad*, the U.S. Supreme Court ruled that workers on the Long Island Railroad and commuter lines operated by a state agency were protected by the Railway Labor Act and had the federally guaranteed right to strike; in another railroad jurisdictional dispute, the court ruled in *Jackson Transit Authority* v. *Amalgamated Transit Union* that public transit workers must settle labor disputes on the state level; and in *Woelke & Romero Framing* v. *NLRB*, the court ruled that a union operating under a collective bargaining agreement can demand that contractors do business only with subcontractors who recognize the union.

In union after union, the leadership agreed to the demands of employers for reductions or concessions on benefit, wages, and work rules, a development called "concessionary bargaining."

After a crippling four-day strike against 117 railroads by locomotive engineers, Congress passed and the President signed a bill (P.L. 97-262) ordering striking engineers to return to work and accept a presidential emergency panel's recommendations.

The Glass Bottle Blowers Association and the International Brotherhood of Pottery and Allied Workers merged to form the Glass, Pottery, Plastics and

Allied Workers Union. The Aluminum, Brick and Clay Workers International Union and the United Glass and Ceramic Workers of North America merged to form the Aluminum, Brick and Glass Workers International Union. The United Hatters, Cap and Millinery Workers International Union merged into the Amalgamated Clothing and Textile Workers Union to become the Headwear Division similar to the already existing Apparel, Textile, and Shoe Divisions, with Nicholas Gyory, former president of the Hatters, as a newly elected Amalgamated vice president.

The NLRB ruled that a union cannot prohibit members from resigning from the union during a strike.

Almost 200 clerical staff members of the United Methodist Church Board of Global Ministries voted to join District 65 of the United Automobile Workers, the first time employees of a church had chosen to join a major American labor union.

During the last half of 1982, it was estimated that AFL-CIO unions lost more than 400,000 dues-paying members because of layoffs, and in many unions it was necessary to reduce staffs.

II

NATIONAL LABOR ORGANIZATIONS

ORGANIZATIONAL LISTING

This listing includes the principal national and regional labor unions, state AFL-CIO labor councils, unions of state government employees, and other general labor-related organizations.

All organizations are listed alphabetically by their official names. For the benefit of those who do not know the exact name of a union, it may be located by consulting the index and looking up the name of the craft, job title, or industry which the union represents. Thus the Brotherhood of Railway, Airline and Steamship Clerks, Freight Handlers, Express and Station Employees is listed alphabetically in this section under "Brotherhood." Readers who look for Railway Clerks, or Airline Clerks, or Steamship Clerks, or Freight Handlers, or Express Employees, or Station Employees will find each of these job titles in its proper alphabetical place in the index, with a reference referring the reader to the main "Brotherhood" listing.

All unions dealing with the same job title, craft, or industry are listed together in the index. A further breakdown shows all of the unions belonging to an industry, such as airlines, government, nursing, railroads, etc.

Each individual listing in this section contains the full name, address, and telephone number of the union and, if provided by the union, its latest membership figure, as well as the names of its principal officers. The presidents, secretaries, treasurers, and executive directors, or their counterparts, are also included in section III, Prominent Labor Leaders.

Actors' Equity Association
165 West Forty-sixth Street
New York, NY 10036
(212) 869-8530
Membership: 27,000
Theodore Bikel, President
Barbara Colton, 1st Vice President
Robert Fitzsimmons, Treasurer
Alan Eisenberg, Executive Secretary

**AFL/CIO-American Library Association
(Reference and Adult Services Division)
Joint Committee on Library Service to
Labor Groups**
50 East Huron Street
Chicago, IL 60611
(312) 944-6780
Andrew M. Hansen, ALA Staff Liaison
  (RASD Executive Director)
Jim Auerbach, AFL/CIO Staff Liaison
  (AFL-CIO Education Department,
  Washington, DC)

Air Line Employees Association, Int'l.
5600 South Central Avenue
Chicago, IL 60638
(312) 767-3333
Membership: 10,000
Victor J. Herbert, President
Robert D. Haskin, Vice President
William A. Schneider, Treasurer
Carolyn Boller, Secretary

Air Line Pilots Association
1625 Massachusetts Avenue, NW
Washington, DC 20036
(202) 797-4000
Membership: 39,685 (1978)
Captain John J. O'Donnell, President
Captain Gerry A. Pryde, 1st Vice
  President
Captain Thomas M. Ashwood, Secretary
Captain John J. Magee, Treasurer

Aircraft Mechanics Fraternal Association
4150 Cypress Road
St. Ann, MO 63074
(314) 423-0449
O. V. Delle-Femine, National Director
Ronald Wirts, Assistant National Director
John Etherton, National Treasurer
Charles Kloepfer, National Secretary

Alabama Labor Council, AFL-CIO
231 West Valley Avenue
Birmingham, AL 35209
(205) 942-5261
Barney Weeks, President
Jim Albright, Vice President
Asa Trammell, Secretary-Treasurer

Alabama State Employees Association
110 North Jackson Street
Montgomery, AL 36104
(205) 834-6965
Membership: 10,500
Robert (Bob) J. Cook, President
Mitchell Owens, Vice President
Annette Patrick, Secretary
Donna Crosby, Treasurer
Paul M. Smith, Jr., Executive Director

Alaska Public Employees Association
340 North Franklin
Juneau, AK 99801
(907) 586-2334
Membership: 9,000
Cherie Shelley, Executive Director
Lynn Harnisch, President

Allied Pilots Association
P.O. Box 5524
Arlington, TX 76011
(817) 261-0261
Membership: 3,700
R. H. Malone, President
F. R. Vogel, Vice President
F. C. Fosdick, Secretary-Treasurer

**Aluminum, Brick and Glass Workers
  International Union**
3362 Hollenberg Drive
Bridgeton, MO 63044
(314) 739-6142
Membership: 70,000
Lawrence A. Holley, President
Joseph Roman, Executive Assistant to the
  President

**Amalgamated Clothing and Textile
  Workers Union**
15 Union Square West
New York, NY 10003
(212) 242-0700
Membership: 526,000 (1978)
Murray H. Finley, President
Jack Sheinkman, Secretary-Treasurer

Amalgamated Lace Operatives of America
4013 Glendale Street
Philadelphia, PA 19124
(215) 743-9358
Membership: 2,100 (1978)
Richard Champagne, Co-President
Edward Zimmerman, Co-President
John Newton, Secretary-Treasurer

Amalgamated Transit Union
5025 Wisconsin Avenue, NW
Washington, DC 20016
(202) 537-1645
Membership: 160,000
  (continued)

John W. Rowland, International President
James LaSala, Executive Vice President
R. C. Wallace, International Secretary-
Treasurer

**American Association of Classified
School Employees**
6805 Oak Creek Drive
Columbus, OH 43229
(614) 890-6448
Membership: 150,000
G. Ray Holt, President
Lawrence V. DeCresce, Vice President
James A. Monroe, Executive Director-
Treasurer

**American Association of University
Professors**
One Dupont Circle
Washington, DC 20036
(202) 466-8050
Membership: 70,000
Victor Stone, President
Paul Strohm, 1st Vice President
Sandra Thornton, 2nd Vice President
Leroy Dubeck, Secretary-Treasurer
Wilfred Kaplan, Chair, Assembly of State
Conferences, AAUP
Norman Kopmeyer, Chair, Collective
Bargaining Congress, AAUP

American Communications Association
111 Broadway
New York, NY 10006
(212) 267-1374

**American Federation of Government
Employees**
1325 Massachusetts Avenue, NW
Washington, DC 20005
(202) 737-8700
Membership: 300,000
Kenneth T. Blaylock, President

**American Federation of Grain Millers
International**
4949 Olson Memorial Highway
Minneapolis, MN 55422
(612) 545-0211
(continued)

Membership: 35,000
Frank T. Hoese, General President
Joseph T. Smisek, General Secretary-
Treasurer

**American Federation of Guards,
Local No. 1**
4157 West Fifth Street
Los Angeles, CA 90020
(213) 387-3127
Membership: 2,000
Ronald Wells, Secretary-Treasurer, Busi-
ness Manager
Ernest McClintock, President

**American Federation of Labor &
Congress of Industrial Organizations**
815 Sixteenth Street, NW
Washington, DC 20006
(202) 637-5000
Membership: 15,000,000
Lane Kirkland, President
Thomas R. Donahue, Secretary-Treasurer

American Federation of Musicians
1500 Broadway
New York, NY 10036
(212) 869-1330
Membership: 330,000 (1978)

**American Federation of School Admin-
istrators, AFL – CIO**
110 East Forty-second Street
New York, NY 10017
(212) 697-5111
Membership: 9,958 (1978)
Peter S. O'Brien, President

**American Federation of State, County
and Municipal Employees**
1625 L Street, NW
Washington, DC 20036
(202) 452-4834
Membership: 1,020,000 (1978)
Gerald W. McEntee, International
President
William Lucy, International Secretary-
Treasurer

American Federation of Teachers, AFL-CIO
11 Dupont Circle, NW
Washington, DC 20036
(202) 797-4400
Membership: 580,000
Albert Shanker, President
Robert G. Porter, Secretary-Treasurer
James Ballard, Vice President
Constance Cabell, Vice President
Paul Cole, Vice President
Antonia Cortese, Vice President
Patrick Daly, Vice President
Kenneth J. Deedy, Vice President
Hugo Dennis, Jr., Vice President
Paul Devlin, Vice President
Sandra Feldman, Vice President
Albert Fondy, Vice President
Robert M. Healey, Vice President
Thomas Y. Hobart, Jr., Vice President
Sandra Irons, Vice President
Lorretta Johnson, Vice President
Eugene G. Kolach, Vice President
Jules Kolodny, Vice President
Nathaniel LaCour, Vice President
Herbert Magidson, Vice President
Richard Manley, Vice President
Edward J. McElroy, Jr., Vice President
James McGarvey, Vice President
John P. Murray, Vice President
Candice Owley, Vice President
Irwin H. Polishook, Vice President
Maria Portalatin, Vice President
Mary Ellen Riordan, Vice President
Flora Rogge, Vice President
Dan Sanders, Vice President
William H. Simons, Vice President
Judy Solkovits, Vice President
Walter Tice, Vice President
Pat Tornillo, Jr., Vice President
Jacqueline Vaughn, Vice President
Samuel Wakshull, Vice President

American Federation of TV and Radio Artists — AFL-CIO
1350 Avenue of the Americas
New York, NY 10019
(212) 265-7700
Membership: 55,000
(continued)

Sanford I. Wolff, National Executive Secretary
John C. Hall, Assistant Executive Secretary
Walter Grinspan, Research Director
Bill Hillman, President

American Flint Glass Workers Union
1440 South Byrne Road
Toledo, OH 43614
(419) 385-6687
Membership: 30,216
George M. Parker, President
Robert W. Newell, 1st Vice President
Eugene F. Bowling, 2nd Vice President
Ben Johnson, Jr., 3rd Vice President
Ivan T. Uncapher, Secretary-Treasurer
Lawrence Bankowski, Assistant Secretary

American Guild of Musical Artists
1841 Broadway
New York, NY 10023
(212) 265-3687
Membership: 5,000
Gene Boucher, President
De Lloyd Tibbs, National Executive Secretary

American Guild of Variety Artists
184 Fifth Avenue
New York, NY 10010
(212) 675-1003
Membership: 4,700
Alan Jan Nelson, Executive President
Rod McKuen, Executive Vice President
Don Phillips, Secretary-Treasurer

American Nurses' Association
2420 Pershing Road
Kansas City, MO 64108
(816) 474-5720
Membership: 187,000 (1978)
Eunice Cole, R.N., President
Judith Yates, R.N., Executive Director

American Postal Workers Union
817 Fourteenth Street, NW
Washington, DC 20005
(202) 842-4200
Membership: 320,000
(continued)

Moe Biller, General President

William Burrus, General Executive Vice President

Douglas Holbrook, General Secretary-Treasurer

John Richards, Industrial Relations Director

Lorenzo Stephens, Human Relations Director

Michael Zullo, Research and Education Director

Ben Zemsky, Organization Director

Patrick Nilan, Legislative Director

Roy Braunstein, Legislative Aide

John Morgen, President, Clerk Craft

Richard Wevodau, President, Maintenance Craft

Leon Hawkins, President, Motor Vehicle Craft

Mike Benner, President, Special Delivery

Kenneth Leiner, President, Mailhandlers Craft

Gerald Anderson, Executive Aide, Clerk Craft

Wallace Baldwin, Administrative Vice President, Clerk Craft

Kenny Wilson, Administrative Aide, Clerk Craft

Jim Adams, Administrative Aide, Maintenance Craft

Tom Freeman, Executive Vice President, Maintenance Craft

James Lingberg, National Representative at Large, Maintenance Craft

Leon Hopton, Administrative Vice President, Motor Vehicle Craft

American Radio Association

270 Madison Avenue

New York, NY 10016

(212) 689-5754

Membership: 1,000 (1978)

The American Railway and Airway Supervisors Association

3 Research Place

Rockville, MD 20850

(301) 948-4910

Membership: 7,054 (1978)

American Train Dispatchers Association

1401 South Harlem Avenue

Berwyn, IL 60402

(312) 795-5656

Membership: 3,300 (1978)

D. E. Collins, President

J. P. Erickson, Secretary-Treasurer

D. V. Chandler, Vice President

R. J. Irvin, Vice President

R. E. Johnson, Vice President

M. H. Kassera, Vice President

American Watch Workers Union

617 West Orange Street

Lancaster, PA 17603

(717) 392-7255

Arizona Public Employees' Association

420 North Fifteenth Avenue

Phoenix, AZ 85007

(602) 252-6501

Membership: 10,000

Luis Arellano, Executive Director

Arizona State AFL-CIO

520 West Adams Street

Phoenix, AZ 85003

(602) 258-3407

Assembly of Governmental Employees

1730 Rhode Island Avenue, NW

Washington, DC 20036

(202) 347-5628

Membership: 30 independent public employee labor organizations

William A. Craib, President

Laura M. Williams, Vice President

Gayle M. Watson, Secretary-Treasurer

Richard F. Dorman, Executive Director

Associated Actors and Artistes of America

165 West Forty-sixth Street

New York, NY 10036

(212) 869-0358

Membership: 78,000 (1978) This international union does not have individual memberships but consists of the following national unions: Actors' Equity Association; American Federation of Television and Radio Artists; American
(continued)

Guild of Musical Artists; American Guild of Variety Artistes; Asociacion Puertorriquena de Artistas y Tecnicos del Espectaculo; Hebrew Actors' Union, Inc.; Italian Actors Union; Screen Actors Guild; Screen Extras Guild.
Frederick O'Neal, President
Harold M. Hoffman, Treasurer
Sanford I. Wolff, Executive Secretary
Kenneth Orsatti, 1st Vice President
De Lloyd Tibbs, 2nd Vice President
Willard Swire, 3rd Vice President
Roy H. Wallack, 4th Vice President
Alan Jan Nelson, 5th Vice President

Association of Civilian Technicians
932 Hungerford Drive
Rockville, MD 20850
(301) 762-5656
Membership: 11,000
John T. Hunter, President
Jack H. Reagor, Executive Vice President
Donald E. Bean, Secretary
James D. Ellis, Vice President
Thomas Bastas, Vice President
William L. Spence, Vice President

Association of Flight Attendants
1625 Massachusetts Avenue, NW
Washington, DC 20036
(202) 328-5400
Membership: 23,000
Linda A. Puchala, President
Susan Bianchi Sand, Vice President
Pamela Casey, Secretary-Treasurer

Association of Labor Relations Agencies
P.O. Box 231
New Brunswick, NJ 08903
(201) 932-9866
Membership: 70
John F. Tesauro, President
Msgr. James A. Healy, President-Elect
John R. Loihl, 1st Vice President
Joan G. Dolan, Vice President—Labor Relations
Edward M. Allen, Vice President— Mediation & Arbitration
Jeffrey B. Tener, Executive Director

Association of Professional Flight Attendants
1220 North State Street
Chicago, IL 60610
(312) 266-9687

Association of Professional Orchestra Leaders
4711 Golf Road
Skokie, IL 60076
(312) 679-5702

Association of Western Pulp and Paper Workers
1430 Southwest Clay
Portland, OR 97201
(503) 228-7486

Atlantic Independent Union
1500 Market Street
Philadelphia, PA 19101
(215) 564-3790
Membership: 3,700
John W. Kerr, President
John W. Hawley, Vice President
Anthony J. Dellaratta, Secretary
Joseph J. Wenke, Treasurer

Bakery, Confectionery and Tobacco Workers International Union
10401 Connecticut Avenue
Kensington, MD 20795
(301) 468-3700
Membership: 166,858 (1978)

Barbers, Beauticians, and Allied Industries International Association
3500 Rockville Road
Indianapolis, IN 46222
(317) 241-6508
Membership: 40,000 (1978)

Brotherhood of Locomotive Engineers
1365 Ontario Street
Cleveland, OH 44114
(216) 241-2630
Membership: 40,000
John F. Sytsma, President
W. J. Wanke, 1st Vice President
John D. Rinehart, General Secretary-Treasurer

Brotherhood of Maintenance of Way Employes
12050 Woodward Avenue
Highland Park, MI 48203
(313) 868-0490
Membership: 119,203 (1978)

Brotherhood of Railroad Signalmen
601 West Golf Road
Mt. Prospect, IL 60056
(312) 439-3732
Membership: 12,972 (1978)

Brotherhood of Railway, Airline and Steamship Clerks, Freight Handlers, Express and Station Employes
3 Research Place
Rockville, MD 20850
(301) 948-4910
Membership: 205,000
R. I. Kilroy, International President
D. A. Bobo, International Secretary-Treasurer

Brotherhood of Railway Carmen of the United States and Canada
4929 Main Street
Kansas City, MO 64112
(816) 561-1112
Membership: 100,000
O. W. Jacobson, General President
W. O. Hearn, Assistant General President
O. P. Channell, Jr., General Secretary-Treasurer
C. W. Hauck, Editor and Manager
Paul Raymond, General Vice President
William G. Fairchild, General Vice President
Sam Bongiovanni, General Vice President
C. C. Bevins, General Vice President
W. D. Crawford, General Vice President
H. O. Crane, General Vice President
W. H. Smith, General Vice President
C. E. Wheeler, General Vice President
J. L. Bailey, General Vice President
J. C. Clementi, General Vice President
N. G. Robison, General Vice President

Brotherhood of Shoe and Allied Craftsmen
838 Main Street
Brockton, MA 02401
(617) 587-2606

Brotherhood of Utility Workers of New England, Inc.
212 Union Street
Providence, RI 02903
(401) 751-6829
Membership: 3,000
Hugh J. Foley, Jr., National President
George P. Fogarty, National Business Representative
Joseph P. Tracy, National Treasurer
Frederick J. Holland, National Secretary
Edmund J. Rourke, National Executive Vice President
Elaine M. Gonsalves, National Vice President
John R. Hayes, National Vice President

California Labor Federation
995 Market Street
San Francisco, CA 94103
(415) 986-3585

California State Employees Association
1108 O Street
Sacramento, CA 95814
(916) 444-8134
Membership: 93,200
Dan L. Western, General Manager
Gerald J. Gress, Controller
Ken Murch, Operations Administrator
Bernard L. Allamano, Chief Counsel
Michael Douglas, Chief Legislative Advocate
Robert Zech, Benefits Administrator
Keith Hearn, Communications Manager

Center for Research in Labor, Business and Community Relations
C & F, Room 2, University of Detroit
4001 West McNichols
Detroit, MI 48221
(313) 927-1355
Dr. Michael Whitty, Research Director

Christian Labor Association of the United States of America
9820 Gordon Street
Zeeland, MI 49464
(616) 772-9153
Don E. Leep, President
Paul Volkers, Vice President
Wayne Becksvoort, Secretary
Murvel Lambers, Treasurer
Byron Fahner, Assistant Secretary-
Treasurer

Civil Service Employees Association, Inc.
33 Elk Street
Albany, NY 12202
(518) 434-0191
Membership: 220,000
William L. McGowan, President
Thomas McDonough, Executive Vice
President
Irene Carr, Secretary
Barbara Fauser, Treasurer

Coalition of American Public Employees
1201 Sixteenth Street, NW
Washington, DC 20036
(202) 223-2267

Coalition of Black Trade Unionists
P.O. Box 13055
Washington, DC 20009
(202) 452-4837
William Lucy, President
Charles Hayes, Executive Vice President
Cleveland Robinson, 1st Vice President
Alzada Clark, 2nd Vice President
William Simons, Treasurer
Horace Sheffield, Secretary
Bob Simpson, Corresponding Secretary

Coalition of Labor Union Women
15 Union Square
New York, NY 10003
(212) 242-0700
Membership: 16,000
Joyce D. Miller, President
Addie Wyatt, Executive Vice President
Clara Day, Vice President
Evelyn Dubrow, Vice President
Pat Halpin, Vice President
(continued)

Georgia McGhee, Vice President
Gwen Newton, Vice President
Gloria Johnson, Treasurer
Odessa Komer, Corresponding Secretary
Patsy Fryman, Recording Secretary
Olga M. Madar, President Emerita

Colorado Association of State Employees
1390 Logan Street, #402
Denver, CO 80203
(303) 832-1001
Membership: 15,500
William J. Maguire, Jr., President
James P. Wilcox, Vice President
Joyce Becker, Secretary
Jean Zagar, Treasurer
Harry C. Reese, Executive Director

Colorado Laborer's District Council
855 Elati Street
Denver, CO 80204
(303) 892-9104

Communications Workers of America
1925 K Street, NW
Washington, DC 20006
(202) 785-6700
Membership: 625,000
Glenn E. Watts, President
Louis B. Knecht, Secretary-Treasurer
John C. Carroll, Executive Vice President
James B. Booe, Executive Vice President
M. E. Nichols, Executive Vice President

Congress of Independent Unions
303 Ridge Street
Alton, IL 62002
(618) 462-2447
Membership: 50,000 (1978)

Connecticut State AFL-CIO
9 Washington Avenue
Hamden, CT 06518
(203) 288-3591
John J. Driscoll, President
Betty L. Tianti, Secretary-Treasurer
Wayne Gilbert, Executive Vice President
Terrence Quinn, General Vice President
Dominic Badolato, Executive Secretary

Coopers International Union of North America, AFL-CIO
400 Sherburn Lane
Louisville, KY 40207
(502) 897-3274
Membership: 1,500
Ernest D. Higdon, President, Secretary-Treasurer
George Sager, Jr., 1st Vice President
Rubel Caldwell, 2nd Vice President
Robert Williams, 3rd Vice President
Robert Herron, 4th Vice President

Delaware State AFL-CIO
301 South Dupont Road
Wilmington, DE 19804
(302) 998-8801
John A. Campanelli, President
Norman L. Tyrie, Vice President
Edward F. Peterson, Secretary-Treasurer

Directors Guild of America, Inc.
7950 Sunset Boulevard
Los Angeles, CA 90046
(213) 656-1220
Membership: 6,500
Michael H. Franklin, National Executive Secretary
Jud Taylor, President
Ira Marvin, 1st Vice President
Gilbert Cates, 2nd Vice President
Enid Roth, 3rd Vice President
Jack Shea, 4th Vice President
Milt Felsen, 5th Vice President
Hal Cooper, Secretary
Marilyn Jacobs, Assistant Secretary
Sheldon Leonard, Treasurer
Max Schindler, Assistant Treasurer

Distillery, Wine and Allied Workers International Union
66 Grand Avenue
Englewood, NJ 07631
(201) 569-9212
Membership: 26,000 (1978)

Engineers and Scientists of California, AFL-CIO
340 Fremont Street
San Francisco, CA 94105
(continued)

(415) 433-7280
Membership: 2,500 (1978)
Peter P. Bartolo, Executive Director
David B. Moore, President
Joyce Thomas, Secretary-Treasurer

Federal Plant Quarantine Inspectors National Association
P.O. Box 73-A
Metairie, LA 70033
Membership: 324 (1978)
Jim Eddy, President

Federation of Westinghouse Independent Salaried Unions
505 Manor Building
Pittsburgh, PA 15219
(412) 471-3815
Membership: 12,000
Francis X. McTiernan, President
Ira J. Matthews, Secretary-Treasurer
William F. Welsh, Vice President
David E. Moses, Vice President
Frank A. Stasio, Vice President
E. W. Papiro, Vice President
Gus A. Geppi, Vice President
Joseph H. Hiltz, Financial Officer
Michael R. Gardinier, Financial Officer
Michael J. Utrata, Financial Officer

Flight Engineers' International Association, AFL-CIO
905 Sixteenth Street, NW
Washington, DC 20006
(202) 347-4511
Membership: 2,500
William A. Gill, Jr., President
Karl F. Anderson, Executive Vice President, Secretary-Treasurer
Donald F. Thielke, Vice President-Technical
Roger C. Brickness, 1st Vice President

Florida AFL-CIO
125 South Monroe Street
Tallahassee, FL 32301
(904) 224-6926
Membership: 350,000
Daniel J. Miller, President
Donald G. Resha, 1st Vice President
Joseph E. Martin, Secretary-Treasurer

Fraternal Order of Police
5613 Belair Road
Baltimore, MD 21206
(301) 488-6880
Membership: 155,000
Leo V. Marchetti, President
Richard Lis, Vice President
Dorothy A. Woods, Secretary
Richard Boyd, Treasurer
James Whaley, Conductor
Anthony Mohatt, Guard
David Green, Chairman of the Board
of Trustees

Glass, Pottery, Plastics and Allied Workers
608 East Baltimore Pike, P.O. Box 607
Media, PA 19063
(215) 565-5051
Membership: 91,000
James E. Hatfield, International President
Lester H. Null, Assistant to the President
Frank W. Carter, International Secretary-
Treasurer

The Graphic Artists Guild
30 East Twentieth Street
New York, NY 10003
(212) 777-7353
Membership: 5,000
Gerald McConnell, Chairman
Diane Dillon, President
Noel Becker, Co-Treasurer
Jeff Feinen, Co-Treasurer
Simms Taback, Co-Secretary
Karen Watkins, Co-Secretary
D. K. Holland, Executive Vice President

Graphic Arts International Union
1900 L Street, NW
Washington, DC 20036
(202) 872-7963
Membership: 120,000
Kenneth J. Brown, President
James J. Norton, Secretary-Treasurer
Eugene M. Boerner, Executive Vice
President
William A. Schroeder, Vice President
Murray McKenzie, Vice President
Leonard Adams, Vice President
(continued)

Felicia Bonelli, Vice President
Joseph H. Gast, Vice President
Leonard Paquette, Vice President
John Greer, Vice President

Hawaii State AFL-CIO
547 Halekauwila Street
Honolulu, HI 96813
(808) 536-4945
Walter H. Kupau, President
John Akana, Vice President
D. Leilani Bush, Vice President
Marvin Ching, Vice President
Nilda Chock, Vice President
Jose Encarnacion, Vice President
Jessica Kirk, Vice President
Emil Lee, Vice President
Dennis Maedo, Vice President
Samson Mamizuka, Vice President
Wallace Mitsunago, Vice President
Pat Nagao, Vice President
Charles Ng, Vice President
John Kramer, Vice President
Fusao Ogoshi, Vice President
Russell Okata, Vice President
Thomas Sing, Vice President
William Smith, Vice President
Thaddeus Tomei, Vice President
Benjamin Toyama, Vice President
Joseph Viela, Vice President
Gordon Yanagawa, Vice President

Hebrew Actors Union, Inc.
31 East Seventh Street
New York, NY 10003
(212) 674-1923

Hotel and Restaurant Employees and Bartenders International Union
120 East Fourth Street
Cincinnati, OH 45202
(513) 621-0300
Membership: 403,890 (1978)
Edward T. Hanley, President
John Gibson, Secretary-Treasurer

Idaho Public Employees Association
1434 West Bannock
Boise, ID 83702
(208) 336-2841
(continued)

Membership: 4,000
Jim Evans, President
Dale McGraw, Vice President
Evelyn Drumheiler, Secretary-Treasurer

Idaho State AFL-CIO
225 North Sixteenth
Boise, ID 83706
(208) 345-8582

Illinois State AFL-CIO
300 North State Street
Chicago, IL 60610
(312) 222-1414

Illinois State Employees Association
2800 South Walnut Street
Springfield, IL 62704
(217) 525-1944

Independent Bakery Employees Union
P.O. Box 188
Alexandria, LA 71301
Irving Ward-Steinman, General Counsel

Independent Hospital Employees Union
P.O. Box 188
Alexandria, LA 71301
Irving Ward-Steinman, General Counsel

**Independent Union of Plant Protection
Employees**
243 Western Avenue
Lynn, MA 01904
(617) 581-0461
Membership: 325
William D. Fallon, President
Robert F. Muchmore, Vice President
Nicholas Petitto, Vice President
Peter A. Colbert, Financial Secretary
Linda Dixon, Recording Secretary

Independent Watchmen's Association
8519 Eighty-sixth Street
Brooklyn, NY 11259
(212) 836-3508
Membership: 4,000 (1978)

Indiana State AFL-CIO
1701 West Eighteenth Street
Indianapolis, IN 46202
(317) 632-9147
Ernest C. Jones, President
Max F. Wright, Secretary-Treasurer

Indiana State Employees Association
17 West Market Street
Indianapolis, IN 46204
(317) 632-7254
Membership: 4,000
Larry D. Kump, Executive Director
Fred Towe, Chief Counsel
Eli Gould, Labor Relations Specialist

**Industrial Union of Marine and Ship-
building Workers of America**
8121 Georgia Avenue
Silver Spring, MD 20910
(301) 589-8820
Membership: 25,000 (1978)

**Institute of Collective Bargaining and
Group Relations, Inc.**
49 East Sixty-eighth Street
New York, NY 10021
(212) 794-3269
Colonel Frank Borman, Chairman
William W. Winpisinger, President
Theodore W. Kheel, Administrative
Director
Ronald W. Haughton, Associate Admin-
istrative Director

**Insurance Workers International Union,
AFL-CIO**
1017 Twelfth Street, NW
Washington, DC 20005
(202) 842-1127
Membership: 20,000 (1978)
Joseph Pollack, President
Nicholas M. Rongione, Secretary-
Treasurer
Andre Henault, Vice President
Pat McGrogan, Vice President
Lawrence Pellegrini, Vice President

International Alliance of Theatrical Stage Employes and Moving Picture Machine Operators of the United States and Canada
1515 Broadway
New York, NY 10036
(202) 730-1770
Membership: 62,000 (1978)

International Allied Printing Trades Association
2710 Hampton Avenue
St. Louis, MO 63139
(314) 647-2266

International Association of Bridge, Structural and Ornamental Iron Workers, AFL-CIO
1750 New York Avenue, NW
Washington, DC 20006
(202) 383-4800
Membership: 182,685
John H. Lyons, General President
Juel D. Drake, General Secretary
Charles R. Anding, General Treasurer

International Association of Fire Fighters
1750 New York Avenue, NW
Washington, DC 20006
(202) 872-8484
Membership: 176,000 (1978)
John A. Gannon, President
Martin E. Pierce, Secretary-Treasurer

International Association of Heat and Frost Insulators and Asbestos Workers
1300 Connecticut Avenue, NW
Washington, DC 20036
(202) 785-2388
Membership: 19,681 (1978)
Andrew T. Haas, General President
William G. Bernard, General Secretary-Treasurer

International Association of Machinists and Aerospace Workers (AFL-CIO)
1300 Connecticut Avenue, NW
Washington, DC 20036
(202) 857-5200
(continued)

Membership: 900,000
William W. Winpisinger, International President
Eugene D. Glover, General Secretary-Treasurer
Thomas Ducy, General Vice President
Sal Iaccio, General Vice President
Stanley E. Jensen, General Vice President
Justin J. Ostro, General Vice President
John F. Peterpaul, General Vice President
George J. Poulin, General Vice President
Merle E. Pryor, General Vice President
Mike Rygus, General Vice President
Roe Spencer, General Vice President

International Association of Tool Craftsmen
1915 Arrowline Court
Bettendorf, IA 52722
(319) 332-6147
Membership: 212
Arthur W. DeKoster, President
Daniel W. Ormsby, Vice President
James J. Ryan, Secretary
Robert F. Moore, Treasurer
Michael Loomis, Trustee
Robert Douglas, Trustee

International Brotherhood of Boilermakers, Iron Shipbuilders, Blacksmiths, Forgers and Helpers
New Brotherhood Building
Eighth Street at State Avenue
Kansas City, KS 66101
(913) 371-2640
Membership: 145,500 (1978)

International Brotherhood of Correctional Officers
2139 Wisconsin Avenue, NW
Washington, DC 20007
(202) 965-4411

International Brotherhood of Electrical Workers
1125 Fifteenth Street, NW
Washington, DC 20005
(202) 833-7000
(continued)

Membership: 1,011,726 (1978)
Charles H. Pillard, President
Ralph A. Leigon, Secretary

International Brotherhood of Firemen and Oilers
200 Maryland Avenue, NE
Washington, DC 20002
(202) 547-7540
Membership: 43,000 (1978)
George J. Francisco, International President
Michael A. Matz, International Secretary-Treasurer

International Brotherhood of Painters and Allied Trades, AFL-CIO
1750 New York Avenue, NW
Washington, DC 20006
(202) 637-0700
Membership: 200,000
S. Frank Raftery, General President
Robert Petersdorg, General Secretary-Treasurer
Bernard A. Sniegowski, General Vice President
A. L. Monroe, General Vice President
James H. Wolford, General Vice President
Jack T. Cox, General Vice President
Guy W. Leber, General Vice President
James B. Cox, General Vice President
William A. Duval, General Vice President

International Brotherhood of Police Officers
2139 Wisconsin Avenue, NW
Washington, DC 20007
(202) 965-4415

International Brotherhood of Teamsters
25 Louisiana Avenue, NW
Washington, DC 20001
(202) 624-6800
Membership: 1,923,896 (1978)
Roy L. Williams, General President
Ray Schoessling, General Secretary-Treasurer

International Chemical Workers Union
1655 West Market Street
Akron, OH 44313
(216) 867-2444
Membership: 60,000
Frank D. Martino, President
William J. Sparks, Secretary-Treasurer
George McDevitt, Vice President
Lawrence J. Ahern, Vice President
W. A. Joiner, Vice President
Ralph Brannon, Vice President
Angelo A. Russo, Vice President
Arthur O. Burns, Vice President
Arthur G. Wood, Vice President

International Confederation of Free Trade Unions (ICFTU)
104 East Fortieth Street
New York, NY 10016
(212) 986-1820
Headquarters: 37-41 rue Montagne aux Herbes Potagères, Brussels, Belgium
Membership: 85,000,000
P. P. Narayanan, President
Otto Kersten, General Secretary
J. Vanderveken, Assistant General Secretary

International Federation of Health Professionals
295 Madison Avenue
New York, NY 10017
(212) 689-7040

International Guards Union of America
1444 Gardiner Lane
Louisville, KY 40213
(502) 454-0278
Membership: 2,500
A. L. McLemore, President
Raymond G. Curtis, Secretary-Treasurer
W. M. Fleming, Trustee
Robert L. Byrd, Trustee
Paul Sartin, Trustee

International Jewelry Workers Union
8 East Fortieth Street
New York, NY 10018
(212) 244-8793

International Labor Office, Washington Branch
1750 New York Avenue, NW
Washington, DC 20006
(202) 376-2315
Membership: This is a specialized agency associated with the United Nations; membership consists of 148 countries.
James H. Quackenbush, Director
David A. Waugh, Deputy Director
Patricia S. Hord, Information Resource Officer

International Labor Press Association, AFL-CIO/CLC
815 Sixteenth Street, NW
Washington, DC 20006
(202) 637-5068
Membership: 700
Diane Curry, President

International Ladies Garment Workers Union
1710 Broadway
New York, NY 10019
(212) 265-7000
Membership: 340,936
Sol C. Chaikin, President
Wilbur Daniels, Executive Vice President
Frederick Siems, Executive Vice President
Shelley Appleton, General Secretary-Treasurer

International Leather Goods, Plastic and Novelty Workers' Union
265 West Fourteenth Street
New York, NY 10011
(212) 675-9240
Membership: 27,000 (1978)

International Longshoremen's & Warehousemen's Union
1188 Franklin
San Francisco, CA 94109
(415) 775-0533
Membership: 55,000
James R. Herman, President
Curtis McClain, Secretary-Treasurer
Rudy Rubio, Vice President
George Martin, Vice President

International Longshoremen's Association
17 Battery Place
New York, 10004
(212) 425-1200
Membership: 77,119 (1978)

International Molders and Allied Workers Union
1225 East McMillan Street
Cincinnati, OH 45206
(513) 221-1526
Membership: 57,000
Carl W. Studenroth, President
Andrew J. Swafford, Secretary-Treasurer
Bernard Butsavage, Executive Vice President
Orian Williams, Vice President
Charles Boyd, Vice President
George Roper, Vice President
Edward Witthames, Vice President
Paul Parker, Vice President
James Rankin, Vice President
Frank Willey, Vice President
Stanley J. Mierzejewski, Financier-Auditor

International Organization of Masters, Mates and Pilots
39 Broadway
New York, NY 10006
(212) 425-3860
Membership: 7,881 (1978)
Robert J. Lowen, President

International Plate Printers, Die Stampers, Engravers Union (AFL-CIO; CLC)
228 South Swarthmore Avenue
Ridley Park, PA 19078
(215) 521-2495
Membership: 400 (1978)
C. Healy, Sr., President
R. Ryan, Vice President
E. Major, Vice President
J. Donegan, Jr., Secretary-Treasurer

International Printing and Graphic Communications Union
1730 Rhode Island Avenue, NW
Washington, DC 20036
(202) 293-2185
Membership: 120,000 (1978)

International Production, Service and Sales Union
100 Livingston Street
Brooklyn, NY 11201
(212) 858-4900
Membership: 21,000 (1978)

International Typographical Union
301 South Union
Colorado Springs, CO 80901
(303) 471-2460
Membership: 80,000
Joe Bingel, President
Thomas W. Kopeck, Secretary-Treasurer

International Union, Allied Industrial Workers of America, AFL-CIO
3520 West Oklahoma Avenue
Milwaukee, WI 53215
(414) 645-9500
Membership: 70,000
Dominick D'Ambrosio, President
William J. Salamone, Secretary-Treasurer
Charles Street, Board Member-at-Large
Nick Serraglio, Region #3 Director
J. B. Arnold, Jr., Region #4 Director
Robert Kellermann, Region #6 Director
Robert Brenner, Region #7 Director
Lyle Daugherty, Region #8 Director
Robert Johnson, Region #9 Director

International Union of Allied, Novelty and Production Workers
147 East Twenty-sixth Street
New York, NY 10010
(212) 889-1212
Membership: 33,500 (1978)

International Union of Bricklayers and Allied Craftsmen
815 Fifteenth Street, NW
Washington, DC 20005
(202) 783-3788
John T. Joyce, President
Edward M. Bellucci, Secretary-Treasurer

International Union of Electrical, Radio and Machine Workers, AFL-CIO, CLC
1126 Sixteenth Street, NW
Washington, DC 20036
(continued)

(202) 296-1200
Membership: 225,000
William H. Bywater, President
Edward Fire, Secretary-Treasurer

International Union of Elevator Constructors
5565 Sterret Place
Columbia, MD 21044
(301) 997-9000
Membership: 17,900 (1978)

International Union of Gas Workers
2424 Pennsylvania Avenue, NW
Washington, DC 20037
(202) 293-4333
Membership: 1,425
Wayne A. Gochenour, President
William A. Coles, Vice President
Kenneth L. Palmer, Financial Secretary-Treasurer
William E. Williams, Jr., Recording Secretary
Michael D. Savin, Trustee
Donald L. Lemon, Trustee
Joe Taylor, Jr., Trustee
Randolph A. Fortune, Sergeant at Arms
John Quade, Guide

International Union of Life Insurance Agents
161 West Wisconsin Avenue
Milwaukee, WI 53203
(414) 273-7849
Membership: 1,200
Robert C. Schuetz, President
C. M. Pulliam, Executive Vice President
Joseph Girard, General Vice President
Donald Ratliff, General Financial Secretary-Treasurer
James A. Wegner, Wisconsin Regional Vice President
Dick Petersen, Minnesota Regional Vice President
Vince Vega, Ohio Regional Vice President
Geraldine A. Gallen, Administrator

International Union of Operating Engineers

1125 Seventeenth Street, NW
Washington, DC 20036
(202) 347-8560
Membership: 411,860 (1978)

International Union of Petroleum and Industrial Workers, SIUNA, AFL-CIO

8131 East Rosecrans Boulevard
Paramount, CA 90723
(213) 630-6232
Membership: 4,000
Carroll G. Clark, International President
Robert H. Madigan, International
    Secretary-Treasurer
George R. Beltz, Senior International
    Representative
Thomas C. Walsh, Sr., International
    Representative
Donald Harris, International
    Representative
Robert Davidson, International
    Representative
Raymond Pounds, Business Agent
Thomas Rincon, Business Agent
Glenn Toon, Senior International
    Representative

International Union of Police Associations, AFL-CIO

422 First Street, SE
Washington, DC 20003
(202) 546-0010
Membership: 30,000
Edward J. Kiernan, President
Robert D. Gordon, Secretary-Treasurer

International Union of Security Officers

2404 Merced Street
San Leandro, CA 94577
(415) 895-9905
Membership: 7,000
Charles A. Plato, International President
Bruce G. Burt, International Secretary-
    Treasurer
Charles A. Newport, International Vice
    President

International Union of Tool, Die and Mold Makers

71 East Cherry Street
Rahway, NJ 07065
(201) 388-3323
Membership: 500
Henry F. Schickling, International
    President
Anthony Calello, Vice President
Albino Jeronimo, Secretary
Julius Puchammer, Treasurer
Edward Chudzinski, Chairman, Executive
    Advisory Committee

International Union, United Automobile, Aerospace and Agricultural Implement Workers of America

8000 East Jefferson
Detroit, MI 48214
(313) 926-5000
Membership: 1,300,000
Owen Bieber, President
Raymond Majerus, Secretary-Treasurer
Donald F. Ephlin, Vice President
Martin Gerber, Vice President
Odessa Komer, Vice President
Marc Stepp, Vice President
Robert White, Vice President
Stephen P. Yokich, Vice President

International Union, United Plant Guard Workers of America

25510 Kelly Road
Roseville, MI 48066
(313) 772-7250
Membership: 27,000
James C. McGahey, President
Francis E. Fitzpatrick, Secretary-
    Treasurer
Henry E. Applen, Vice President
Albert L. Ross, Director, Region 1
Donald G. Roehl, Director, Region 2
Gerry E. Hartlage, Director, Region 3
Donal E. Bray, Director, Region 4
John J. Baumler, Director, Region 6
Jack Russell, Director, Region 10
Robert F. Voie, Director, Region 11

International Woodworkers of America, AFL-CIO & CLC
1622 North Lombard Street
Portland, OR 97217
(503) 285-5281
Membership: 115,000
Keith W. Johnson, President
Fernie J. Viala, 1st Vice President
Bud Rahberger, 2nd Vice President
Robert Gerwig, Secretary-Treasurer

Iowa Federation of Labor, AFL-CIO
2000 Walker Street
Des Moines, IA 50317
(515) 262-9571
James J. Wengert, President
Mark L. Smith, Secretary-Treasurer
Donald P. Rowen, Executive Vice
  President
Leo Ruth, Vice President
Patricia Marshall, Vice President
Gene Redman, Vice President
Perry Chapin, Vice President
Joan Little, Vice President
Ken Rains, Vice President
William Fenton, Vice President
Steve Elliott, Vice President
Lloyd Freilinger, Vice President

Italian Actors Union
184 Fifth Avenue
New York, NY 10010
Sal Carollo, Executive Secretary

Kansas State Federation of Labor
110 West Sixth
Topeka, KS 66601
(913) 357-0396

Kentucky State AFL-CIO
706 East Broadway
Louisville, KY 40202
(502) 589-1360

Labor Policy Association, Inc.
1015 Fifteenth Street, NW
Washington, DC 20005
(202) 789-8670
Kenneth C. McGuiness, Vice President
  and General Counsel

Labor Research Associates, Institute for Technological Humanism
C & F, Room 2, University of Detroit
4001 West Nichols
Detroit, MI 48221
(313) 927-1355
Dr. Michael Whitty, Research Director

Labor Research Association, Inc.
80 East Eleventh Street
New York, NY 10003
(212) 473-1042
Sidney Gluck, President
Ernest DeMaio, Vice President
Frank Goldsmith, Secretary-Treasurer

Laborers' International Union of North America
905 Sixteenth Street, NW
Washington, DC 20006
(202) 737-8320
Membership: 610,000 (1978)
Angelo Fosco, President
Arthur E. Coia, Secretary-Treasurer

Laundry and Dry Cleaning International Union
307 Fourth Avenue
Pittsburgh, PA 15215
(412) 281-8105
Membership: 17,365 (1978)

Leather Workers International Union, AFL-CIO
11 Peabody Square
Peabody, MA 01960
(617) 531-5605
Membership: 2,110 (1978)
James L. Sawyer, President
Albano Quadros, Secretary-Treasurer

Louisiana AFL-CIO
429 Government Street
Baton Rouge, LA 70821
(504) 383-5741

Machine Printers and Engravers Association of the United States
690 Warren Avenue
East Providence, RI 02914
(continued)

(401) 438-3911
Membership: 500
John J. Phillips, President
David J. Bernier, Secretary-Treasurer
Joseph F. Hodge, 1st Vice President
Robert P. Whinlow, 2nd Vice President
John A. Nex, 3rd Vice President
Pierce C. Owens, 4th Vice President
Earl T. Whitmire, 5th Vice President

Maine AFL-CIO
72 Center Street
Brewer, ME 04412
(207) 989-3630

Maine State Employees Association
65 State Street
Augusta, ME 04330
(207) 622-3151
Membership: 12,000
Richard Trahey, President
Gerry Stanton, Vice President
John Oliver, Executive Director
Jack Finn, Chief Counsel
Joseph Mackey, Assistant Executive
  Director

**Major League Baseball Players
  Association**
1370 Avenue of the Americas
New York, NY 10019
(212) 581-8484
Marvin J. Miller, Executive Director
Donald M. Fehr, General Counsel
Peter Rose, Associate Counsel

**Marine Firemen's Union (Pacific Coast
  Marine Firemen, Oilers, Watertenders
  and Wipers Association)**
240 Second Street
San Francisco, CA 94105
(415) 362-4592
Membership: 627
Henry Disley, President
B. C. Shoup, Vice President
Joel E. McCrum, Treasurer

**Maryland Classified Employees
  Association, Inc.**
7127 Rutherford Road
Baltimore, MD 21207
(301) 298-8800
Membership: 27,000
Joseph Adler, Executive Director

Maryland State and D.C. AFL-CIO
93 Main Street
Annapolis, MD 21401
(301) 269-1940 (Baltimore)
(202) 261-1400 (DC)
Membership: 500,000
Thomas M. Bradley, President
Edward A. Mohler, Secretary-Treasurer

Massachusetts AFL-CIO
6 Beacon Street
Boston, MA 02108
(617) 227-8260
Membership: 500,000
Arthur R. Osborn, President
George E. Carpenter, Jr., Secretary-
  Treasurer
Joseph P. Lydon, Executive Vice
  President
Russell P. Campbell, Executive Vice
  President

**Mechanics Educational Society of
  America**
15300 East Seven Mile Road
Detroit, MI 48205
(313) 372-5700
Membership: 25,000 (1978)

**Metal Polishers, Buffers, Platers and
  Allied Workers International Union**
5578 Montgomery Road
Cincinnati, OH 45212
(513) 531-2500
Membership: 10,000 (1978)

Michigan State AFL-CIO
419 South Washington Avenue
Lansing, MI 48933
(517) 487-5966
William C. Marshall, President
Walter L. Oliver, Secretary-
  Treasurer

Michigan State Employees Association
P.O. Box 13158
Lansing, MI 48901
(517) 372-9104
Membership: 18,872 (1978)

Minnesota AFL-CIO
175 Aurora Avenue
St. Paul, MN 55103
(612) 227-7647

Mississippi AFL-CIO
P.O. Box 2010
Jackson, MS 39205
(601) 948-0517
Claude Ramsay, President
Thomas Knight, Secretary-Treasurer

Missouri State Labor Council
208 Madison Street
Jefferson City, MO 65101
(314) 634-2115

Montana Public Employees Association
P.O. Box 5600
Helena, MT 59601
(406) 442-4600
Membership: 6,700 (1978)

Montana State AFL-CIO
P.O. Box 1176
Helena, MT 59624
(406) 442-1708
Membership: 26,000
James W. Murry, Executive Secretary
Jerry Driscoll, President
Nadiean Jensen, Vice President

National Alliance of Postal and Federal Employees
1644 Eleventh Street, NW
Washington, DC 20001
(202) 332-4313
Membership: 20,000 (1978)

National Association of Air Traffic Specialists
Wheaton Plaza North
Wheaton, MD 20902
(301) 946-0882
Membership: 2,200
(continued)

Lawrence C. Cushing, President-Executive Director
Donald Leatherman, Treasurer-Budget Director
Mary J. Carter, National Secretary

National Association of ASCS County Office Employees
P.O. Box 242
Gettysburg, PA 17325

National Association of Broadcast Employees and Technicians, AFL-CIO
7101 Wisconsin Avenue
Bethesda, MD 20814
(301) 657-8420
Membership: 7,300 (1978)
Edward M. Lynch, International President
James P. Nolan, International Vice President
Duane R. Corder, International Secretary-Treasurer

National Association of Government Employees
2139 Wisconsin Avenue, NW
Washington, DC 20007
(202) 965-4411
Membership: 200,000 (1978)

National Association of Governmental Labor Officials
c/o Al Meier, 307 East Seventh Street
Des Moines, IA 50319
(515) 281-3447
Membership: 48
Lias B. Steen, President
William Shipps, Vice President
Allen J. Meier, Secretary-Treasurer

National Association of Letter Carriers
100 Indiana Avenue, NW
Washington, DC 20001
(202) 393-4695
Membership: 240,000
Vincent R. Sombrotto, President
Tony R. Huerta, Executive Vice President
Francis J. Conners, Vice President
Richard P. O'Connell, Secretary-Treasurer
(continued)

Halline Overby, Assistant Secretary-
Treasurer
Joseph H. Johnson, Jr., Director of
City Delivery
William M. Dunn, Jr., Director, Life
Insurance
Robert J. Buntz, Director, Health
Insurance
Anthony B. Morell, Assistant Director,
Health Insurance
Mark Roth, Director of Retired Members
George Davis, Jr., Trustee
James G. Souza, Jr., Trustee
James Worsham, Trustee

**National Association of Municipal
Employees**
2139 Wisconsin Avenue, NW
Washington, DC 20007
(202) 965-4411

**National Association of Postal
Supervisors**
490 L'Enfant Plaza, SW
Washington, DC 20024-2120
(202) 484-6070
Membership: 35,000
Donald N. Ledbetter, President
Maurice J. Twomey, Executive
Vice President
Rubin Handelman, Secretary

**National Association of Public
Employees**
1730 Rhode Island Avenue, NW
Washington, DC 20005
(202) 232-2626

**National Brotherhood of Packinghouse
and Industrial Workers**
3855 Bellcrossing Drive
Kansas City, KS 66104
(913) 342-4117
Membership: 1,400 (1978)

National Child Labor Committee
1501 Broadway
New York, NY 10036
(212) 840-1801
Membership: 5,000
Jeffrey Newman, Executive Director

National Council for Labor Reform
406 South Plymouth Court
Chicago, IL 60605
(312) 427-0206
Membership: 3,000
James Pluymert, President
Thomas H. Latimer, Executive Vice
President
Hon. Frank Angalone, Vice President
Frederick A. Faville, Vice President
Richard A. Thompson, Vice President
Carol Ann Arthur, Secretary
Robert J. Cassidy, Treasurer

National Education Association
1201 Sixteenth Street, NW
Washington, DC 20036
(202) 822-7000
Membership: 1,700,000
Willard H. McGuire, President
Bernie Freitag, Vice President
Mary H. Futrell, Secretary-Treasurer
Terry E. Herndon, Executive Director

**National Federation of Federal
Employees**
1016 Sixteenth Street, NW
Washington, DC 20036
(202) 862-4440
Membership: 150,000
James M. Peirce, Jr., National President
Abraham Orlofsky, National Secretary-
Treasurer
Paul C. McNaught, National Vice
President, Region 1
J. Richard Hall, National Vice President,
Region 2
A. B. Reynolds, National Vice President,
Region 3
Richard Reiman, National Vice President,
Region 4
Prospero Chavez, National Vice
President, Region 5
Marlene S. Steffen, National Vice
President, Region 6
Albert W. Lampton, National Vice
President, Region 7
Gary W. Divine, National Vice
President, Region 8
Charles G. Smith, National Vice
President, Region 9

National Federation of Independent Unions
1166 South Eleventh Street
Philadelphia, PA 19147
(215) 336-3300
F. J. Chiappardi, President
F. W. Tittle, Secretary-Treasurer

National Federation of Licensed Practical Nurses
888 Seventh Avenue
New York, NY 10019
(212) 246-6629
Membership: 18,000 (1978)

National Football League Players Association
1300 Connecticut Avenue, NW
Washington, DC 20036
(202) 463-2200
Membership: 1,475
Gene Upshaw, President
Jeff Van Note, Vice President
Dan Jiggetts, Vice President
Ed Garvey, Executive Director

National Industrial Workers Union
514 North Main Street
Lima, OH 45802
(419) 224-1031
Membership: 850
Duard Bellamy, President
Alonzo Wheeler, Business Manager
Douglas P. Suman, Vice President
Danny Spears, Vice President
Mrs. Alma Sherpe, Vice President
Ron Wilson, Vice President
Karin Jandt, Secretary-Treasurer

National Labor Law Center
2000 P Street, NW
Washington, DC 20036
(202) 785-2035

National Labor-Management Foundation
1901 L Street, NW
Washington, DC 20036
(202) 296-8577

National Labor Reform Committee
1430 K Street, NW
Washington, DC 20005
(202) 638-2921

National Labor Relations Board Professional Association
1717 Pennsylvania Avenue, NW
Washington, DC 20006
(202) 254-9156
Membership: 200
Martha R. Houser, President
Lafe Solonon, Vice President
Sue Gunter, Secretary
Genevieve Pluhowski, Treasurer

National Labor Relations Board Union
450 Golden Gate Avenue
San Francisco, CA 94102
(415) 556-3197
Membership: 1,350 (1978)

National League of Postmasters of the United States
1023 North Royal Street
Alexandria, VA 22314-1569
(703) 548-5922
Membership: 20,000 (1978)
R. Fain Hambright, President
Dale Alvestad, Executive Vice President
Barbara Veech, Secretary
Donald M. Gray, Treasurer
Gil V. Montanez, Vice President
Harvey Moritz, Vice President
Dorothy Van Beck, Vice President
Mary Worcester, Vice President

National Marine Engineers Beneficial Association
444 North Capitol Street
Washington, DC 20001
(202) 347-8585
Membership: 13,490 (1978)

National Maritime Union
346 West Seventeenth Street
New York, NY 10011
(212) 620-5700
Membership: 35,000
Shannon J. Wall, President
(continued)

Thomas Martinez, Secretary-Treasurer
James F. Paterson, Vice President
Rene Lioeanjie, Vice President
Louis Parise, Vice President

National Organization of Industrial Trade Unions
148-06 Hillside Avenue
Jamaica, NY 11435
(212) 291-3434

National Post Office Mail Handlers, Watchmen, Messengers and Group Leaders Division of the Laborers' International Union of North America, AFL-CIO
1225 Nineteenth Street, NW
Washington, DC 20036
(202) 833-9095
Membership: 40,000
Lonnie L. Johnson, National Director
Vito P. Magrino, Financial Officer
Aaron Preston, Member, Policy and Steering Committee
Al Walker, Member, Policy and Steering Committee
Michael Mathias, Jr., Member, Policy and Steering Committee
Jackie E. Lee, Member, Policy and Steering Committee
Alfred Harrington, Member, Policy and Steering Committee

National Right to Work Committee
8001 Braddock Road
Springfield, VA 22160
(703) 321-9820

National Rural Letter Carriers' Association
1750 Pennsylvania Avenue, NW
Washington, DC 20006
(202) 393-5840
Membership: 64,778
Wilbur S. Wood, President
Tom W. Griffith, Vice President
Olin F. Armentrout, Secretary-Treasurer
Dallas N. Fields, Director of Labor Relations

National Treasury Employees Union
1730 K Street, NW
Washington, DC 20006
(202) 785-4411
Membership: 70,000
Vincent L. Connery, National President
Robert M. Tobias, National Executive Vice President

National Union of Hospital and Health Care Employees
310 West Forty-third Street
New York, NY 10036
(212) 582-1890
Henry Nicholas, President
Jerome P. Brown, Secretary-Treasurer
Doris Turner, Secretary
Moe Foner, Executive Secretary
Robert Muehlenkamp, Executive Vice President for Organization
Leon J. Davis, President Emeritus

National Weather Service Employees Organization
444 North Capitol Street
Washington, DC 20001
(202) 783-3131
Membership: 1,300
Leo R. Harrison, Jr., President
Joseph V. Knack, Executive Vice President
Stanley Marczewski, National Vice President
Robert Frazier, Secretary-Treasurer

Nebraska Association of Public Employees
1302 J Street
Lincoln, NE 68508
(402) 475-5221
Membership: 1,330 (1978)

Nebraska State AFL-CIO
4660 South Sixtieth Avenue
Omaha, NE 68117
(402) 734-1300

Nevada State AFL-CIO
P.O. Box 2115
Carson City, NV 89701
(continued)

(702) 882-7490
Mark Tully Massagli, President
Claude Evans, Executive Secretary-
 Treasurer

**New Hampshire State Employees
 Association**
163 Manchester Street
Concord, NH 03301
(603) 271-3411
Membership: 5,300 (1978)

New Hampshire State Labor Council
P.O. Box 1305
Portsmouth, NH 03801
(603) 431-7155

New Jersey State AFL-CIO
106 West State Street
Trenton, NY 08608
(609) 392-1006

New Mexico State AFL-CIO
5905 Marble NE
Albuquerque, NM 87110
(505) 262-2629
Membership: 36,000
Neal Gonzalez, Executive Secretary-
 Treasurer
Mary Sue Gutierrez, COPE Director
C. M. Norris, President
Frutoso Chavez, 1st Vice President

New York State AFL-CIO
451 Park Avenue South
New York, NY 10016
(212) 689-9320

The Newspaper Guild
1125 Fifteenth Street, NW
Washington, DC 20005
(202) 296-2990
Membership: 33,000
Charles A. Perlik, Jr., President
Charles Dale, Secretary-Treasurer
Harry S. Culver, International
 Chairperson

North Carolina State AFL-CIO
P.O. Box 10805
Raleigh, NC 27605
(919) 833-6678

**North Carolina State Employees
 Association**
P.O. Drawer 27727
Raleigh, NC 27611
(919) 833-6436
Membership: 25,000
Emmett W. Burden, Executive Director
Graham Goodwin, Assistant Director
Leonard W. S. Wilson, Assistant Director

North Dakota AFL-CIO
1533 North Twelfth Street
Bismarck, ND 58501
(701) 223-0784
Membership: 15,500-16,500
James Gerl, President
Robert A. Donegan, Secretary-
 Treasurer
Raymond Such, 1st Vice President
James Robillard, Vice President
John Gefroh, Vice President
Ronald Vetsch, Vice President
William Couchigian, Vice President
Alton Schuette, Vice President
James McLaughlin, Vice President

**Office and Professional Employees
 International Union**
265 West Fourteenth Street
New York, NY 10011
(212) 675-3210
Membership: 105,000 (1978)
John Kelly, President

Ohio AFL-CIO
271 East State Street
Columbus, OH 43215
(614) 224-8271
Milan Marsh, President
Warren J. Smith, Secretary-Treasurer

Ohio Civil Service Employees Association
991 Goodale Boulevard
Columbus, OH 43212
(614) 221-2409
 (continued)

Membership: 25,800 (1978)
Leslie Best, President
Ronald Alexander, President-Elect
Betty Lyrds, Immediate Past-President
Arthur Evans, Executive Director
Margaret Penn, Comptroller

Oil, Chemical and Atomic Workers International Union

1636 Champa Street
Denver, CO 80201
(303) 893-0811
Membership: 145,000
Robert F. Goss, President
Michael Ricigliano, Secretary-Treasurer
Joseph Misbrener, Vice President
L. Calvin Moore, Vice President
John Tadlock, General Counsel

Oklahoma State AFL-CIO

501 Northeast Twenty-seventh Street
Oklahoma City, OK 73105
(405) 528-2409

Operative Plasterers' and Cement Masons' International

Association of the United States and Canada
1125 Seventeenth Street, NW
Washington, DC 20036
(202) 393-6569
Membership: 57,000 (1978)
Melvin H. Roots, General President
Robert J. Holton, Secretary-Treasurer
James J. Boyle, Executive Vice President
Edward J. Leonard, General President Emeritus
Frank G. Rossetti, Vice President
Pat J. Christiano, Vice President
Warner Sevander, Vice President
Donald B. Johnston, Vice President
James W. Thomas, Vice President
Harry D. Martinez, Jr., Vice President
Michael Canuso, Vice President
Frank Saffel, Vice President
Con O'Shea, Vice President
Robert T. Beam, Vice President
William E. McMynn, Vice President
James Clayman, Vice President

Oregon Public Employes Union (Local 503 SEIU, AFL-CIO, CLC)

1127 Twenty-fifth Street, SE
Salem, OR 97309
(503) 581-1505
Membership: 13,000
D. H. Petry, President
John Clapp, Vice President
Carol Laizure-Jellison, Secretary-Treasurer
Thomas J. Gallagher, Executive Director

Overseas Education Association, Inc.

1201 Sixteenth Street, NW
Washington, DC 20036
(202) 833-4276
Membership: 3,971 (1978)

Patent Office Professional Association

P.O. Box 2745
Arlington, VA 22202
(703) 557-3107
Membership: 1,100
Edward S. Bauer, President
Ronald Stern, Vice President & General Counsel
James L. Ridgill, Jr., Secretary
Richard Fisher, Treasurer
Lawrence Oresky, Assistant Secretary

Pattern Makers' League of North America

1925 North Linn
Arlington, VA 22209
(703) 525-9234
Membership: 9,600 (1978)

Pennsylvania AFL-CIO

101 Pine Street
Harrisburg, PA 17101
(717) 238-9351
Membership: 1,500,000
Julius Uehlein, President
Judith Heh, Secretary-Treasurer
Robert T. McIntyre, Executive Vice President

Public Employment Relations Board
50 Wolf Road
Albany, NY 12205
(518) 457-2676
Harold R. Newman, Chairman
Ida Klaus, Member
David C. Randles, Member
Ralph Vatalano, Executive Director

**Puerto Rico Federation of Labor
  (AFL-CIO)**
Avenida Central 274
Bajos, Hyde Park, Rio Piedras 00918
(809) 754-5353

Railroad Yardmasters of America
1411 Peterson Avenue
Park Ridge, IL 60068
(312) 696-2510
Membership: 3,500
A. T. Otto, Jr., Grand President
R. J. Culver, Grand Secretary-
  Treasurer

Railway Labor Executives' Association
400 First Street, NW
Washington, DC 20001
(202) 737-1541
Membership: 20
Fred A. Hardin, Chairman
O. M. Berge, Vice Chairman
R. I. Kilroy, Executive Secretary

**Retail, Wholesale, and Department
  Store Union, AFL-CIO**
30 East Twenty-ninth Street
New York, NY 10016
(212) 684-5300
Membership: 250,000
Alvin E. Heaps, President
Lenore Miller, Secretary-Treasurer

Rhode Island AFL-CIO
15 Jefferson Street
Providence, RI 02908
(401) 751-7100
Edward J. McElroy, Jr., President
Edwin C. Brown, Secretary-Treasurer

Sailors' Union of the Pacific
450 Harrison Street
San Francisco, CA 94105
(415) 362-8363
Membership: 2,000
Paul Dempster, President and Secretary-
  Treasurer
Jack Ryan, Vice President and Assistant
  Secretary-Treasurer

Screen Actors Guild
7750 Sunset Boulevard
Hollywood, CA 90046
(213) 876-3030
Membership: 51,000
Edward Asner, President
Ken Orsatti, National Executive
  Secretary
Kim Fellner, Director of Information

Screen Extras Guild, Inc.
3629 Cahuenga Boulevard, West
Los Angeles, CA 90068
(213) 851-4301
Membership: 5,079
Roy Wallack, President
Paul Deceglie, Vice President
Josephine Parra, Vice President
Kathryn Janssen, Secretary
Leland Sun, Treasurer
Leonard Chassman, National Executive
  Secretary

Seafarers International Union
815 Sixteenth Street, NW
Washington, DC 20006
(202) 628-6300
Membership: 100,000
Frank Drozak, President
Joe DiGiorgio, Secretary-Treasurer
Ed Turner, Executive Vice President
Mike Sacco, Vice President-Lakes and
  Rivers
Joe Sacco, Vice President-Gulf
George McCartney, Vice President-West
  Coast
Leon Hall, Vice President-East Coast
Jack Caffey, Assistant to the President
Marianne Rogers, Political Director

Service Employees International Union, AFL-CIO, CLC
2020 K Street, NW
Washington, DC 20006
(202) 452-8750
Membership: 700,000
John J. Sweeney, International President
Richard W. Cordtz, International Secretary-Treasurer
Martell F. Blake, U.S. Vice President
Walter J. Butler, U.S. Vice President
Eugene P. Moats, U.S. Vice President
Joseph E. Murphy, U.S. Vice President
William Stodghill, U.S. Vice President
Rosemary Trump, U.S. Vice President
Timothy Twomey, U.S. Vice President
Stanley E. Roscoe, Canadian Vice President
Aime Gohier, Canadian Vice President

Sheet Metal Workers International Association
1750 New York Avenue, NE
Washington, DC 20006
(202) 783-5880
Membership: 158,528 (1978)

Socialist Labor Party
914 Industrial Avenue
Palo Alto, CA 94303
(415) 494-1532
Robert Bills, National Secretary
Nathan Karp, Financial Secretary

South Carolina AFL-CIO
1625 Charleston Highway
West Columbia, SC 29171
(803) 794-9025
Randy Kiser, President
R. H. Harmon, Secretary-Treasurer
Harry Wilson, Vice President
David Richardson, Vice President

South Dakota State Employees Organization
P.O. Box 1021
Pierre, SD 57501
(605) 224-8241
Membership: 1,600
Dave Merrill, President
(continued)

Robert Harter, 1st Vice President
Judy Toelle, 2nd Vice President
Della Andre, Secretary
Mary Haviland, Treasurer
Ken Balgeman, Executive Secretary
Marcia Knight, Office Manager
Gary Colwill, Legislative Counsel

South Dakota State Federation of Labor, AFL-CIO
P.O. Box 58
Huron, SD 57350
(605) 352-1949
Jack E. Dudley, President and Financial Secretary
Ben J. Aning, 1st Vice President
Doris Mowry, 2nd Vice President
Charles Murray, Vice President
Dallas Tinnell, Vice President
John E. Hansen, Vice President
Charles Good, Vice President
Gerald Podoll, Vice President
Ralph Pearl, Vice President
Peter Knowlton, Vice President

Southern Labor Union
P.O. Box 479
Oneida, TN 37841
(615) 569-8335
Membership: 3,200
Johnnie Joseph, President
Mack Dilbeck, 1st Vice President
Bryan Fultz, 2nd Vice President
Jim Polly, Secretary
Delmas Layton, Treasurer

State of Nevada Employees Association
P.O. Box 1016
Carson City, NV 89702
(702) 882-3910
Membership: 4,800
Robert J. Gagnier, Executive Director
Karon Brewster, President
Bill Cassell, Vice President
Morris Kanowitz, Director-at-Large
Phonon Reddicks, Director-at-Large
John Hutchings, Immediate Past President

Stove, Furnace and Allied Appliance Workers' International Union of North America
2929 South Jefferson Avenue
St. Louis, MO 63118
(314) 664-3736
Membership: 6,400 (1978)

Technical Engineers Association
4701 North Seventy-sixth Street
Milwaukee, WI 53218
(414) 462-1234

Telecommunications International Union
2341 Whitney Avenue
Hamden, CT 06518
(203) 281-7945
Membership: 50,000
John W. Shaughnessy, Jr., President
Joan H. Noonan, Vice President
Kay K. Dresler, Secretary-Treasurer

Tennessee State Labor Council, AFL-CIO
535 Church Street
Nashville, TN 37219
(615) 256-5687
James G. Neeley, President
Eddie Bryan, Secretary-Treasurer
H. T. Powell, 1st Vice President
Charlie Dunning, 2nd Vice President

Texas AFL-CIO
P.O. Box 12727
Austin, TX 78711
(512) 477-6195
Membership: 298,000
Harry Hubbard, President
Joe D. Gunn, Secretary-Treasurer

Textile Processors, Service Trades, Health Care, Professional and Technical Employees International Union
360 North Michigan
Chicago, IL 60601
(312) 726-9416
Membership: 45,000
John J. Fagan, General President
Charles Naddeo, General Secretary-Treasurer
E. L. Abercrombie, 1st Vice President
(continued)

Charles M. Jackson, 2nd Vice President
Frank A. Scalish, 3rd Vice President
Martin A. White, Jr., 4th Vice President
Thomas Corrigan, 5th Vice President
Albert J. Rogers, 6th Vice President

Tile, Marble, Terrazzo, Finishers, Shopworkers and Granite Cutters International Union, AFL-CIO
801 North Pitt Street
Alexandria, VA 22314
(703) 549-3050
Membership: 8,000
Pascal DiJames, General President, Secretary-Treasurer
Frank Iarrobino, 1st Vice President
Frank Fiano, 2nd Vice President
Dennis Murphy, 3rd Vice President
Alfred Buono, 4th Vice President
Gerald Bombassaro, 5th Vice President
Joseph DiGiulian, Jr., 6th Vice President
Robert Horner, 7th Vice President
Harvey C. Krohn, 8th Vice President
Luciano Busnardo, 9th Vice President
Patrick Calhoun, 10th Vice President
Joseph Ricciarelli, Director, Granite Cutters

Transport Workers Union of America
1980 Broadway
New York, NY 10014
(212) 873-6000
Membership: 100,000+
William G. Lindner, International President
Roosevelt Watts, International Secretary-Treasurer
John E. Lawe, International Executive Vice President

Union of American Physicians and Dentists
1730 Franklin Street
Oakland, CA 94612
(415) 839-0193
Sanford A. Marcus, M.D., President
Charles L. Allen, M.D., Vice President
John L. Eicholz, M.D., Vice President
Deane Hillsman, M.D., Secretary
Truman A. Newberry, M.D., Treasurer

United Association of Journeymen and Apprentices of the Plumbing and Pipe Fitting Industry of the United States and Canada
901 Massachusetts Avenue, NW
Washington, DC 20001
(202) 628-5823
Membership: 337,055 (1978)
Marvin Boede, President

United Brotherhood of Carpenters and Joiners of America
101 Constitution Avenue, NW
Washington, DC 20001
(202) 546-6206
Membership: 800,000
Patrick Campbell, General President
Sigurd Lucassen, First General Vice President
John S. Rogers, General Secretary
Charles E. Nichols, General Treasurer

United Cement, Lime, Gypsum and Allied Workers International Union
7830 West Lawrence
Norridge, IL 60656
(312) 774-2217
Membership: 33,000
Thomas F. Miechur, President
Richard A. Northrip, Secretary-Treasurer
August Clavier, Jr., Vice President (DC-9)
Henry W. Bechtholdt, Vice President (DC-2)
Kent Weaver, Vice President (DC-3)
Paul H. Balliet, Vice President (DC-4)
Bernard Martinez, Vice President (DC-6)
Tyrone C. Perkins, Vice President (DC-5)
Marvin Wright, Vice President (DC-1)
Joseph B. Granich, Vice President (DC-8)
Ross Seaman, Vice President (DC-10, 11)

United Electrical, Radio and Machine Workers of America (UE)
11 East Fifty-first Street
New York, NY 10022
(212) 753-1960
Membership: 166,000 (1978)
James M. Kane, General President
(continued)

Boris H. Block, General Secretary-Treasurer
Hugh Harley, Director of Organization

United Farm Workers of America, AFL-CIO
P.O. Box 62
Keene, CA 93531
(805) 822-5571
Membership: 25,000 (1978)
Cesar E. Chavez, President
Peter G. Velasco, Secretary-Treasurer
Dolores Huerta, 1st Vice President
Frank Ortiz, 2nd Vice President
Richard E. Chavez, 3rd Vice President

United Food & Commercial Workers International Union
1775 K Street, NW
Washington, DC 20006
(202) 223-3111
Membership: 1,235,000 (1978)
William H. Wynn, International President
Anthony J. Lutty, International Secretary-Treasurer

United Furniture Workers of America
1910 Airlane Drive
Nashville, TN 37210
(615) 889-8860
Membership: 27,042 (1978)

United Garment Workers of America
200 Park Avenue South
New York, NY 10003
(212) 677-0573
Membership: 22,000
William O'Donnell, General President
Calvina S. Little, General Secretary-Treasurer

United Mine Workers of America
900 Fifteenth Street, NW
Washington, DC 20005
(202) 842-7200
Membership: 225,000
Richard L. Trumka, President
Cecil Roberts, Vice President
John Banovic, Secretary-Treasurer

United Paperworkers International Union
702 Church Street
Nashville, TN 37202
(615) 254-6666
Membership: 300,000
Wayne E. Glenn, President
Nicholas C. Vrataric, Secretary-Treasurer
George H. O'Bea, Jr., Vice President/
National Director-PEP
John M. Defee, Vice President/Director
of Special Projects
Raymond J. Laplante, Vice President/
Director, Region I
Christopher J. Jackman, Vice President/
Director, Region II
Marshall A. Smith, Vice President/
Director, Region III
Arnold E. Brown, Vice President/
Director, Region IV
Jesse W. Whiddon, Sr., Vice President/
Director, Region V
David W. Gordon, Jr., Vice President/
Director, Region VI
Joe J. Bradshaw, Vice President/Director,
Region VII
John H. Jamison, Vice President/
Director, Region VIII
Glenn B. Goss, Vice President/Director,
Region IX
Raymond W. Klescewski, Vice President/
Director, Region X
William W. Bergren, Vice President/
Director, Region XI
J. Gilbert Hay, Vice President/Director,
Canada, Region XII

**United Retail Workers Union Local 881
(Chartered by UFCW)**
9865 West Roosevelt Road
Westchester, IL 60153
(312) 681-1000
Membership: 22,000
Fred A. Burki, President
Frank Koukl, Secretary-Treasurer
Tom Walsh, Recorder

**United Rubber, Cork, Linoleum and
Plastic Workers of America, AFL-CIO,
CLC**
87 South High Street
Akron, OH 44308
(continued)

(216) 376-6181
Membership: 130,000
Milan Stone, International President
Joseph H. Johnston, International
Vice President
Donald C. Tuckee, International
Secretary-Treasurer

United Scenic Artists
1540 Broadway
New York, NY 10036
(212) 575-5120

**United Steelworkers of America,
AFL-CIO**
Five Gateway Center
Pittsburgh, PA 15222
(412) 562-2400
Membership: 1,300,000
Lloyd McBride, International President
Lynn R. Williams, International Secretary
Frank S. McKee, International Treasurer
Joseph Odorcich, Vice President
(Administration)
Leon Lynch, Vice President (Human
Affairs)

United Telegraph Workers, AFL-CIO
701 East Gude Drive
Rockville, MD 20850
(301) 762-4444
Membership: 12,000
Richard C. Brockert, International
President
Jerry Grim, International Secretary-
Treasurer

United Textile Workers of America
420 Common Street
Lawrence, MA 01842
(617) 686-2901
Membership: 40,000 (1978)

United Transportation Union
14600 Detroit Avenue
Cleveland, OH 44107
(216) 228-9400
Membership: 175,500 (1978)
Fred A. Hardin, President
R. R. Bryant, Assistant President
(continued)

John H. Shepherd, General Secretary and Treasurer
Kenneth Moore, Vice President, Business Department
James Amerson, Trustee

United Union of Roofers, Waterproofers and Allied Workers
1125 Seventeenth Street, NW
Washington, DC 20036
(202) 638-3228

Upholsterers' International Union of North America—AFL-CIO
25 North Fourth Street
Philadelphia, PA 19106
(215) 923-5700
Membership: 39,000
John Serembus, President
Duane Giesler, 1st Vice President
Paul Heaton, Treasurer
Earl Graves, Vice President
Jess Gonzales, Vice President
Gary Walston, Vice President
Ernest Shock, Vice President
Wardell Lamberson, Vice President
Roger Murray, Vice President
Kenneth McAvoy, Vice President
Donat Theriault, Vice President

Utah Public Employees Association
438 South 600 East
Salt Lake City, UT 84110
(801) 328-4995
Membership: 10,000
Dr. Clark L. Puffer, Executive Director
Marty Cutler, President
Joyce Blankenship, 1st Vice President

Utah State AFL-CIO
2261 South Redwood Road
Salt Lake City, UT 84119
(801) 972-2771
Ed Mayne, President, Secretary-Treasurer
Clifford Green, Vice President
Beverly Saathoff, VIP Director-COPE
John Timothy Rice, Public Relations Director

Utility Workers Union of America, AFL-CIO
815 Sixteenth Street, NW
Washington, DC 20006
(202) 347-8105
Membership: 55,000 (1978)
James Joy, Jr., President
Valentine P. Murphy, Executive Vice President
C. Joseph Luciano, Vice President
Marshall M. Hicks, Secretary-Treasurer

Vermont State Employees' Association, Inc.
P.O. Box 518
Montpelier, VT 05602
(802) 223-5247
Membership: 3,700
Ruth Watson, President
Roy Farmer, 1st Vice President
Frank Schlosser, 2nd Vice President
Judy P. Rosenstreich, Executive Director

Vermont State Labor Council, AFL-CIO
149 State Street
Montpelier, VT 05602
(802) 223-5229
Robert Clark, President
Carla Thomas, Secretary-Treasurer
Maurice Fortier, Executive Vice President

Virginia State AFL-CIO
3315 West Broad Street
Richmond, VA 23230
(804) 355-7444
Membership: 108,000
Julian F. Carper, President
Leander V. Lewis, Vice President
David H. Laws, Secretary-Treasurer

Washington Public Employees Association
124 West Tenth Street
Olympia, WA 98501
(206) 943-1121
Membership: 2,515 (1978)

Washington State Labor Council,
  AFL-CIO
2815 Second Avenue
Seattle, WA 98121
(206) 682-6002
Marvin L. Williams, President
Lawrence Kenney, Secretary-Treasurer

West Virginia Labor Federation,
  AFL-CIO
501 Broad Street
Charleston, WV 25301
(304) 344-3557

Wisconsin State AFL-CIO
6333 West Bluemound Road
Milwaukee, WI 53213
(414) 771-0700
Membership: 320,000
John W. Schmitt, President
Joseph A. Gruber, Executive Vice
  President
Jack B. Reihl, Secretary-Treasurer

Writers Guild of America, East, Inc.
555 West Fifty-seventh Street
New York, NY 10019
(212) 245-6180
Membership: 2,400 (1978)

Writers Guild of America, West, Inc.
8955 Beverly Boulevard
Los Angeles, CA 90048
(213) 550-1000
Membership: 6,000
Frank Pierson, President
William Ludwig, Secretary-Treasurer
Naomi Gurian, Executive Director

Wyoming Public Employees Association
408 West Twenty-third Street
Cheyenne, WY 82001
(307) 635-7901
Membership: 3,400 (1978)

Wyoming State AFL-CIO
1904 Thomes Avenue
Cheyenne, WY 82001
(307) 635-2823
Membership: 17,000
L. Keith Henning, Executive Secretary
Tom Lee, President
Bill Newman, Vice President

UNION CODES

To facilitate reference to individual unions, many of which have lengthy names, the U.S. Department of Labor assigns standard abbreviations and a Union Code Number to each. This list is divided into four parts: AFL-CIO Union Codes, Independent Union Codes, Organizations of Federal Employees, and Professional and State Employee Associations.

AFL-CIO UNION CODES—
NUMERICAL LISTING

Abbreviations	Union Codes	Name of Unions
AFL-CIO	100	TWO OR MORE AFL-CIO UNIONS
	101	DIRECTLY AFFILIATED UNIONS OF THE AFL-CIO, formerly referred to as Federal Labor Union (FLU) or Local Industrial Unions (LIU)

Abbreviations	Union Codes	Name of Unions
AAAA	102	ACTORS
AEA		Actors' Equity
AFTRA		TV & Radio Artists
AGMA		Musical Artists
AGVA		Variety Artists
HAU		Hebrew Actors
IAU		Italian Actors
SAG		Screen Actors
SEG		Screen Extras
ALPA	104	AIR LINE PILOTS
ALEA		Air Line Employees
UPA		Professional Airmen
PTE	105	PROFESSIONAL AND TECHNICAL ENGINEERS
HFIA	106	ASBESTOS WORKERS
AIW	107	INDUSTRIAL WORKERS; ALLIED
BCTW	108	BAKERY, CONFECTIONERY AND TOBACCO WORKERS
BBAI	109	BARBERS
BBF	112	BOILERMAKERS
UBCW	114	BRICK AND CLAY WORKERS
BAC	115	BRICKLAYERS
BSIW	116	IRON WORKERS
SEIU	118	SERVICE EMPLOYEES
CJA	119	CARPENTERS
CLGW	120	CEMENT WORKERS
ICW	121	CHEMICAL WORKERS
CIU	124	COOPERS
DWW	126	DISTILLERY WORKERS
IBEW	127	ELECTRICAL WORKERS
IUEC	128	ELEVATOR CONSTRUCTORS
IUOE	129	OPERATING ENGINEERS
IAFF	131	FIRE FIGHTERS
IBFO	132	FIREMEN AND OILERS
UGW	133	GARMENT WORKERS; UNITED
ILGWU	134	LADIES GARMENT WORKERS
GBBA	135	GLASS BOTTLE BLOWERS
AFGW	137	GLASS WORKERS; FLINT
AFGE	139	GOVERNMENT EMPLOYEES
GCIA	140	GRANITE CUTTERS
LGPN	141	LEATHER, PLASTIC AND NOVELTY WORKERS
HCMW	142	HATTERS
LIUNA	143	LABORERS
UJH	144	HORSESHOERS
HREU	145	HOTEL AND RESTAURANT EMPLOYEES
JWU	146	JEWELRY WORKERS
WWML	147	LATHERS
NALC	150	LETTER CARRIERS
BMWE	152	MAINTENANCE OF WAY EMPLOYEES

Abbreviations	Union Codes	Name of Unions
TMTF	153	TILE, MARBLE, TERRAZZO, FINISHERS
MMP	154	MASTERS, MATES, AND PILOTS
MCBW	155	MEAT CUTTERS
MPBP	158	METAL POLISHERS
IMAW	161	MOLDERS
AFM	162	MUSICIANS
OPEIU	163	OFFICE EMPLOYEES
PAT	164	PAINTERS
PML	166	PATTERN MAKERS
OPCM	168	PLASTERERS AND CEMENT MASONS
PPDSE	169	PLATE PRINTERS
PPF	170	PLUMBERS
IBPAW	174	POTTERS
BRS	178	RAILROAD SIGNALMEN
RYA	180	RAILROAD YARDMASTERS
BRC	181	RAILWAY CARMEN
BRAC	183	RAILWAY CLERKS
RCIU	184	RETAIL CLERKS
RWAW	185	ROOFERS
SIU	186	SEAFARERS
AGLIW		Atlantic, Gulf, Lakes
IUP		Inland Boatmen's
IUPW		Petroleum Workers
MFOW		Pacific Coast Marine Firemen
SUP		Sailors
TSAW		Transportation Services
SMW	187	SHEET METAL WORKERS
IAS	189	SIDEROGRAPHERS
IATSE	192	THEATRICAL STAGE EMPLOYEES
AFSCME	193	STATE, COUNTY, AND MUNICIPAL EMPLOYEES
SFAAW	196	STOVE WORKERS
ATU	197	TRANSIT UNION; AMALGAMATED
AFT	199	TEACHERS
UTW	201	TELEGRAPH WORKERS
UTWA	202	TEXTILE WORKERS; UNITED
ITU	204	TYPOGRAPHICAL UNION
UIU	205	UPHOLSTERERS
AFGM	208	GRAIN MILLERS
FEIA	215	FLIGHT ENGINEERS
IAM	218	MACHINISTS
AWU	220	ALUMINUM WORKERS
NPW	221	NOVELTY AND PRODUCTION WORKERS
UPIU	231	PAPERWORKERS
TDA	232	TRAIN DISPATCHERS
RASA	233	RAILWAY AND AIRWAY SUPERVISORS
LDC	236	LAUNDRY AND DRY CLEANING UNION
IWIU	238	INSURANCE WORKERS
ILA	239	LONGSHOREMEN'S ASSOCIATION

Abbreviations	Union Codes	Name of Unions
UFW	241	FARM WORKERS; UNITED
GAIU	243	GRAPHIC ARTS
PGCU	244	PRINTING AND GRAPHIC
ACTWU	305	CLOTHING AND TEXTILE WORKERS
UFWA	312	FURNITURE WORKERS
UGCW	314	GLASS AND CERAMIC WORKERS
MEBA	319	MARINE ENGINEERS
IUMSW	320	MARINE AND SHIPBUILDING WORKERS
NMU	321	MARITIME UNION; NATIONAL
TNG	323	NEWSPAPER GUILD
RWDSU	332	RETAIL, WHOLESALE, AND DEPARTMENT STORE UNION
URW	333	RUBBER WORKERS
USA	335	STEELWORKERS
TWU	341	TRANSPORT WORKERS
UWU	342	UTILITY WORKERS
IWA	343	WOODWORKERS
ARA	345	RADIO ASSOCIATION
CWA	346	COMMUNICATIONS WORKERS
IUE	347	ELECTRICAL WORKERS
NABET	352	BROADCAST EMPLOYEES AND TECHNICIANS
MESA	354	MECHANICS EDUCATIONAL SOCIETY
LWU	356	LEATHER WORKERS
OCAW	357	OIL, CHEMICAL, AND ATOMIC WORKERS
UTU	358	TRANSPORTATION UNION; UNITED
APWU	360	POSTAL WORKERS
AFSA	361	SCHOOL ADMINISTRATORS
ALPA-AFA	362	FLIGHT ATTENDANTS
MEBA-PATCO	363	AIR TRAFFIC CONTROLLERS

INDEPENDENT UNION CODES

Abbreviations	Union Codes	Name of Unions
(I)	400	TWO OR MORE INDEPENDENT UNIONS (I)
DSC (I)	404	DIE SINKERS
ALO (I)	412	LACE OPERATIVES
LIA (I)	414	INSURANCE AGENTS
BLE (I)	415	LOCOMOTIVE ENGINEERS
MPEA (I)	417	MACHINE PRINTERS
DWA (I)	423	DISTRIBUTIVE WORKERS
NMD (I)	425	NEWSPAPER AND MAIL DELIVERERS
BSAC (I)	442	SHOE CRAFTSMEN
AWWU (I)	449	WATCH WORKERS
UMW (I)	454	MINE WORKERS
APA (I)	459	ALLIED PILOTS ASSOCIATION
PGW (I)	461	GUARD WORKERS; PLANT
CLA (I)	465	CHRISTIAN LABOR ASSOCIATION

Abbreviations	Union Codes	Name of Unions
UWNE (I)	469	UTILITY WORKERS OF NEW ENGLAND
AIU (I)	470	ATLANTIC INDEPENDENT UNION
BEU (I)	471	BAKERY EMPLOYEES UNION; INDEPENDENT
ILWU (I)	480	LONGSHOREMEN AND WAREHOUSEMEN
UE (I)	484	ELECTRICAL WORKERS
PPE (I)	490	PROTECTION EMPLOYEES; PLANT
WA (I)	494	WATCHMEN'S ASSOCIATION
(I)	500	SINGLE FIRM INDEPENDENT UNION
NFIU (I)	514	NATIONAL FEDERATION OF INDEPENDENT UNIONS
TIU (I)	516	TELECOMMUNICATIONS INTERNATIONAL UNION
MLBPA (I)	517	BASEBALL PLAYERS
NBPA (I)	518	BASKETBALL PLAYERS
NHLPA (I)	519	HOCKEY PLAYERS
NFLP (I)	520	FOOTBALL PLAYERS
MLU (I)	521	UMPIRES
NBPW (I)	524	PACKINGHOUSE AND INDUSTRIAL WORKERS
WPPW (I)	527	PULP AND PAPER; WESTERN
SLU (I)	528	SOUTHERN LABOR UNION
WSSS (I)	529	WESTERN STATES SERVICE STATIONS EMPLOYEES
WGA (I)	530	WRITERS GUILD (EAST AND WEST)
IBT (I)	531	TEAMSTERS
IBT-LWIU (I)	533	LAUNDRY, DRY CLEANING, AND DYEHOUSE WORKERS
IATC (I)	534	TOOL CRAFTSMEN
NIW (I)	535	INDUSTRIAL WORKERS; NATIONAL
IT (I)	536	INDUSTRIAL TRADE
COIU (I)	538	INDEPENDENT UNIONS; CONGRESS OF
RWU (I)	539	RETAIL WORKERS
DGA (I)	540	DIRECTORS GUILD
GUA (I)	541	GUARDS UNION
CTD (I)	542	TRUCK DRIVERS; CHICAGO
AWIU (I)	543	ALLIED WORKERS
GLLO (I}	547	LICENSED OFFICERS' ORGANIZATION; GREAT LAKES
TFG (I)	551	TEXTILE FOREMEN'S GUILD
UAW (I)	553	AUTO WORKERS
PNHA (I)	555	PHYSICIANS NATIONAL HOUSESTAFF ASSOCIATION
RIWU (I)	556	RHODE ISLAND WORKERS UNION
PLSA (I)	557	LOG SCALERS
TDMN (I)	558	TOOL DIE AND MOLD MAKERS
IUSO (I)	559	SECURITY OFFICERS
IWRS (I)	560	INTERNATIONAL WESTERN RAILWAY SUPERVISORS
WIIU (I)	561	WAREHOUSE INDUSTRIAL INTERNATIONAL UNION
CLGA (I)	562	COMPOSERS AND LYRICISTS GUILD

Abbreviations	Union Codes	Name of Unions
IPSS	563	INTERNATIONAL PRODUCTION, SERVICE AND SALES UNION
UAPD	565	AMERICAN PHYSICIANS AND DENTISTS
MULTI	600	TWO OR MORE UNIONS – DIFFERENT AFFILIATIONS [i.e., AFL-CIO and INDEPENDENT UNION(S)]

Independent Unions Having Agreements with More Than One Employer, but Confined within a Single State (Not Listed in Directory)

EAA (I)	701	ENGINEERS AND ARCHITECTS
ITUA (I)	702	INDUSTRIAL TRADES
OSTE (I)	704	OFFICE, SALES AND TECHNICAL EMPLOYEES
L-A-ASPA (I)	705	SHOEWORKERS PROTECTIVE ASSOCIATION
FITU (I)	708	TEXAS UNIONS
AIU (I)	715	INDUSTRIAL UNION; AMALGAMATED
PMW (I)	717	MINE WORKERS; PROGRESSIVE

ORGANIZATIONS OF FEDERAL EMPLOYEES

	800	TWO OR MORE FEDERAL EMPLOYEE ORGANIZATIONS
ASCSE (I)	802	ASCS COUNTY OFFICE EMPLOYEES
FEA (I)	803	FEDERAL EMPLOYEES
FPQI (I)	804	QUARANTINE INSPECTORS
NAGE (I)	807	GOVERNMENT EMPLOYEES
NAGI (I)	808	GOVERNMENT INSPECTORS
NTE (I)	809	TREASURY EMPLOYEES
NAPEP (I)	810	PLANNER-ESTIMATORS AND PROGRESSMEN
NAPFE (I)	811	POSTAL AND FEDERAL EMPLOYEES
NAPS (I)	812	POSTAL SUPERVISORS
NFFE (I)	814	FEDERAL EMPLOYEES
NLP (I)	815	POSTMASTERS LEAGUE
NLRBP (I)	817	NLRB PROFESSIONAL ASSOCIATION
NLRBU (I)	818	NLRB UNION
POPA (I)	821	PATENT OFFICE PROFESSIONAL ASSOCIATION
RLCA (I)	822	RURAL LETTER CARRIERS
TRSOC (I)	823	TRADEMARK SOCIETY
TSA (I)	824	TECHNICAL SKILLS ASSOCIATION
AAE (I)	825	AERONAUTICAL EXAMINERS
APCA (I)	826	AERONAUTICAL CONTROLMEN
CTA (I)	828	CIVILIAN TECHNICIANS ASSOCIATION
FPSP (I)	829	POSTAL SECURITY POLICE
ICCP (I)	830	INTERSTATE COMMERCE COMMISSION PRO-FESSORS ASSOCIATION

PROFESSIONAL AND STATE EMPLOYEE ASSOCIATIONS

Abbreviations	Union Codes	Name of Unions
FOP (I)	901	POLICE; FRATERNAL ORDER OF
CSEA (I)	902	CIVIL SERVICE EMPLOYEES ASSOCIATION (excluding N.Y. State and Ohio)
ANA (I)	903	NURSES; AMERICAN
LPN (I)	904	LICENSED PRACTICAL NURSES
NA (I)	905	NURSES' ASSOCIATIONS (other than ANA and LPN)
DA (I)	906	DOCTORS' ASSOCIATIONS
(I)	907	SINGLE INDEPENDENT ASSOCIATIONS
AU (I)	908	ASSOCIATION AND UNION
NEA (I)	909	EDUCATION ASSOCIATION; NATIONAL
AACSE (I)	962	CLASSIFIED SCHOOL EMPLOYEES
CEU (I)	963	CONNECTICUT EMPLOYEES UNION
NCSGEA (I)	964	NORTH CAROLINA STATE GOVERNMENT EMPLOYEES ASSOCIATION
AAUP (I)	970	UNIVERSITY PROFESSORS
PA (I)	971	POLICE ASSOCIATIONS (other than FRATERNAL ORDER OF POLICE)
ASSNS (I)	972	TWO OR MORE INDEPENDENT ASSOCIATIONS
FAA (I)	975	FIRE FIGHTERS (other than INTERNATIONAL ASSOCIATION OF FIRE FIGHTERS)

III

PROMINENT
LABOR LEADERS

INCUMBENT OFFICERS
AND LEADERS

Most of the names included in this listing appear in section II, National Labor Organizations. In addition, there are a few prominent government officials and recent retirees who were selected because of their importance to the labor movement.

Those union labor leaders chosen for this listing include the current president, secretary, treasurer, and executive director or their corresponding positions. Names of all other union officials are included in the index to facilitate finding the union affiliation of each.

Abel, I. W., Past President, United Steelworkers of America. Retired.

Adler, Joseph, Executive Director, Maryland Classified Employees Association, Inc.

Allen, Edward M., Vice President-Labor Relations, Association of Labor Relations Agencies.

Alvestad, Dale, Executive Vice President, National League of Postmasters of the U.S.

Anderson, Karl F., Executive Vice President, Secretary-Treasurer, Flight Engineers International Association.

Anding, Charles R., General Treasurer, International Association of Bridge, Structural and Ornamental Iron Workers.

Andre, Della, Secretary, South Dakota State Employees Organization.

Appleton, Shelley, General Secretary-Treasurer, International Ladies Garment Workers Union.

Arellano, Luis, Executive Director, Arizona Public Employees' Association.

Armentrout, Olin F., Secretary-Treasurer, National Rural Letter Carriers' Association.

Arthur, Carol Ann, Secretary, National Council for Labor Reform.

Ashwood, Thomas M., Secretary, Air Line Pilots Association.

Asner, Edward, President, Screen Actors Guild.

Auerbach, Jim, AFL/CIO Staff Liaison, AFL-CIO American Library Association, Joint Committee on Library Service to Labor Groups.

Badolato, Dominic, Executive Secretary, Connecticut State AFL-CIO.

Balgeman, Ken, Executive Secretary, South Dakota State Employees Organization.

Banovic, John, Secretary-Treasurer, United Mine Workers of America.

Bartolo, Peter P., Executive Director, Engineers and Scientists of California.

Bauer, Edward S., President, Patent Office Professional Association.

Bean, Donald E., Secretary, Association of Civilian Technicians.

Beck, David, Past President, International Brotherhood of Teamsters; imprisoned for tax evasion and larceny.

Becker, Joyce, Secretary, Colorado Association of State Employees.

Becker, Noel, Co-Treasurer, The Graphic Artists Guild.

Becksvoort, Wayne, Secretary, Christian Labor Association of the U.S.A.

Bellamy, Duard, President, National Industrial Workers Union.

Bellucci, Edward M., Secretary-Treasurer, International Union of Bricklayers and Allied Craftsmen.

Bernard, William G., General Secretary-Treasurer, International Association of Heat and Frost Insulators and Asbestos Workers.

Bernier, David J., Secretary-Treasurer, Machine Printers and Engravers Association of the U.S.

Best, Leslie, President, Ohio Civil Service Employees Association.

Beyer, Clara, U.S. Department of Labor, primarily with Bureau of Labor Statistics. Retired.

Bieber, Owen, President, International Union, United Automobile, Aerospace and Agricultural Implement Workers of America.

Bikel, Theodore, President, Actors' Equity Association.

Biller, Moe, General President, American Postal Workers Union.

Bills, Robert, National Secretary, Socialist Labor Party.

Bingel, Joe, President, International Typographical Union.

Blaylock, Kenneth T., President, American Federation of Government Employees.

Block, Boris, General Secretary-Treasurer, United Electrical, Radio and Machine Workers of America.

Bobo, D. A., International Secretary-Treasurer, Brotherhood of Railway, Airline and Steamship Clerks.

Boede, Marvin, President, United Association of Journeymen and Apprentices of the Plumbing and Pipe Fitting Industry of the United States and Canada.

Boller, Carolyn, Secretary, Air Line Employees Association, International.

Borman, Frank, Chairman, Institute of Collective Bargaining and Group Relations, Inc.

Boucher, Gene, President, American Guild of Musical Artists.

Boyd, Richard, Treasurer, Fraternal Order of Police.

Boyle, James J., Executive Vice President, Operative Plasterers' and Cement Masons' International Association of U.S. and Canada.

Bradley, Thomas M., President, Maryland State and D.C. AFL-CIO.

Brewster, Karon, President, State of Nevada Employees Association.

Bridges, Harry, Founder and President, International Longshoremen's Association. Retired.

Brockert, Richard C., International President, United Telegraph Workers.

Brown, Edwin C., Secretary-Treasurer, Rhode Island AFL-CIO.

Brown, Jerome P., Secretary-Treasurer, National Union of Hospital and Health Care Employees.

Brown, Kenneth J., President, Graphic Arts International Union.

Bryan, Eddie, Secretary-Treasurer, Tennessee State Labor Council.

Burden, Emmett W., Executive Director, North Carolina State Employees Association.

Burki, Fred A., President, United Retail Workers Union.

Burt, Bruce G., International Secretary-Treasurer, International Union of Security Officers.

Butsavage, Bernard, Executive Vice President, International Molders and Allied Workers Union.

Bywater, William H., President, International Union of Electrical, Radio and Machine Workers.

Campanelli, John A., President, Delaware State AFL-CIO.

Campbell, Patrick, General President, United Brotherhood of Carpenters and Joiners of America.

Carollo, Sal, Executive Secretary, Italian Actors Union.

Carpenter, George E., Jr., Secretary-Treasurer, Massachusetts AFL-CIO.

Carper, Julian F., President, Virginia State AFL-CIO.

Carr, Irene, Secretary, Civil Service Employees Association, Inc.

Carter, Frank W., International Secretary-Treasurer, Glass, Pottery, Plastics and Allied Workers.

Carter, Mary J., National Secretary, National Association of Air Traffic Specialists.

Casey, Pamela, Secretary-Treasurer, Association of Flight Attendants.

Cassidy, Robert J., Treasurer, National Council for Labor Reform.

Chaikin, Sol C., President, International Ladies Garment Workers Union.

Champagne, Richard, Co-President, Amalgamated Lace Operatives of America.

Channell, O. P., Jr., General Secretary-Treasurer, Brotherhood Railway Carmen of the U.S. and Canada.

Chavez, Cesar E., President, United Farm Workers of America.

Chiappardi, F. J., President, National Federation of Independent Unions.

Church, Sam, Jr., Past President, United Mine Workers of America.

Clark, Carroll G., International President, International Union of Petroleum and Industrial Workers.

Clark, Robert, President, Vermont State Labor Council AFL-CIO.

Coia, Arthur E., Secretary-Treasurer, Laborers' International Union of North America.

Colbert, Peter A., Financial Secretary, Independent Union of Plant Protection Employees.

Cole, Eunice, President, American Nurses' Association.

Collins, D. E., President, American Train Dispatchers Association.

Connery, Vincent L., National President, National Treasury Employees Union.

Cook, Robert J., President, Alabama State Employees Union.

Cooper, Hal, Secretary, Directors Guild of America, Inc.

Corder, Duane R., International Secretary-Treasurer, National Association of Broadcast Employees and Technicians.

Cordtz, Richard W., International Secretary-Treasurer, Service Employees International Union.

Craib, William A., President, Assembly of Governmental Employees.

Crosby, Donna, Treasurer, Alabama State Employees Association.

Culver, R. J., Grand Secretary-Treasurer, Railroad Yardmasters of America.

Curry, Diane, President, International Labor Press Association.

Curtis, Raymond G., Secretary-Treasurer, International Guards Union of America.

Cushing, Lawrence C., President-Executive Director, National Association of Air Traffic Specialists.

Cutler, Marty, President, Utah Public Employees Association.

Dale, Charles, Secretary-Treasurer, The Newspaper Guild.

D'Ambrosio, Dominick, President, International Union, Allied Industrial Workers of America.

DeKoster, Arthur W., President, International Association of Craftsmen.

Dellaratta, Anthony J., Secretary, Atlantic Independent Union.

Delle-Femine, O. V., National Director, Aircraft Mechanics Fraternal Association.

Dempster, Paul, President and Secretary-Treasurer, Sailors' Union of the Pacific.

DiGiorgio, Joe, Secretary-Treasurer, Seafarers' International Union.

DiJames, Pascal, General President, Secretary-Treasurer, Tile, Marble, Terrazzo, Finishers, Shopworkers and Granite Cutters International Union.

Dillon, Diane, President, The Graphic Artists Guild.

Disley, Henry, President, Marine Firemen's Union (Pacific Coast Marine Firemen, Oilers, Watertenders and Wipers Association).

Dixon, Linda, Recording Secretary, Independent Union of Plant Protection Employees.

Dolan, Joan G., Vice President-Labor Relations, Association of Labor Relations Agencies.

Donahue, Thomas R., Secretary-Treasurer, American Federation of Labor and Congress of Industrial Organizations.

Donegan, J., Jr., Secretary-Treasurer, International Plate Printers, Die Stampers, Engravers Union.

Donegan, Robert A., Secretary-Treasurer, North Dakota AFL-CIO.

Donovan, William, Secretary of Labor.

Dorman, Richard F., Executive Director, Assembly of Governmental Employees.

Dotson, Donald, Chairman, National Labor Relations Board.

Drake, Juel D., General Secretary, International Association of Bridge, Structural and Ornamental Iron Workers.

Dresler, Kay K., Secretary-Treasurer, Telecommunications International Union.

Driscoll, Jerry, President, Montana State AFL-CIO.

Driscoll, John J., President, Connecticut State AFL-CIO.

Drozak, Frank, President, Seafarers International Union.

Drumheiler, Evelyn, Secretary-Treasurer, Idaho Public Employees Association.

Dubeck, Leroy, Secretary-Treasurer, American Association of University Professors.

Dubrow, Evelyn, Vice President, International Ladies Garment Workers Union.

Dudley, Jack E., President and Financial Secretary, South Dakota State Federation of Labor.

Eddy, Jim, President, Federal Plant Quarantine Inspectors National Association.

Eisenberg, Alan, Executive Secretary, Actors' Equity Association.

Erickson, J. P., Secretary-Treasurer, American Train Dispatchers Association.

Etherton, John, National Treasurer, Aircraft Mechanics Fraternal Association.

Evans, Arthur, Executive Director, Ohio Civil Service Employees Association.

Evans, Claude, Executive Secretary-Treasurer, Nevada State AFL-CIO.

Evans, Jim, President, Idaho Public Employees Association.

Fagan, John J., General President, Textile Processors, Service Trades, Health Care, Professional and Technical Employees International Union.

Fallon, William D., President, Independent Union of Plant Protection Employees.

Fauser, Barbara, Treasurer, Civil Service Employees Association, Inc.

Feinen, Jeff, Co-Treasurer, The Graphic Artists Guild.

Finley, Murray H., President, Amalgamated Clothing and Textile Workers Union.

Fire, Edward, Secretary-Treasurer, International Union of Electrical, Radio and Machine Workers.

Fisher, Richard, Treasurer, Patent Office Professional Association.

Fitzpatrick, Francis E., Secretary-Treasurer, International Union, United Plant Guard Workers of America.

Fitzsimmons, Robert, Treasurer, Actors' Equity Association.

Foley, Hugh J., Jr., National President, Brotherhood of Utility Workers of New England, Inc.

Foner, Moe, Executive Secretary, National Union of Hospital and Health Care Employees.

Fortier, Maurice, Executive Vice President, Vermont State Labor Council AFL-CIO.

Fosco, Angelo, President, Laborers' International Union of North America.

Fosdick, F. C., Secretary-Treasurer, Allied Pilots Association.

Francisco, George J., International President, International Brotherhood of Firemen and Oilers.

Franklin, Michael H., National Executive Secretary, Directors Guild of America, Inc.

Fraser, Douglas A., Past President, International Union, United Automobile, Aerospace and Agricultural Implement Workers of America.

Frazier, Robert, Secretary-Treasurer, National Weather Service Employees Organization.

Fryman, Patsy, Recording Secretary, Coalition of Labor Union Women.

Futrell, Mary H., Secretary-Treasurer, National Education Association.

Gagnier, Robert J., Executive Director, State of Nevada Employees Association.

Gallagher, Thomas J., Executive Director, Oregon Public Employees Union.

Gannon, John A., President, International Association of Firefighters.

Garvey, Ed, Executive Director, National Football League Players Association.

Gerl, James, President, North Dakota AFL-CIO.

Gerwig, Robert, Secretary-Treasurer, International Woodworkers of America.

Gibson, John, Secretary-Treasurer, Hotel and Restaurant Employees and Bartenders International Union.

Gill, William A., Jr., President, Flight Engineers' International Association.

Glenn, Wayne E., President, United Paperworkers International Union.

Glover, Eugene D., General Secretary-Treasurer, International Association of Machinists and Aerospace Workers.

Gluck, Sidney, President, Labor Research Association, Inc.

Gochenour, Wayne A., President, International Union of Gas Workers.

Goldberg, Arthur J., labor lawyer, instrumental in bringing about AFL-CIO merger; former Secretary of Labor and former justice on the U.S. Supreme Court.

Goldsmith, Frank, Secretary-Treasurer, Labor Research Association, Inc.

Gonzalez, Neal, Executive Secretary-Treasurer, New Mexico State AFL-CIO.

Gordon, Robert D., Secretary-Treasurer, International Union of Police Associations.

Goss, Robert F., President, Oil, Chemical and Atomic Workers International Union.

Gray, Donald M., Treasurer, National League of Postmasters of the U.S.

Grim, Jerry, International Secretary-Treasurer, United Telegraph Workers.

Gruber, Joseph A., Executive Vice President, Wisconsin State AFL-CIO.

Gunn, Joe D., Secretary-Treasurer, Texas AFL-CIO.

Gunter, Sue, Secretary, National Labor Relations Board Professional Association.

Gurian, Naomi, Executive Director, Writers Guild of America, West, Inc.

Haas, Andrew T., General President, International Association of Heat and Frost Insulators and Asbestos Workers.

Hambright, R. Fain, President, National League of Postmasters of the U.S.

Handelman, Rubin, Secretary, National Association of Postal Supervisors.

Hanley, Edward T., President, Hotel and Restaurant Employees and Bartenders International Union.

Hansen, Andrew M., ALA Staff Liaison, AFL-CIO American Library Association, Joint Committee on Library Service to Labor Groups.

Hardin, Fred A., Chairman, Railway Labor Executives Association; President, United Transportation Union.

Harmon, R. H., Secretary-Treasurer, South Carolina AFL-CIO.

Harnisch, Lynn, President, Alaska Public Employees Association.

Harris, Robert O., Chairman, National Mediation Board.

Harrison, Lee R., Jr., President, National Weather Service Employees Organization.

Hatch, Orrin G., Chairman, Senate Labor and Human Resources Committee.

Hatfield, James E., International President, Glass, Pottery, Plastics and Allied Workers.

Haughton, Ronald W., Chairman, Federal Labor Relations Authority.

Haviland, Mary, Treasurer, South Dakota State Employees Organization.

Healy, C., Sr., President, International Plate Printers, Die Stampers, Engravers Union.

Healy, Msgr. James A., President-Elect, Association of Labor Relations Agencies.

Heaps, Alvin E., President, Retail, Wholesale, and Department Store Union.

Heaton, Paul, Treasurer, Upholsterers' International Union of North America.

Heh, Judith, Secretary-Treasurer, Pennsylvania AFL-CIO.

Henning, L. Keith, Executive Secretary, Wyoming State AFL-CIO.

Herbert, Victor J., President, Air Line Employees Association, International.

Herman, James R., President, International Longshoremen's and Warehousemen's Union.

Herndon, Terry E., Executive Director, National Education Association.

Hicks, Marshall, Secretary-Treasurer, Utility Workers Union of America.

Higdon, Ernest D., President, Secretary-Treasurer, Coopers International Union of North America.

Hillman, Bill, President, American Federation of TV and Radio Artists.

Hillsman, Deane, Secretary, Union of American Physicians and Dentists.

Hoese, Frank T., General President, American Federation of Grain Millers International.

Hoffman, Harold M., Treasurer, American Actors and Artistes of America.

Holbrook, Douglas, General Secretary-Treasurer, American Postal Workers Union.

Holland, Frederick J., National Secretary, Brotherhood of Utility Workers of New England, Inc.

Holley, Lawrence A., President, Aluminum, Brick and Glass Workers International Union.

Holt, G. Ray, President, American Association of Classified School Employees.

Holton, Robert J., Secretary-Treasurer, Operative Plasterers' and Cement Masons' International Association of the U.S. and Canada.

Houser, Martha R., President, National Labor Relations Board Professional Association.

Hubbard, Harry, President, Texas AFL-CIO.

Hunter, John T., President, Association of Civilian Technicians.

Jacobson, O. W., General President, Brotherhood Railway Carmen of the U.S. and Canada.

Jandt, Karin, Secretary-Treasurer, National Industrial Workers Union.

Janssen, Kathryn, Secretary, Screen Extras Guild, Inc.

Jeronimo, Albino, Secretary, International Union of Tool, Die and Mold Makers.

Johnson, Gloria, Director of Education and Women's Activities, International Union of Electrical, Radio and Machine Workers; Treasurer, Coalition of Labor Union Women.

Johnson, Keith W., President, International Woodworkers of America.

Johnson, Lonnie L., National Director, National Post Office Mail Handlers, Watchmen, Messengers and Group Leaders Division of the Laborers' International Union of North America.

Jones, Ernest C., President, Indiana State AFL-CIO.

Joseph, Johnnie, President, Southern Labor Union.

Joy, James, Jr., President, Utility Workers Union of America.

Joyce, John T., President, International Union of Bricklayers and Allied Craftsmen.

Kane, James M., General President, United Electrical, Radio and Machine Workers of America.

Karp, Nathan, Financial Secretary, Socialist Labor Party.

Kelly, John, President, Office and Professional Employees International Union.

Kemp, (Mrs.) Maida Springer, Representative, African-American Labor Center; member, International Ladies Garment Workers Union; active in many phases of labor movement.

Kenney, Lawrence, Secretary-Treasurer, Washington State Labor Council AFL-CIO.

Kerr, John W., President, Atlantic Independent Union.

Kersten, Otto, General Secretary, International Confederation of Free Trade Unions.

Kheel, Theodore W., Administrative Director, Institute of Collective Bargaining and Group Relations, Inc.

Kiernan, Edward J., President, International Union of Police Associations.

Kilroy, R. I., Executive Secretary, Railway Labor Executives Association; President, Brotherhood of Railway, Airline and Steamship Clerks.

Kirkland, Lane, President, American Federation of Labor and Congress of Industrial Organizations.

Kiser, Randy, President, South Carolina AFL-CIO.

Kloepfer, Charles, National Secretary, Aircraft Mechanics Fraternal Association.

Knack, Joseph V., Executive Vice President, National Weather Service Employees Organization.

Knecht, Louis B., Secretary-Treasurer, Communications Workers of America.

Knight, Thomas, Secretary-Treasurer, Mississippi AFL-CIO.

Komer, Odessa, Corresponding Secretary, Coalition of Labor Union Women.

Kopeck, Thomas W., Secretary-Treasurer, International Typographical Union.

Koukl, Frank, Secretary-Treasurer, United Retail Workers Union.

Kump, Larry D., Executive Director, Indiana State Employees Association.

Kupau, Walter H., President, Hawaii State AFL-CIO.

Laizure-Jellison, Carol, Secretary-Treasurer, Oregon Public Employees Union.

Lambers, Muriel, Treasurer, Christian Labor Association of the U.S.A.

Latimer, Thomas H., Executive Vice President, National Council for Labor Reform.

Lane, John E., International Executive Vice President, Transport Workers Union of America.

Laws, David H., Secretary-Treasurer, Virginia State AFL-CIO.

Layton, Delmas, Treasurer, Southern Labor Union.

Leatherman, Donald, Treasurer-Budget Director, National Association of Air Traffic Specialists.

Ledbetter, Donald N., President, National Association of Postal Supervisors.

Lee, Tom, President, Wyoming State AFL-CIO.

Leep, Don E., President, Christian Labor Association of the U.S.A.

Leigon, Ralph A., Secretary, International Brotherhood of Electrical Workers.

Leonard, Sheldon, Treasurer, Directors Guild of America.

Lindner, William G., International President, Transport Workers Union of america.

Little, Calvina S., General Secretary-Treasurer, United Garment Workers of America.

Loihl, John R., 1st Vice President, Association of Labor Relations Agencies.

Lowen, Robert J., President, International Organization of Masters, Mates and Pilots.

Lucassen, Sigurd, 1st General Vice President, United Brotherhood of Carpenters and Joiners of America.

Lucy, William, President, Coalition of Black Trade Unionists, International Secretary-Treasurer, American Federation of State, County and Municipal Employees.

Ludwig, William, Secretary-Treasurer, Writers Guild of America, West, Inc.

Lutty, Anthony J., International Secretary-Treasurer, United Food and Commercial Workers International Union.

Lynch, Edward M., International President, National Association of Broadcast Employees and Technicians.

Lyons, John H., General President, International Association of Bridge, Structural and Ornamental Iron Workers.

Madar, Olga, Past President, Coalition of Labor Union Women.

Madigan, Robert, International Secretary-Treasurer, International Union of Petroleum and Industrial Workers.

Magee, John J., Treasurer, Air Line Pilots Association.

Magrino, Vito P., Financial Officer, National Post Office Mail Handlers, Watchmen, Messengers and Group Leaders Division of the Laborers' International Union of North America.

Maguire, William J., Jr., President, Colorado Association of State Employees.

Majerus, Raymond, Secretary-Treasurer, International Union, United Automobile, Aerospace and Agricultural Implement Workers of America.

Malone, R. H., President, Allied Pilots Association.

Marchetti, Leo V., President, Fraternal Order of Police.

Marcus, Dr. Sanford A., President, Union of American Physicians and Dentists.

Marsh, Milan, President, Ohio AFL-CIO.

Marshall, William C., President, Michigan State AFL-CIO.

Martin, Joseph E., Secretary Treasurer, Florida AFL-CIO.

Martinez, Thomas, Secretary-Treasurer, National Maritime Union.

Martino, Frank D., President, International Chemical Workers Union.

Massagli, Mark Tully, President, Nevada State AFL-CIO.

Matthews, Ira J., Secretary-Treasurer, Federation of Westinghouse Independent Salaried Unions.

Matz, Michael A., International Secretary-Treasurer, International Brotherhood of Firemen and Oilers.

Mayne, Ed, President, Secretary-Treasurer, Utah State AFL-CIO.

McBride, Lloyd, International President, United Steelworkers of America.

McClain, Curtis, Secretary-Treasurer, International Longshoremen's and Warehousemen's Union.

McClintock, Ernest, President, American Federation of Guards, Local No. 1.

McCrum, Joel E., Treasurer, Marine Firemen's Union (Pacific Coast Marine Firemen, Oilers, Watertenders and Wipers Association).

McElroy, Edward J., Jr., President, Rhode Island AFL-CIO.

McEntee, Gerald W., International President, American Federation of State, County and Municipal Employees.

McGahey, James C., President, International Union, United Plant Guard Workers of America.

McGowan, William L., President, Civil Service Employees Association, Inc.

McGrawth, J. Paul, Assistant Attorney General, Civil Division, U.S. Department of Justice.

McGuiness, Kenneth C., Vice President and General Counsel, Labor Policy Association, Inc.

McGuire, Willard H., President, National Education Association.

McIntyre, Robert T., Executive Vice President, Pennsylvania AFL-CIO.

McKee, Frank S., International Treasurer, United Steelworkers of America.

McLemore, A. L., President, International Guards Union of America.

McMurray, Kay, Director, Federal Mediation and Conciliation Service.

McTiernan, Francis, President, Federation of Westinghouse Independent Salaried Unions.

Meier, Allen J., Secretary-Treasurer, National Association of Governmental Labor Officials.

Merrill, Dave, President, South Dakota State Employees Organization.

Miechur, Thomas F., President, United Cement, Lime, Gypsum and Allied Workers International Union.

Miller, Daniel J., President, Florida AFL-CIO.

Miller, Joyce, National President, Coalition of Labor Union Women; Vice President and Director of Social Services, Amalgamated Clothing and Textile Workers Union.

Miller, Lenore, Secretary-Treasurer, Retail, Wholesale, and Department Store Union.

Miller, Marvin J., Executive Director, Major League Baseball Players Association.

Mohler, Edward A., Secretary-Treasurer, Maryland State and D.C. AFL-CIO.

Monroe, James A., Executive Director-Treasurer, American Association of Classified School Employees.

Moore, David B., President, Engineers and Scientists of California.

Moore, Kenneth, Vice President, Business Department, United Transportation Union.

Moore, Robert F., Treasurer, International Association of Tool Craftsmen.

Murry, James W., Executive Secretary, Montana State AFL-CIO.

Naddeo, Charles, General Secretary-Treasurer, Textile Processors, Service Trades, Health Care, Professional and Technical Employees International Union.

Narayanan, P. P., President, International Confederation of Free Trade Unions.

Neeley, James G., President, Tennessee State Labor Council.

Nelson, Alan Jan, Executive President, American Guild of Variety Artists.

Newberry, Dr. Truman A., Treasurer, Union of American Physicians and Dentists.

Newman, Harold R., Public Employment Relations Board.

Newman, Jeffrey, Executive Director, National Child Labor Committee.

Newman, Pauline, first woman organizer for International Ladies Garment Workers Union; co-founder and Educational Director, Union Health Center of the ILGWU. Retired.

Newton, John, Secretary-Treasurer, Amalgamated Lace Operatives of America.

Nichols, Charles E., General Treasurer, United Brotherhood of Carpenters and Joiners of America.

Nichols, Henry, President, National Union of Hospital and Health Care Employees.

Norris, C. M., President, New Mexico State AFL-CIO.

Northrip, Richard A., Secretary-Treasurer, United Cement, Lime, Gypsum and Allied Workers International Union.

Norton, James J., Secretary-Treasurer, Graphic Arts International Union.

Norwood, Janet L., U.S. Commissioner of Labor Statistics, U.S. Department of Labor.

Null, Lester H., Assistant to the President, Glass, Pottery, Plastics and Allied Workers.

O'Bea, George H., Jr., National Director, United Paperworkers International Union.

O'Brien, Peter S., President, American Federation of School Administrators.

O'Connell, Richard P., Secretary-Treasurer, National Association of Letter Carriers.

O'Donnell, John J., President, Air Line Pilots Association.

O'Donnell, William, General President, United Garment Workers of America.

Odorcich, Joseph, Vice President (Administration), United Steelworkers of America.

Oliver, John, Executive Director, Maine State Employees Association.

Oliver, Walter L., Secretary-Treasurer, Michigan State AFL-CIO.

O'Neal, Frederick, President, Associated Actors and Artistes of America.

Orlofsky, Abraham, National Secretary-Treasurer, National Federation of Federal Employees.

Orsatti, Ken, National Executive Secretary, Screen Actors Guild.

Osborn, Arthur R., President, Massachusetts AFL-CIO.

Otto, A. T., Jr., Grand President, Railroad Yardmasters of America.

Palmer, Kenneth, Financial Secretary-Treasurer, International Union of Gas Workers.

Parker, George M., President, American Flint Glass Workers Union.

Patrick, Annette, Secretary, Alabama State Employees Association.

Peirce, James M., Jr., National President, National Federation of Federal Employees.

Perkins, Carl D., Chairman, House Committee on Education and Labor.

Perlik, Charles A., Jr., President, The Newspaper Guild.

Peterson, Edward F., Secretary-Treasurer, Delaware State AFL-CIO.

Peterson, Esther, active in labor movement since 1930; legislative representative for Amalgamated Clothing Workers and AFL-CIO; director, Women's Bureau, U.S. Department of Labor; Assistant Secretary of Labor for Labor Standards. Retired.

Petrillo, James C., Past President, American Federation of Musicians. Retired.

Petry, D. H., President, Oregon Public Employees Union.

Phillips, Don, Secretary-Treasurer, American Guild of Variety Artists.

Phillips, John J., President, Machine Printers and Engravers Association of the U.S.

Pierce, Martin E., Secretary-Treasurer, International Association of Fire Fighters.

Pierson, Frank, President, Writers Guild of America, West, Inc.

Pillard, Charles H., President, International Brotherhood of Electrical Workers.

Plato, Charles A., International President, International Union of Security Officers.

Pluhowski, Genevieve, Treasurer, National Labor Relations Board Professional Association.

Pluymert, James, President, National Council for Labor Reform.

Pollack, Joseph, President, Insurance Workers International Union.

Polly, Jim, Secretary, Southern Labor Union.

Porter, Robert G., Secretary-Treasurer, American Federation of Teachers.

Puchala, Linda A., President, Association of Flight Attendants.

Puchammer, Julius, Treasurer, International Union of Tool, Die and Mold Makers.

Puffer, Clark L., Executive Director, Utah Public Employees Association.

Quackenbush, James H., Director, International Labor Office (Washington Branch).

Quadros, Albano, Secretary-Treasurer, Leather Workers International Union.

Ramsay, Claude, President, Mississippi AFL-CIO.

Ratliff, Donald, General Financial Secretary-Treasurer, International Union of Life Insurance Agents.

Reese, Harry C., Executive Director, Colorado Association of State Employees.

Reihl, Jack B., Secretary-Treasurer, Wisconsin State AFL-CIO.

Ricigliana, Michael, Secretary-Treasurer, Oil, Chemical and Atomic Workers International Union.

Ridgill, James L., Jr., Secretary, Patent Office Professional Association.

Rinehart, John D., General Secretary-Treasurer, Brotherhood of Locomotive Engineers.

Rogers, John S., General Secretary, United Brotherhood of Carpenters and Joiners of America.

Roman, Joseph, Executive Assistant to the President, Aluminum, Brick and Glass Workers International Union.

Rongione, Nicholas M., Secretary-Treasurer, Insurance Workers International Union.

Roots, Melvin H., General President, Operative Plasterers' and Cement Masons' International Association of the U.S. and Canada.

Rosenstreich, Judy P., Executive Director, Vermont State Employees Association, Inc.

Rowland, John W., International President, Amalgamated Transit Union.

Rowland, Robert A., Chairman, Occupational Safety and Health Review Commission.

Ryan, James J., Secretary, International Association of Tool Craftsmen.

Salamone, William J., Secretary-Treasurer, International Union, Allied Industrial Workers of America.

Sawyer, James L., President, Leather Workers International Union.

Schickling, Henry F., International President, International Union of Tool, Die and Mold Makers.

Schmitt, John W., President, Wisconsin State AFL-CIO.

Schneider, William A., Treasurer, Air Line Employees Association International.

Schoessling, Ray, General Secretary-Treasurer, International Brotherhood of Teamsters.

Schuetz, Robert C., President, International Union of Life Insurance Agents.

Serembus, John, President, Upholsterers' International Union of North America.

Shanker, Albert, President, American Federation of Teachers.

Shattuck, Cathie A., Acting Chairman, Equal Employment Opportunity Commission.

Shaughnessy, John W., Jr., President, Telecommunications International Union.

Sheffield, Horace, Secretary, Coalition of Black Trade Unionists.

Sheinkman, Jack, Secretary-Treasurer, Amalgamated Clothing and Textile Workers Union.

Shelley, Cherie, Executive Director, Alaska Public Employees Association.

Shepherd, John H., General Secretary-Treasurer, United Transportation Union.

Shields, Dorothy, Head, Education Department, AFL-CIO.

Simons, William, Treasurer, Coalition of Black Trade Unionists.

Smisek, Joseph T., General Secretary-Treasurer, American Federation of Grain Millers International.

Smith, Mark L., Secretary-Treasurer, Iowa Federation of Labor.

Smith, Paul M., Jr., Executive Director, Alabama State Employees Association.

Smith, Warren J., Secretary-Treasurer, Ohio AFL-CIO.

Sombrotto, Vincent R., President, National Association of Letter Carriers.

Sparks, William J., Secretary-Treasurer, International Chemical Workers Union.

Steen, Lias B., President, National Association of Governmental Labor Officials.

Stone, Milan, International President, United Rubber, Cork, Linoleum and Plastic Workers of America.

Stone, Victor, President, American Association of University Professors.

Studenroth, Carl W., President, International Molders and Allied Workers Union.

Sun, Leland, Treasurer, Screen Extras Guild, Inc.

Swafford, Andrew J., Secretary-Treasurer, International Molders and Allied Workers Union.

Sweeney, John J., International President, Service Employees International Union.

Systema, John F., President, Brotherhood of Locomotive Engineers.

Taback, Simms, Co-Secretary, The Graphic Artists Guild.

Taylor, Jud, President, Directors Guild of America, Inc.

Tener, Jeffrey B., Executive Director, Association of Labor Relations Agencies.

Tesauro, John F., President, Association of Labor Relations Agencies.

Thomas, Carla, Secretary-Treasurer, Vermont State Labor Council, AFL-CIO.

Thomas, Joyce, Secretary-Treasurer, Engineers and Scientists of California.

Tianti, Betty L., Secretary-Treasurer, Connecticut State AFL-CIO.

Tibbs, De Lloyd, National Executive Secretary, American Guild of Musical Artists.

Tittle, F. W., Secretary-Treasurer, National Federation of Independent Unions.

Tobias, Robert N., National Executive Vice President, National Treasury Employees Union.

Tracy, Joseph P., National Treasurer, Brotherhood of Utility Workers of New England, Inc.

Trahey, Richard, President, Maine State Employees Association.

Trammell, Asa, Secretary-Treasurer, Alabama Labor Council, AFL-CIO.

Trumka, Richard L., President, United Mine Workers of America.

Tucker, Donald C., International Secretary-Treasurer, United Rubber, Cork, Linoleum and Plastic Workers of America.

Turner, Doris, President, National Union of Hospital and Health Care Employees, District 1199.

Turner, Ed, Executive Vice President, Seafarers International Union.

Twomey, Maurice J., Executive Vice President, National Association of Postal Supervisors.

Uehlein, Julius, President, Pennsylvania AFL-CIO.

Uncapher, Ivan T., Secretary-Treasurer, American Flint Glass Workers Union.

Upshaw, Gene, President, National Football League Players Association.

Vatalano, Ralph, Executive Director, Public Employment Relations Board.

Veech, Barbara, Secretary, National League of Postmasters of the U.S.

Velasco, Peter G., Secretary-Treasurer, United Farm Workers of America.

Vrataric, Nicholas C., Secretary-Treasurer, United Paperworkers International Union.

Wall, Shannan J., President, National Maritime Union.

Wallace, R. C., International Secretary-Treasurer, Amalgamated Transit Union.

Wallack, Roy, President, Screen Extras Guild, Inc.

Ward-Steinman, Irving, General Counsel: Independent Bakery Employees Union and the Independent Hospital Employees Union.

Watkins, Karen, Co-Secretary, The Graphic Artists Guild.

Watson, Gayle M., Secretary-Treasurer, Assembly of Governmental Employees.

Watson, Ruth, President, Vermont State Employees Association, Inc.

Watts, Glenn E., President, Communications Workers of America.

Watts, Roosevelt, International Secretary-Treasurer, Transport Workers Union of America.

Webster, H. Max, Secretary-Treasurer, Aluminum, Brick and Clay Workers International Union.

Weeks, Barney, President, Alabama Labor Council, AFL-CIO.

Wells, Ronald, Secretary-Treasurer, Business Manager, American Federation of Guards, Local No. 1.

Wengert, James J., President, Iowa Federation of Labor.

Wenke, Joseph J., Treasurer, Atlantic Independent Union.

Western, Dan L., General Manager, California State Employees Association.

Wheeler, Alonzo, Business Manager, National Industrial Workers Union.

Whitty, Dr. Michael, Research Director: Labor Research Associates, Institute for Technological Humanism and the Center for Research in Labor, Business and Community Relations.

Williams, Lynn R., International Secretary, United Steelworkers of America.

Williams, Marvin L., President, Washington State Labor Council AFL-CIO.

Williams, Roy L., General President, International Brotherhood of Teamsters.

Winpisinger, William W., President, Institute of Collective Bargaining and Group Relations, Inc.; International President, International Association of Machinists and Aerospace Workers.

Wolff, Sanford I., National Executive Secretary: American Federation of TV and Radio Artists and the Associated Actors and Artistes of America.

Wood, Wilbur S., President, National Rural Letter Carriers' Association.

Woodcock, Leonard, Past President, International Union, United Automobile, Aerospace and Agricultural Implement Workers of America.

Woods, Dorothy A., Secretary, Fraternal Order of Police.

Wright, Max F., Secretary-Treasurer, Indiana State AFL-CIO.

Wyatt, Addie, Director, Women's Affairs, United Food and Commercial Workers International Union.

Wynn, William H., International President, United Food and Commercial Workers International Union.

Yates, Judith, Executive Director, American Nurses' Association.

Zagar, Jean, Treasurer, Colorado Association of State Employees.

Zimmerman, Edward, Co-President, Amalgamated Lace Operatives of America.

DECEASED OFFICERS AND LEADERS

This listing, compiled from several histories of the labor movement and recent newspaper indexes, is limited to outstanding personalities who in one way or another figured prominently in the history of the labor movement. They may have worked to advance the cause of unionism, fought for workingmen's rights, established and/or built up a major union, or otherwise achieved recognition or notoriety.

Berger, Victor L., b. February 28, 1860, Nieder Rehbach, Austria-Hungary. d. August 7, 1929. Socialist leader; a founder of the Social Democratic Party; first Socialist elected to the U.S. House of Representatives.

Curran, Joseph F., b. March 1, 1906, New York, New York. d. August 14, 1981. Founder and president, National Maritime Union.

Debs, Eugene V., b. November 5, 1855, Terre Haute, Indiana. d. October 20, 1926. Labor leader and founder of Socialist Party.

DeLeon, Daniel, b. December 14, 1852, Curacao, Netherlands Antilles. d. May 11, 1914. Socialist leader; established Socialist Trade and Labor Alliance.

Dubinsky, David, b. February 22, 1892, Brest Litovsk, Poland. d. September 17, 1982. President, International Ladies Garment Workers' Union.

Evans, George H., b. March 25, 1805, Bromyard, England. d. February 2, 1856. Publisher, *The Working Man's Advocate*.

Fitzsimmons, Frank E., b. April 7, 1908, Jeanette, Pennsylvania. d. May 6, 1981. President, International Brotherhood of Teamsters.

Foster, William Z., b. February 25, 1881, Taunton, Massachusetts. d. September 1, 1961. Left-wing socialist and labor leader; General Secretary of Communist Party (U.S.).

Gompers, Samuel, b. January 27, 1850, London, England. d. December 13, 1924. Labor leader; first president of the American Federation of Labor.

Green, William, b. March 3, 1873, Coshocton, Ohio. d. November 21, 1952. Labor leader; president of American Federation of Labor.

Haywood, William D., b. February 4, 1869, Salt Lake City, Utah. d. May 18, 1928. Labor leader; co-founder, Industrial Workers of the World.

Hillman, Sidney, b. 1887, Zagare, Lithuania. d. July 10, 1946. President, Amalgamated Clothing Workers; founder, American Labor Party.

Hoffa, James R., b. February 14, 1913, Brazil, Indiana. d. 1980 (?). Controversial labor leader; president, Teamsters Union, imprisoned for wiretapping and perjury; disappeared in 1980 and thought to have been murdered.

Hutchinson, Maurice, b. May 7, 1897, Saginaw, Michigan. d. January 9, 1983. President, United Brotherhood of Carpenters and Joiners of America, from 1952-1972, succeeding his father, William L. Hutchinson.

Hutchinson, William L., b. February 7, 1874, Saginaw, Michigan. d. October 20, 1953. President, United Brotherhood of Carpenters and Joiners of America.

LaFollette, Robert M., b. June 14, 1855, Primrose, Wisconsin. d. June 18, 1925. Governor of Wisconsin; then U.S. senator and leader of liberals and progressives; sponsor of LaFollette Seamen's Act of 1915.

Lewis, John L., b. February 12, 1880, Lucas, Iowa. d. June 11, 1969. President, United Mine Workers.

McDonald, David J., b. Pittsburgh, Pennsylvania, November 22, 1902. d. August 8, 1979. President, United Steelworkers of America.

Meany, George, b. August 16, 1894, New York, New York. d. January 10, 1980. President AFL-CIO.

Mitchell, John, b. February 4, 1870, Braidwood, Illinois. d. September 9, 1919. Early president of United Mine Workers.

Murray, Philip, b. May 25, 1886, Blantyre, Scotland. d. November 9, 1952. President of Congress of Industrial Organizations and United Steelworkers of America.

Perkins, Frances, b. April 10, 1882, Boston, Massachusetts. d. May 14, 1965. Secretary of Labor from 1933 to 1945.

Potofsky, Jacob S., b. November 16, 1894, Radomisi, Russia. d. August 5, 1979. President, Amalgamated Clothing and Textile Workers Union; senior member, AFL-CIO Executive Council.

Powderly, Terence V., b. January 22, 1849, Carbondale, Pennsylvania. d. June 24, 1924. Grand Master Workman (president), Noble Order of the Knights of Labor.

Quill, Michael J., b. September 18, 1905, Gourtloughera, Ireland. d. January 28, 1966. Founder and president, Transport Workers Union of America.

Randolph, A. Philip, b. April 15, 1889, Crescent City, Florida. d. May 16, 1979. President, Brotherhood of Sleeping Car Porters.

Reuther, Walter, b. September 1, 1907, Wheeling, West Virginia. d. May 9, 1970. President, United Automobile Workers.

Schneiderman, (Mrs.) Rose, b. April 1884, Poland. d. August 11, 1972. President of National and New York Women's Trade Union League; held offices in United Hatters, Cap & Millinery Workers International Union; early labor activist.

Shaw, Lemuel, b. January 9, 1781, Barnstable, Massachusetts. d. March 30, 1861. Famous jurist and chief justice of the Massachusetts Supreme Court (1830-1860); most famous case was *Commonwealth* v. *Hunt*.

Stephens, Uriah S., b. August 3, 1821, near Cape May, New Jersey. d. February 13, 1882. Founder and Grand Master Workman (president), Noble Order of the Knights of Labor.

Wagner, Robert F., b. Nastatten, Hesse-Nassan, Germany, June 8, 1877. d. May 5, 1953. U.S. senator responsible for introducing important labor and social legislation in the 1930s.

Wurf, Jerry, b. May 19, 1919, Bronx, New York. d. December 10, 1981. President, American Federation of State, County and Municipal Employees.

IV

PRINCIPAL FEDERAL LABOR LAWS AND EXECUTIVE ORDERS AFFECTING LABOR

This section contains citations to and summaries of laws affecting the more important aspects of labor relations through 1982, together with pertinent Presidential Executive Orders.

Section I, Labor History Highlights, which is arranged chronologically, indicates what legislation was adopted at a specific time; this section gives additional data on the more important laws and executive orders relating to the labor movement. The laws are arranged alphabetically by their best-known titles, but the alternative titles may be found in the index.

For current information about federal and state labor legislation and the regulations promulgated by the administrative agencies responsible for enforcing the laws, consult either the *Labor Law Reports*, published by Commerce Clearing House, or the *Labor Relations Guide*, published by Prentice-Hall. These may be found in many large public libraries, municipal, state or federal law libraries, as well as college or university libraries. Your public librarian can probably help you find the location of the nearest library which subscribes to these loose-leaf reports or other guides to federal and state legislation.

It should be pointed out that some of the laws included in this section have been amended, repealed, reenacted, or partially amended by subsequent legislation. Therefore, if the current status of a law is required, it is recommended that those unfamiliar with the use of the various guides to legislation seek the assistance of counsel, a knowledgeable librarian, or someone familiar with the subject.

All of the laws enacted by Congress are contained in a volume titled, the *United States Code*, 1976 edition, which is kept up to date through annual cumulative supplements. Proceedings of Congress, speeches, debates, and actions of the legislative body and its committees are published daily in the *Congressional Record*.

All federal agency regulations and other legal documents of the executive branch are published daily in the *Federal Register*. It also carries proposed changes in regulated areas. The *Code of Federal Regulations* is the annual cumulation of executive agency regulations issued previously and still in effect. This serves as a convenient reference for those desiring a comprehensive source of general and permanent federal regulations.

LEGISLATION

Adamson Act of 1916 (C436, 39 Stat. 721)

This law was passed to avert a threatened nationwide railroad strike, established the eight-hour day for all railroad employees, and stipulated there must be no reduction in pay for a shorter working day. Its constitutionality was upheld in 1917 by the U.S. Supreme Court in the case of *Wilson* v. *New.*

Age Discrimination in Employment Act of 1967 (PL 90-202, 81 Stat. 602)

The act made it illegal for employers, unions, and employment agencies in interstate commerce to discharge, refuse to hire or otherwise discriminate against persons aged 40 to 65.

Apprentice Training Service Act of 1937 (C663, 50 Stat. 664)

Also known as the Fitzgerald Act of 1937, this law set the pattern for today's system of federal government assistance in apprenticeship programs and established the Bureau of Apprenticeship in the U.S. Department of Labor.

Bituminous Coal Conservation Act of 1935 (C824, 49 Stat. 991)

This law, also known as the Guffey Act, was passed to stabilize the coal industry and to improve labor conditions. The labor relations provisions of the law were declared unconstitutional on May 18, 1936.

Child Labor Act of 1916 (C432, 39 Stat. 675)

Also known as the Owen-Keating Act, this law prohibited a company from shipping its products in interstate commerce if it employed any children under 14 or worked children 14 to 16 years of age more than eight hours a day or six days a week, or from 7:00 p.m. to 6:00 a.m. The U.S. Supreme Court ruled the law unconstitutional two years later, on June 3, 1918. Another act adopted in 1919 was also declared unconstitutional on May 15, 1922, and an amendment to the Constitution was proposed on June 2, 1924, but only 28 of the necessary 36 states ratified it.

Civil Rights Act of 1964 (PL 88-352, 78 Stat. 241)

This law aimed to eliminate all employment discrimination based on color, sex, and religion in industries engaged in interstate commerce. After its fourth year, the law covered all employers of at least 25 workers.

The act established the Equal Employment Opportunity Commission (EEOC) to administer and enforce the fair employment practice sections of the statute, although it was not given any power to enforce the act. It could investigate complaints of job discrimination, but the best it could do was try to bring about a voluntary settlement of a dispute. If that failed, the individual who sought justice had to file suit in court. The EEOC could recommend that the U.S. Attorney General file suits against violators, but this did not prove practical.

Civil rights groups and women's organizations pressed Congress to give EEOC authority to enforce the law; a new act, the Equal Employment Opportunity Act, was passed in 1972. (See Equal Employment Opportunity Act.)

Civil Service Reform Act of 1978 (PL 95 454, 92 Stat. 1111)

Among the key features of this law were an independent appeals process, protection against abuse of the merit system, and incentives and rewards for good work and skilled management. A new agency, the Federal Labor Relations Authority, was to administer the federal labor relations program and investigate unfair labor practices. This was the most comprehensive reform of the civil service rules since the system was established in 1883 by the Pendleton Act.

Clayton Act of 1914 (C323, 38 Stat. 730)

Samuel Gompers, president of the AFL, hailed this act as labor's "Magna Carta." The law strengthened previous antitrust laws and added important sections which affected the rights of labor.

The language read in part: "The labor of a human being is not a commodity or article of commerce," and therefore antitrust laws should not be used to forbid the existence of labor unions. The law also outlawed the use of injunctions in disputes between management and labor "unless necessary to prevent irreparable injury to property or to a property right ... for which injury there is no adequate remedy at law."

Comprehensive Employment and Training Act of 1973 (CETA) (PL 93-203, 87 Stat. 839)

Under this act, the Secretary of Labor awarded grants to about 450 state and local units of government if they could identify employment and training needs in their areas and provide job training and other services required to meet these needs. The goal of the programs provided under CETA was to encourage and develop the employment potential of the disadvantaged, unemployed, and underemployed. The Office of Comprehensive Employment Development Program had major responsibility for implementing the CETA Act.

Contract Labor Act of 1864

This law was adopted to obtain additional labor during the Civil War. The act provided that Europeans might be brought into the country if they promised to sign over not more than 12 months wages to repay the cost of bringing them here. The American Emigrant Company was then formed to import workingmen "for manufacturers, railroad companies and other employers." Although the aliens were unskilled and inefficient, they were very useful to manufacturers who lacked workers to operate machines and to companies which sought muscle power.

Davis-Bacon Act of 1931 (C411, 46 Stat. 1491)

This law provided for the payment of prevailing wage rates to laborers and mechanics employed by contractors and subcontractors on public construction.

Economic Opportunity Act of 1964 (PL 88, 452, 78 Stat. 508)

This law formed the cornerstone of President Lyndon Johnson's "War on Poverty," which included a number of programs providing jobs and job training, as well as a variety of projects revolving around education, housing, welfare, and vocational rehabilitation. The Job Corps which provided employment to 16-21-year-olds was one of the best known of the Office of Economic Opportunity programs.

Economic Stabilization Act of 1942 (C578, 56 Stat. 765)

The law required the War Labor Board to limit all subsequent wage increases to 15% except when unusual conditions prevailed. This was known as the "Little Steel Formula" because it was patterned on a settlement of the same amount awarded by the War Labor Board to Little Steel companies (Bethlehem Steel Corp., Inland Steel Co., Republic Steel Corp., and Youngstown Sheet and Tube Co.), the 15% being the cost-of-living increase which occurred between January 1941 and May 1942.

Emergency Railroad Transportation Act of 1933 (C91, 48 Stat. 211)

The act recognized the various railway unions as proper bargaining agents and guaranteed all railroad employees the right to organize and bargain collectively.

The law also established the office of Federal Coordinator of Transportation. The Coordinator was directed to conduct various studies and report to the President on elimination of duplication and waste, reorganization of railroad financing, labor matters, means of improving transportation, and other matters.

Employee Retirement Income Security Act of 1974 (PL 93-406, 88 Stat. 829)

This act regulated all private pension plans and, to a more limited extent, all private welfare plans.

Administrators of pension plans were required to observe certain funding standards to assure the payment of adequate contributions and to purchase termination insurance. The insurance, provided by the Pension Benefit Guaranty Corporation headed by the Secretary of Labor, was to pay pensions up to $750 a month if a plan terminated without sufficient funds to pay all of its nonforfeitable benefits.

Equal Employment Opportunity Act of 1972 (PL 92-412, 86 Stat. 644)

The law granted the Equal Employment Opportunity Commission authority to take court complaints of discrimination on the basis of race, religion, or sex which it could not resolve under mediation and conciliation. Employment practices in state and local governments were brought under federal equal employment opportunity standards, with authority given the U.S. Department of Justice to bring cases against states and local governmental bodies.

Equal Pay Act of 1963 (PL 88-38, 77 Stat. 56)

This act prohibited wage differentials based on sex after June 10, 1963, for all workers covered by the Fair Labor Standards Act.

Erdman Act of 1898 (C370, 30 Stat. 421)

Congress enacted this law as a result of the 1894 Pullman strike, its purpose being to establish mediation machinery for railroads. The law provided that the chairman of the Interstate Commerce Commission and the Commissioner of Labor would comprise a permanent mediation board whose services would be available to railroad labor and management in any dispute. If settlement could not be reached, the mediators would set up a special three-member board to propose arbitration, and if the proposal were accepted, the board's decision would be binding on both parties.

The law also outlawed use of all "yellow-dog" contracts by railroads, but in 1908 the U.S. Supreme Court declared that this provision was unconstitutional in the case of *Adair* v. *United States*, holding that the law was unwarranted interference with the freedom to make a contract, as well as an invasion of liberty and rights of property. In 1915 in *Coppage* v. *Kansas*, the same court struck down a comparable state statute.

Fair Labor Standards Act of 1938 (C676, 52, Stat. 1060)

Known also as the Wages and Hours Law, the act covered all workers in businesses engaged in interstate commerce or producing goods for interstate commerce. A milestone in labor relations legislation, its purpose was to eliminate "labor conditions detrimental to the maintenance of the minimum standards of living necessary for health, efficiency and well being of workers."

A Wages and Hour Division was set up in the Department of Labor, and provision was made for the administrator of the new division to appoint committees to determine proper rates of pay for various industries. The act has been amended several times to increase minimum wages ($3.35 an hour in 1983).

Federal Mine Safety and Health Act of 1977 (PL 95-164, 91 Stat. 1290)

This act placed more than 20,000 underground and surface coal and noncoal mining operations under a single federal law which protects the safety and health of almost a million miners. It repealed the Federal Metal and Nonmetallic Mine Safety Act and amended the Federal Coal Mine Health and Safety Act of 1969 to contain strong provisions and cover both coal and noncoal mines. The act also created the Mine Safety and Health Administration, headed by an Assistant Secretary of Labor.

Full Employment Act of 1946 (C33, 60 Stat. 23)

Following the end of World War II, Congress adopted this act to forestall any chance of a postwar depression. Essentially the law stated that hereafter the federal government would be responsible for the nation's economic growth and stability. It established a congressional Joint Committee on the Economic Report, made up of seven senators and as many representatives. The law required the committee to evaluate the President's annual economic report and propose stabilization measures.

Section 2 of the act stated: "It is the continuing policy and responsibility of the federal government ... to promote maximum employment production and purchasing power." To accomplish this, the law established the Council of Economic Advisers with the following duties: to analyze the national economy and its various segments; to advise the President on economic developments; to appraise the economic programs and policies of the federal government; to recommend to the President policies for economic growth and stability; to assist in the preparation of economic reports of the President to Congress. Once Congress has received and considered the President's annual economic report, it may adopt such legislation as is desirable or required.

Full Employment and Balanced Growth Act of 1978 (PL 95-523, 92 Stat. 1887)

Reduction of unemployment to 4% over a five-year period was established as a priority under this act, with corollary goals of lowering inflation rates and federal budget and foreign trade deficits, and maintaining economic growth. The act also provided for periodic reviews of programs and policies of the President, Congress, Federal Reserve System, and many other agencies at all government levels.

Hobbs Anti-Racketeering Act (C537, 60 Stat. 420)

The law was adopted in 1946 to restrain the illegal activities of the Teamsters Union which had been brought to the attention of Congress.

LaFollette Seamen's Act of 1915 (C153, 38 Stat. 1164)

This was essentially a reform bill which abolished imprisonment for desertion in a safe harbor, gave sailors the right to obtain half their earned wages in any port, established standards for food allowances and living conditions, set a nine-hour day when in port, protected seamen from abuse by crimps, made shipowners responsible for any corporal punishment administered at sea, and set new safety rules.

Landrum-Griffin Act of 1959 (PL 86-257, 73 Stat. 519)

Following the McClellan Hearings which disclosed violence and corruption in certain labor union tactics, Congress passed the Labor-Management Reporting and Disclosure act of 1959, also known as the Landrum-Griffin Act, designed to eliminate improper activities by management and labor.

The law aimed to safeguard the interests of each union member by forcing union leadership to run the unions in a democratic manner. Officials who misused union funds would be fined and imprisoned. Communists and political prisoners who sought to serve as union officials could not be elected until five years after they had resigned their Communist membership or been released from prison. The law also declared it a federal crime for anyone to interfere with the rights of a union member.

The act contains what has been called a "Bill of Rights" for labor because it 1) guarantees union members freedom of assembly and speech, control over union dues, fees and assessments, plus the right to sue their union and have protection against unwarranted disciplinary actions; 2) requires that reports be filed by union officers and employees as well as employers, and lists the records which unions and employers must keep and file with the Secretary of Labor; 3) regulates union elections, financial accounting, the qualifications of officers and employees; and 4) sets up penalties for embezzlement and making loans over $2,000 to union officers and employees.

Union leaders were infuriated by sections of the act which strengthened what unionists considered the antilabor provisions of the Taft-Hartley Act. These pertained to secondary boycotts and picketing of companies where another union was recognized. The Landrum-Griffin Act also permitted states to step into labor disputes if the National Labor Relations Board refused to do so. The Department of Labor administers all sections of the act except those which amend the Taft-Hartley Act, these portions being under the jurisdiction of the NLRB.

Lea Act (C138, 60 Stat. 89)

This law, adopted in 1946, was intended to curb the featherbedding practices of James C. Petrillo's American Federation of Musicians.

Manpower Development and Training Act of 1962 (PL 87-415, 76 Stat. 23)

This law required the federal government to determine manpower requirements and resources and to "deal with the problems of unemployment resulting from automation and technological changes and other types of persistent unemployment."

MultiEmployer Pension Plan Amendments Act of 1980 (PL 96-364, 94 Stat. 1208)

This act was passed to discourage companies from withdrawing from multiemployer pension plans which were in financial trouble. These plans were used frequently by coal mining, construction, entertaining, and trucking industries. The law made employers liable for a share of future pension benefits due workers covered by these plans.

National Industrial Recovery Act of 1933 (C90, 48 Stat. 195)

To spur industrial recovery during the Depression of the 1930s, this act, popularly known as the NIRA or NRA, became law on June 16, 1933. The statute provided for "self-regulation" of business through industry codes to eliminate overproduction and cutthroat competition. Prices could be increased to produce a reasonable profit, and labor was protected by guarantees of a minimum wage, reasonable hours of work, and the right of collective bargaining. Under the law, each division of commerce and industry established a committee representing labor, management, and the public to draw up and adopt a code which would be observed by all who signed its provisions. (Antitrust laws were temporarily suspended.) Each employer was given a Blue Eagle emblem to display. To get the program under way, Congress appropriated $3.3 billion for a public works program to stimulate the economy and put men to work.

The most famous and important part of the NIRA was its Section 7(a) which stipulated that every code should contain three guarantees: 1) that employees could organize and bargain collectively; 2) that no employee could be prevented from joining a labor union or forced to join a company union; and 3) that employers must pay minimum wage rates and observe maximum hours of work and other employment rules set forth in the code adopted by the industry.

To administer this section, Congress established the National Labor Board, which was replaced on July 9, 1934, by the National Labor Relations Board which operated independently of the National Recovery Administration headed by General Hugh S. Johnson.

On "Black Monday"—May 25, 1935, in the case of *Schechter Poultry Corporation* v. *United States*, the U.S. Supreme Court declared the NIRA unconstitutional because Congress had extended its authority beyond interstate commerce to intrastate commerce and had delegated authority without spelling out how it should be exercised. The NIRA was superseded by the National Labor Relations Act which did not include the Blue Eagle industry codes but concentrated on giving labor the protections it had sought for a long time. (See below.)

National Labor Relations Act of 1935 (C372, 49 Stat. 449)

Known also as the Wagner Act, the NLRA has been called the cornerstone of President Franklin D. Roosevelt's New Deal program for labor. Once it was apparent that the NIRA was a failure, Senator Robert Wagner introduced his bill which retained and tightened the controversial Section 7(a).

The new law established a three-member National Labor Relations Board (later increased by the Taft-Hartley Act to five members) to administer its provisions in accordance with the principle that employees have the "right to self-organization, to form, join or assist labor organizations to bargain collectively through representatives of their own choosing, and to engage in concerted activities for the purpose of collective bargaining or other mutual aid or protection."

The NLRA guaranteed workers the right to organize, join labor unions, and bargain collectively with employers. It also defined unfair labor practices committed by employers and which were thereafter declared illegal.

In *National Labor Relations Board* v. *Jones and Laughlin Steel Company*, the U.S. Supreme Court upheld the constitutionality of the law and subsequently supported the numerous rulings which the National Labor Relations Board handed down to enforce the law.

Newlands Act of 1913 (C6, 38 Stat. 103)

Because of union hostility to the Erdman Act, Congress adopted the Newlands Act which established a Board of Mediation and Conciliation to offer its services as a mediator. If the disputing parties did not accept the board's help, the board was authorized to increase its membership from three members to a larger board of arbitration which could act as an arbitrator if requested by both parties. This agency achieved a fair measure of success in adjusting disputes and avoiding strikes.

Norris-LaGuardia Act of 1932 (C90, 47 Stat. 70)

This law prohibited federal courts from issuing injunctions against labor unions unless certain procedures were followed. The union had to be given opportunity to state its case fully; there had to be proof that all possible efforts had been made to reach a peaceful settlement by mediation or other means; and it had to be shown that if no injunction were granted, more hardship would be caused one party than granting the injunction would cause the other.

(Under the Taft-Hartley Act of 1957 and amendments thereto, injunctions may be issued in three types of situations, and under the Fair Labor Standards Act of 1938 the Secretary of Labor may seek injunctions to enforce the law's provisions.)

Occupational Safety and Health Act of 1970 (PL 91-596, 84 Stat. 1590)

This law authorized the Secretary of Labor to establish occupational safety and health standards and gave him an independent review commission (appointed by the President) with authority to impose civil penalties and fines. Criminal action was sanctioned in the cases of willful violation resulting in death and in certain other instances. The act also provided for development and enforcement of occupational safety and health standards by the states, subject to the approval of the Secretary of Labor.

Portal-to-Portal Act of 1947 (C52, 61 Stat. 84)

In the *Mount Clemens Pottery Company* decision handed down on June 10, 1946, the U.S. Supreme Court ruled that under the Fair Labor Standards Act employers were liable for portal-to-portal pay. So many companies faced bankruptcy from claims filed by employee groups and unions for back pay amounting to billions of dollars that Congress passed this law to relieve employers of past liabilities for portal-to-portal pay. The law also stipulated that employers did not have to make such payments unless they were provided for in union contracts or by the tradition of the job or industry.

Railroad Arbitration Act of 1963 (PL 88-108, 77 Stat. 132)

This law was passed to help solve a long-standing railroad dispute and called for arbitration of the two principal issues: the use of firemen on diesel locomotives in freight and yard service, and the makeup of train crews. On November 26, 1963, the report of the arbitrators called for gradual elimination of firemen in 90% of freight and yard service, and the other issue was returned to the railroads and their unions for further negotiations, and arbitration, if necessary.

Railway Labor Act of 1926 (C347, 44 Stat. 577)

Known also as the Watson-Parker Act, the law abolished the former Railway Labor Board and provided for a National Mediation Board of five members empowered to mediate any dispute which had not been settled by direct negotiation or by boards of adjustment. If a board failed to settle a disagreement, it tried to induce the parties to submit to a court of arbitration, whose decision would be binding. If this court failed, the President was authorized to appoint an emergency board to investigate and report to him. The act proved to be ineffective.

Railway Labor Act of 1934 (June 21, 1934, Ch. 691, 48 Stat. 1185)

Also known as the Crosser-Dill Act, it abolished the five-member National Mediation Board and provided for a three-man board. The act also made it unlawful for carriers to interfere with any organizing of employees, to compel employees to join or not join a union, or force employees to sign "yellow-dog" contracts.

Rehabilitation Act of 1973 (PL 93-112, Sec. 503, 87 Stat. 355)

Section 503 of this law requires government contractors and subcontractors to take affirmative action to employ and to advance in employment qualified handicapped individuals.

Service Contract Act of 1965 (PL 89-286, 79 Stat. 1034)

This law pertains to employees performing work under federal contracts and subcontracts which are principally for services. It includes: 1) Contracts of $2,500 or less, payment of not less than the minimum wage provided for by the Fair Labor Standards Act; 2) Contracts over $2,500, payment of not less than the wage rates and fringe benefits found by the Department of Labor to be prevailing in the locality or, in certain cases, wage rates and fringe benefits contained in a predecessor contractor's collective bargaining agreement. The act also contains certain recordkeeping and safety and health requirements.

Smith-Connally Act of 1943 (C144, 57 Stat. 163)

Also known as the War Labor Disputes Act, Congress passed this law to reduce the number of strikes which had erupted during the early months of World War II. President Roosevelt vetoed the bill because he felt it ran counter to labor's no-strike pledge and would make labor more restive.

The law provided: 1) that strikes could not be called until a vote had been conducted by the National Labor Relations Board during a 30-day cooling-off period; 2) the government could seize any plant if workers stopped production and threatened war efforts; 3) anyone who started or promoted a strike in a seized plant might be subject to criminal penalties; and 4) that unions could not contribute to political campaign funds.

Social Security Act of 1935 (C531, 49 Stat. 620)

The Social Security Act established a national old-age insurance program and an agency, the Social Security Administration, to administer it. The original law has since been amended to increase benefits and broaden the types of assistance which include the following:

Unemployment insurance for workers who have been unemployed or released from work for more than a week. This is administered by the states and financed by a special payroll tax.

Old-age retirement insurance administered by the Social Security Administration and financed by contributions from employers, employees, and the federal government.

Workmen's compensation or disability insurance for those who are disabled by industrial injuries or diseases and unable to work for even as short a time as a year.

Hospitalization insurance for those over 65, this program being known as Medicare.

Supplementary medical insurance for those over 65 to cover payment of doctors' and related bills, costs being shared by the insured and the federal government. This is a voluntary plan known as Medicaid.

Assistance to the blind, needy, aged, and needy families with children who are deprived of parental support. The states receive matching grants-in-aid to help pay for this.

Aid to crippled, needy, and dependent children.

Aid to those who have become permanently disabled.

Vocational and health programs.

An amendment adopted in 1950 extended benefits to some 10 million additional men and women (C809, 64 Stat. 477).

Taft-Hartley Act of 1947 (C120, 61 Stat. 136)

Also known as the Labor-Management Relations Act, President Harry Truman vetoed the bill but it was passed over his veto. The act reflected the public's concern that unions had become too powerful under the Wagner Act and that management should be able to "manage" its employees.

The act permitted employers to sue unions for breach of contract; provided for "cooling off" periods and presidential use of 80-day injunctions in strikes that imperiled the national health and safety; prohibited closed and preferential shops and union hiring halls; permitted union shops only on a vote of a majority of the employees*; forbade union contributions to national elections or primaries; forbade secondary boycotts** and jurisdictional strikes; guaranteed employers the right to express opinions on unions without reprisal or use of force against their employees; forbade employers to contribute to health and welfare funds unless they were administered by a board of trustees on which employers and employees were represented; exempted employers from bargaining with unions of supervisors or foremen unless they chose to do so; and restricted many unfair union practices.

In addition, the National Labor Relations Board was enlarged to five members and a presidentially appointed general counsel was added to handle prosecution of unfair labor practices. The services of the NLRB would be available only to unions which filed certain financial reports with the Secretary of Labor and distributed them to their own members. In addition, a new independent Federal Mediation and Conciliation Service was authorized to mediate disputes threatening interstate commerce. Finally, each official of a national or international union had to file an affidavit stating he was not a Communist, a provision upheld by the U.S. Supreme Court on May 8, 1950.

Trade Act of 1974 (PL 93-618, 88 Stat. 1978)

Growing unemployment, especially in the shoe industry from imports, caused Congress to examine with sympathy the plight of workers who suffered from foreign competition, while the nation's trade policy looked with disfavor on protective tariffs. The act provides special benefits for workers adversely affected by such competition: 70% of their regular wages for one year, 80% of their moving costs up to a maximum of $500, job search funds, and up to three years of job training.

---

*On October 22, 1951, an amendment permitted union shop contracts without voting permission of employees.

**The Landrum-Griffin Act of 1959 amended this act with respect to boycotts and picketing, even further limiting the economic power of unions.

Wagner-Peyser Act of 1933 (C49, 48 Stat. 113)

The law established a joint federal-state administration of the public employment services, to be financed by matching federal and state funds, the federal contributions to be based on population. A system of national employment offices was to be established wherever no public offices existed, and assistance would be given in maintaining offices already functioning. The states would be required to observe federal regulations and standards regarding operation of the employment offices, as well as certain policies for handling applicants.

The act also provided for creation of the United States Employment Service in the Department of Labor. In 1939 the service was transferred to the Federal Security Agency and then was abolished in 1969 by reorganization of the Manpower Administration, and its functions were assigned to the U.S. Training and Employment Service. The Comprehensive Employment and Training Act of 1973 established the Employment and Training Administration within which the United States Employment Service operates.

Walsh-Healey Act of 1936 (C881, 49 Stat. 2036)

Also known as the Public Contract Act, the law provides that government contractors must pay their workers no less than prevailing minimum wage scales for comparable work; observe the 40-hour week with an eight-hour day; employ no boys under 16 or girls under 18 years of age; hire no convict labor; and eliminate all unhealthy working conditions.

The act covers employers holding government contracts in excess of $10,000, whereas the Davis-Bacon Act calls for paying prevailing wages to mechanics and laborers hired to work on contracts over $2,000 for the alteration, construction, or repair of public buildings or public works.

Welfare and Pension Plans Disclosure Act of 1958 (PL 85-836, 72 Stat. 997)

This law requires administrators of all health, pension, insurance, and supplementary unemployment compensation programs covering more than 25 workers to file descriptions and annual financial reports with the Secretary of Labor, to be available for public inspection, as well as by those participating in the plan.

EXECUTIVE ORDERS

Executive Order	Date	Subject
President Dwight D. Eisenhower		
10640	October 10, 1955	President's Committee on Employment of the Handicapped.
10689	November 22, 1956	Board of inquiry to report on a labor dispute affecting the maritime industry.
10842	October 6, 1959	Board of inquiry to report on a labor dispute affecting the maritime industry.
10843	October 9, 1959	Board of inquiry to report on a labor dispute affecting the steel industry.
10848	October 14, 1959	Amendment to Executive Order 10843.

Executive Order	Date	Subject
President John F. Kennedy		
10994	February 14, 1961	President's Committee on Employment of the Handicapped.
11013	April 7, 1962	Board of inquiry to report on a labor dispute affecting the maritime industry.
11025	June 7, 1962	Board of inquiry to report on a labor dispute affecting the aircraft industry.
11026	June 8, 1962	Amendment to Executive Order 11025.
11029	June 13, 1962	Board of inquiry to report on a labor dispute affecting the aircraft industry.
11054	October 1, 1962	Board of inquiry to report on a labor dispute affecting the maritime industry.
11078	January 23, 1963	Board of inquiry to report on a labor dispute affecting the ballistics missiles, space vehicles, and military aircraft industry.
President Lyndon B. Johnson		
11181	September 30, 1964	Board of inquiry to report on a labor dispute affecting the maritime industry.
11276	April 21, 1966	Emergency board to investigate a labor dispute between the Five Carriers' Negotiating Committee and certain of their employees.
11291	July 27, 1966	Emergency board to investigate a labor dispute between American Airlines, Inc., and certain of its employees.
11308	September 30, 1966	Emergency board to investigate a labor dispute between Pan American World Airways, Inc. and certain of its employees.
11324	January 28, 1967	Emergency board to investigate a labor dispute between carriers represented by the National Railway Labor Conference and certain of their employees.
11329	March 2, 1967	Board of inquiry to report on a labor dispute affecting the shipbuilding and repair industries.
11343	April 12, 1967	Emergency board to investigate a labor dispute between the Long Island Railroad and certain of its employees.
11362	July 16, 1967	Provisions for use of transportation priorities and allocations during current railroad strike.
11431	September 30, 1968	Board of inquiry to report on a labor dispute affecting the maritime industry.
11433	November 6, 1968	Emergency board to investigate a labor dispute between the Illinois Central Railroad, Louisville & Nashville Railroad, and Belt Railway Company of Chicago and certain of their employees.
11442	December 27, 1968	Emergency board to investigate a labor dispute between the Long Island Railroad and certain of its employees.

Executive Order	Date	Subject
11443-44	January 13, 1969	Emergency board to investigate a labor dispute between carriers represented by the National Railway Labor Conference and certain employees.

President Richard M. Nixon

11486	October 3, 1969	Emergency board to investigate a labor dispute between carriers represented by the National Railway Labor Conference and certain employees.
11543	July 7, 1970	Emergency board to investigate a labor dispute between carriers represented by the National Railway Labor Conference and certain employees.
11558-9	September 18, 1970	Emergency board to investigate a labor dispute between carriers represented by the National Railway Labor Conference and certain employees.
11572	December 10, 1970	Provisions for use of transportation priorities and allocations during current railroad strike.
11621	September 25, 1971	Board of inquiry to report on a labor dispute affecting the maritime industry.
11622	October 4, 1971	Amendment to Executive Order 11621.

President James Earl Carter

12042	March 6, 1978	Board of inquiry to report on a labor dispute affecting the bituminous coal industry.
12196	February 26, 1980	Occupational Safety and Health Program for federal employees.
12223	June 30, 1980	Amendment to Executive Order 12196.

V

FEDERAL GOVERNMENT AGENCIES
CONCERNED WITH LABOR RELATIONS

The following federal government agencies are concerned with labor relations: Department of Labor, Equal Employment Opportunity Commission, Federal Labor Relations Authority, Federal Mediation and Conciliation Service, National Labor Relations Board, National Mediation Board, and the Occupational Safety and Health Review Commission.

At the end of each agency description which follows, the name, address, and telephone number of the agency's public information office are included so that users of this almanac may know whom to contact for further information.

Federal Information Centers. If other information about the federal government is required, Federal Information Centers may be telephoned or visited in 41 major metropolitan areas throughout the country. Another 43 cities are connected to the nearest center by toll-free telephone tielines. The address and telephone number of each center is listed under UNITED STATES GOVERNMENT, Federal Information Center.

These centers offer many additional services. For non-English-speaking persons, many centers have specialists who can offer assistance in other languages. Often, centers can help answer questions about state and local government as well, and a number of useful government publications can be found at the centers.

Standard Federal Administrative Regions. Ten Standard Federal Administrative Regions were established to achieve more uniformity in the local and geographic jurisdiction of federal field offices as well as better coordination between agencies. All agencies do not have structures which conform to this uniform system, however, and deviations are noted hereafter for those agencies which are not strictly conforming.

Listed below are the addresses of the regional office locations and the states included in each (see also regional map on page 110):

Region	Address	States Included
1	John F. Kennedy Federal Bldg., Boston, MA 02203	Ct., Me., Mass., N.H., R.I., Vt.
2	1515 Broadway, New York, NY 10036	N.J., N.Y., Virgin Islands, Puerto Rico

Region	Address	States Included
3	3535 Market Street, Philadelphia, PA 19104	Del., D.C., Md., Pa., Va., W.Va.
4	1371 Peachtree Street, NE, Atlanta, GA 30309	Ala., Fla., Ga., Ky., Miss., N.C., S.C., Tenn.
5	230 South Dearborn Street, Chicago, IL 60604	Ill., Ind., Mich., Minn., Ohio, Wis.
6	555 Griffin Square Bldg., Dallas, TX 75202	Ark., La., N.M., Okla., Texas
7	911 Walnut Street, Kansas City, MO 64106	Iowa, Kans., Mo., Nebr.
8	1961 Stout Street, Denver, CO 80294	Colo., Mont., N.D., S.D., Utah, Wyo.
9	450 Golden Gate Avenue, San Francisco, CA 94102	Ariz., Calif., Hawaii, Nev.
10	909 First Avenue, Seattle, WA 98174	Alaska, Idaho, Oreg., Wash.

STANDARD FEDERAL REGIONS

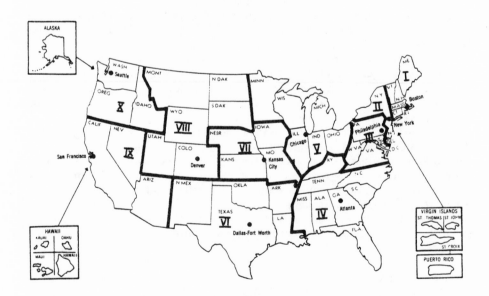

DEPARTMENT OF LABOR*
200 Constitution Avenue NW
Washington, DC 20210
(202) 523-8165

Authorization. Created as the ninth executive department by act approved March 4, 1913 (37 Stat. 736; 5 U.S.C. 611). In 1884 a Bureau of Labor was created by Congress in the Interior Department, but the bureau later became independent as a Department of Labor without executive rank. It again returned to a bureau status in the Department of Commerce and Labor which was created by act of February 14, 1903 (32 Stat. 827; 5 U.S.C. 591).

Purpose. The department's purpose is to foster, promote, and develop the welfare of wage earners of the United States, to improve their working conditions, and to advance their opportunities for profitable employment. To carry out this mission the Department administers more than 130 federal labor laws guaranteeing workers' rights to safe and healthful working conditions, a minimum hourly wage and overtime pay, freedom from employment discrimination, unemployment insurance, and workers' compensation. The department also protects workers' pension rights; sponsors job training programs; helps workers find jobs; works to strengthen free collective bargaining; and keeps track of changes in employment, prices, and other national economic measurements.

Principal Officials.
Raymond J. Donovan, Secretary of Labor
Donald L. Rosenthal, Chief of Staff and Counselor to the Secretary
Kathy Regan, Special Assistant to the Secretary for Public Affairs
Vernon R. Louviere, Special Assistant to the Secretary
Earl Cox, Director, Office of Information and Public Affairs
Thomas McBride, Inspector General, Office of the Inspector General
Lenora Cole-Alexander, Director, Women's Bureau
Malcolm R. Lovell, Jr., Under Secretary
Richard C. Breden, Executive Assistant to the Under Secretary
Walter Terry, Director, Office of Small and Disadvantaged Business Utilization
E. Gerald Lamboley, Chairman, Employees' Compensation Appeals Board
Robert L. Ramsey, Chairman, Benefits Review Board
Nahum Litt, Chief Administrative Law Judge
T. Timothy Ryan, Jr., Solicitor
Francis X. Lilly, Deputy Solicitor, National Operations
Ronald G. Whiting, Deputy Solicitor, Regional Operations
William Du Ross, III, Associate Solicitor, Division of Employment and Training Legal Services
Beate Bloch, Associate Solicitor, Division of Fair Labor Standards
Seth D. Zinman, Associate Solicitor, Division of Legislation and Legal Counsel
John F. Depenbrock, Associate Solicitor, Division of Labor-Management Laws
Donald S. Shire, Associate Solicitor, Division of Employee Benefits
Benjamin W. Mintz, Associate Solicitor, Division of Occupational Safety and Health
James D. Henry, Associate Solicitor, Division of Labor Relations and Civil Rights

---

*For organizational chart, see page 116.

Monica Gallagher, Associate Solicitor, Division of Plan Benefits Security
Cynthia Attwood, Associate Solicitor, Division of Mine Safety and Health
David H. Feldman, Associate Solicitor, Division of Special Litigation
Donald J. Shasteen, Deputy Under Secretary for Legislation and Intergovern-
    mental Relations
Debbie K. Williams, Executive Assistant to the Deputy Under Secretary
Robert W. Searby, Deputy Under Secretary for International Affairs
George Bensema, Executive Assistant to the Deputy Under Secretary
James F. Taylor, Associate Deputy Under Secretary for International Affairs
John F. Cogan, Assistant Secretary for Policy, Evaluation and Research
Alfred M. Zuck, Assistant Secretary for Administration and Management
Betty Bolden, Deputy Assistant Secretary
William R. Reise, Comptroller
Donald E. Lemmon, Director of Management Policy and Systems
Nathaniel Baccus, III, Director, Office of Civil Rights
W. Spence Filleman, Director, Administrative Programs and Services
John Dinneen, Directorate of Information Technology
Frank A. Yeager, Director, Personnel Management
Robert Hastings, Director, Office of Labor-Management Relations
Julius G. Hansen, Director, Office of Safety and Health
William C. Plowden, Jr., Assistant Secretary for Veteran's Employment
Albert Angrisani, Assistant Secretary for Employment and Training
Joyce Kaiser, Associate Assistant Secretary for Employment and Training
Roberts T. Jones, Administrator, Office of Comprehensive Employment and
    Training
William B. Lewis, Administrator, Office of Employment Security
Thomas J. Hague, Administrator, Office of Strategic Planning and Policy
    Development
Thomas C. Komarek, Administrator, Office of Financial Control and Manage-
    ment Systems
T. James Walker, Administrator, Office of Administration and Regional
    Management
James T. Hashian, Director, Public Affairs
Donald L. Dotson, Assistant Secretary for Labor-Management Relations and
    Administrator, Labor-Management Services Administration
Ronald J. St. Cyr, Deputy Assistant Secretary and Deputy Administrator
Frederic M. Haas, Assistant Administrator for Field Operations
Jeffrey Clayton, Administrator, Pension and Welfare Benefit Program
Richard G. Hunsucker, Director, Office of Labor-Management Standards
    Enforcement
George O. Gonzalez, Director, Office of Veterans Reemployment Rights
John R. Stepp, Director, Office of Labor-Management Relations Services
Ernest J. German, Director, Office of Management
Robert Burns Collyer, Deputy Under Secretary for Employment Standards
Craig Berrington, Associate Deputy Under Assistant Secretary
Robert Cuccia, Office of Information and Consumer Affairs
William M. Otter, Acting Wage and Hour Administrator
Ellen M. Shong, Director, Office of Federal Contract Compliance Programs
Ralph M. Hartman, Director, Office of Workers' Compensation Programs
Lawrence W. Rogers, Director, Office of Management, Administration, and
    Planning

June M. Robinson, Director, Office of State Liaison and Legislative Analysis
Thorne G. Auchter, Assistant Secretary for Occupational Safety and Health
Mark D. Cowan, Deputy Assistant Secretary
James Foster, Director, Office of Information and Consumer Affairs
Anthony Goldin, Director, Office of Policy Analysis, Integration and Evaluation
John Miles, Director, Office of Field Coordination and Experimental Programs
Leonard Vance, Director, Health Standards Programs
Barry White, Director, Safety Standards Programs
David C. Zeigler, Director, Administrative Programs
Patrick Tyson, Director, Federal Compliance and State Programs
Janet L. Norwood, Commissioner of Labor Statistics
Henry Lowenstern, Associate Commissioner for Publications
William G. Barron, Jr., Associate Commissioner for Administrative Management
William M. Eisenberg, Associate Commissioner for Statistical Operations
Ford B. Ford, Assistant Secretary for Mine Safety and Health
Thomas J. Shepich, Deputy Assistant Secretary
Harrison Combs, Jr., Director, Office of Congressional and Legislative Affairs
Wayne E. Veneman, Director, Office of Information
Madison McCulloch, Director of Technical Support
David L. Harris, Director of Administration and Management
Joseph A. Amonica, Administrator for Coal Mine Safety and Health
Roy L. Bernard, Administrator for Metal and Nonmetal Mine Safety and Health

COMMISSIONERS AND SECRETARIES OF LABOR

Agency	Title	Incumbent	Period of Service	Served under President
Bureau of Labor (in the Department of the Interior)	Commissioner of Labor	Carroll D. Wright	January 31, 1885- January 31, 1905	Chester A. Arthur Grover Cleveland Benjamin Harrison
Department of Labor (without Cabinet rank)	Commissioner of Labor	Carroll D. Wright		Grover Cleveland William McKinley Theodore Roosevelt
Department of Commerce and Labor*	Secretary of Commerce and Labor	George B. Cortelyou Victor H. Metcalf Oscar S. Straus Charles Nagel	1903-1904 1904-1906 1906-1909 1909-1913	Theodore Roosevelt Theodore Roosevelt Theodore Roosevelt William H. Taft
Department of Labor	Secretary of Labor	William B. Wilson	March 6, 1913- March 4, 1921	Woodrow Wilson
		James J. Davis	March 5, 1921- November 30, 1930	Warren G. Harding Calvin Coolidge Herbert Hoover
		William N. Doak	December 9, 1930- March 4, 1933	Herbert Hoover
		Frances Perkins	March 4, 1933- June 30, 1945	Franklin D. Roosevelt
		Lewis B. Schwellenbach	July 1, 1945- June 10, 1948 (Died in office)	Harry S. Truman Harry S. Truman

	Acting Secretary of Labor	Secretary of Labor	
David A. Morse	June 11, 1948-		Harry S. Truman
Maurice J. Tobin	August 12, 1948	August 13, 1948-	Harry S. Truman
Martin P. Durkin	January 20, 1953	January 21, 1953-	Dwight D. Eisenhower
James P. Mitchell	September 10, 1953	October 9, 1953-	Dwight D. Eisenhower
Arthur J. Goldberg	January 20, 1961	January 21, 1961-	John F. Kennedy
W. Willard Wirtz	September 20, 1962	September 25, 1962-	John F. Kennedy / Lyndon B. Johnson / Richard M. Nixon
George P. Shultz	January 20, 1969	January 22, 1969-	Richard M. Nixon
James D. Hodgson	July 1, 1970	July 2, 1970-	Richard M. Nixon
Peter J. Brennan	February 1, 1973	February 2, 1973-	Richard M. Nixon
John T. Dunlop	March 15, 1975	March 18, 1975-	Gerald R. Ford
W. J. Usery, Jr.	January 31, 1976	February 10, 1976-	Gerald R. Ford
Ray Marshall	January 20, 1977	January 27, 1977-	James E. Carter
Raymond J. Donovan	January 20, 1981	February 4, 1981-	Ronald Reagan

*From 1903 to 1913 the Bureau of Labor was under the Department of Commerce and Labor. During this time, Carroll Wright was Commissioner from 1903 to January 31, 1905, and Charles P. Neill was Commissioner from February 1, 1905 to March 3, 1913.

DEPARTMENT OF LABOR

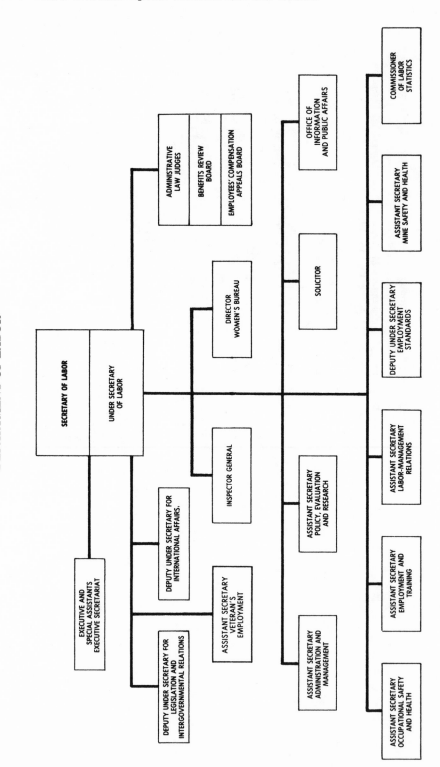

OFFICE OF THE SECRETARY OF LABOR

The **Secretary** is the head of the Department of Labor and principal adviser to the President on the development and execution of policies and the administration and enforcement of laws relating to wage earners, their working conditions, and their employment opportunities.

The **Wage Appeals Board** acts on behalf of the Secretary of Labor in deciding appeals on questions of law and fact, taken at the discretion of the board from wage determinations issued under the Davis-Bacon Act and its related prevailing wage statutes; debarments under the department's regulations; disputes concerning payment of prevailing wage rates which involve significant sums of money, large groups of employees, or novel or unusual situations; and recommendations by federal agencies for appropriate adjustments of liquidated damages which are assessed under the Contract Work Hours and Safety Standards Act.

The **Office of Inspector General** is responsible for providing comprehensive, independent, and objective audits and investigations programs to identify and report program deficiencies and improve the economy, efficiency, and effectiveness of operations. The office is also responsible for ensuring program integrity through prevention and detection of criminal activity, unethical conduct, and program fraud and abuse. Regional offices of the Inspector General conform to the Standard Federal Regions, except for Region 9, 1375 Sutter Street, San Francisco, CA 94109.

The **Office of Information and Public Affairs** is responsible for providing the department with a comprehensive information program designed to inform the public about the department's policies, programs and activities. Regional Information Offices conform to the Standard Federal Regions.

The **Women's Bureau** is responsible for formulating standards and policies which promote the welfare of wage-earning women, improve their working conditions, increase their efficiency, and advance their opportunities for profitable employment; it also investigates and reports on all matters pertinent to the welfare of women in industry. Regional offices of the Women's Bureau conform to the Standard Federal Regions.

OFFICE OF THE UNDER SECRETARY OF LABOR

The **Under Secretary of Labor** is the principal advisor to the Secretary and serves as Acting Secretary in his absence.

The **Employees' Compensation Appeals Board** considers and decides appeals from final decisions in cases arising under the Federal Employees' Compensation Act (5 U.S.C. 8101).

The **Office of Administrative Law Judges** provides administrative law judges who preside over formal hearings to determine violations of minimum wage requirements, overtime payments, compensation benefits, employee discrimination, grant performance, alien certification, employee protection, and health and safety regulations set forth under numerous laws.

The **Benefit Review Board** decides appeals raising substantial questions of law or fact from decisions of administrative law judges with respect to cases arising under the Longshoremen's and Harbor Workers' Compensation Act and its extensions and the Black Lung Benefits Act of 1972.

The **Solicitor of Labor** is responsible for all the legal activities of the department and its legislative program and also serves as legal adviser to the Secretary and other officials of the department. The regional offices of the Solicitor are as follows:

Region	Address	States Included
1	John F. Kennedy Federal Bldg., Boston, MA 02203	Ct., Mass., Me., N.H., R.I., Vt.
2	1515 Broadway, New York, NY, 10036 Branch Office: Federal Office Bldg., Hato Rey, PR 00918	N.J., N.Y., Virgin Islands, Puerto Rico
3	3535 Market Street, Philadelphia, PA 19104	D.C., Del., Md., Pa., Va., W.Va.
4	1371 Peachtree Street, NE, Atlanta, GA 30309 Branch Offices: 1929 Ninth Avenue, S., Birmingham, AL 35205; U.S. Courthouse Bldg., Nashville, TN 37203; Court House Federal Bldg., NE Third Avenue, Ft. Lauderdale, FL 33301	Ala., Fla., Ga., Ky., Miss., N.C., S.C., Tenn.
5	230 South Dearborn Street, Chicago, IL 60604 Branch Offices: Federal Office Bldg., Cleveland, OH 44199; 234 State Street, Detroit, MI 48226	Ill., Ind., Mich., Minn., Ohio, Wis.
6	555 Griffin Square Bldg., Dallas, TX 75202	Ark., La., N.M., Okla., Texas
7	Federal Office Bldg., Kansas City, MO 64106 Branch Office: Federal Office Bldg., Denver, CO 80294	Colo., Iowa, Kans., Mo., Mont., Nebr., N.D., S.D., Utah, Wyo.
8	450 Golden Gate Avenue, San Francisco, CA 94102 Branch Offices: Federal Bldg., Los Angeles, CA 90012; 909 First Avenue, Seattle, WA 98104	Alaska, Ariz., Calif., Hawaii, Idaho, Nev., Oreg., Wash.

The **Assistant Secretary for Administration and Management** is responsible for administrative policy. The **Assistant Secretary for Policy, Evaluation, and Research** is responsible for coordinating and providing leadership to the department's activities in policy and program planning, program evaluation, and economic and social research, bearing on the welfare of all workers. The **Deputy Under Secretary for Legislation and Intergovernmental Relations** coordinates, supervises, and directs all legislative activities of the department, including contacts with Congress. He also maintains liaison with state and local officials and federal agencies and relations with community, labor, minority, and business groups. Regional representatives are located in the 10 Standard Federal Regions. They maintain liaison with local, state, and other federal agencies and handle relations with community, labor, minority, and business groups and governmental bodies in their regions.

The **Deputy Under Secretary for International Affairs** supervises the Bureau of International Labor Affairs and is responsible for the department's international responsibilities. The bureau assists in formulating international economic and trade policies affecting American workers, represents the United States in multilateral and bilateral trade negotiations and various international organizations, helps administer the U.S. labor attaché program at embassies abroad, carries out overseas technical assistance projects, and arranges trade union exchange and other programs for foreign visitors to the United States.

EMPLOYMENT AND TRAINING ADMINISTRATION

The responsibilities of this administration relate to employment services, work experience, job training, and unemployment insurance. Component offices and services administer a federal/state employment security system; fund and oversee programs to provide work experience and training for groups having difficulty entering or returning to the work force; formulate and promote apprenticeship standards and programs, and conduct continuing programs of research, development, and evaluation. The **Assistant Secretary for Employment and Training** is responsible for directing and overseeing the programs.

OFFICE OF EMPLOYMENT SECURITY

Unemployment Insurance. The federal/state unemployment compensation program is the basic program of income support for the nation's unemployed workers. The **Federal Unemployment Insurance Service** provides leadership and policy guidance to state employment security agencies for the development, improvement, and operation of the unemployment insurance system and of related wage-loss, worker dislocation, and adjustment assistance compensation programs, including to ex-service personnel and federal civilian workers, and supplemental or extended benefits programs.

Employment Service. The **United States Employment Service** provides assistance to states in establishing and maintaining a system of nearly 2,500 local public employment offices in the states and territories. The federal/state employment service is responsible for providing unemployed individuals and other job-seekers with job placement and other employment services, and for providing employers and workers with job development, placement services, recruitment, and similar assistance, including employment counseling and related supportive services.

The Employment Service also disseminates national, area, and local labor market information and administers the work incentive program designed to help persons receiving Aid to Families with Dependent Children become self-supporting. The service provides other subsidiary services, such as certifying aliens who seek to enter the country for permanent employment as immigrants or temporary workers; providing employment services and adjustment assistance to American workers adversely affected by foreign imports under the Trade Act of 1974; administering with the Internal Revenue Service a program providing tax credits for employers who hire workers from certain target groups; and providing other specialized services to the public and the federal and state agencies responsible for employment activities.

Trade Adjustment Assistance. American workers adversely affected by foreign imports may appeal to the **Office of Trade Adjustment Assistance** for certification for adjustment assistance under the Trade Act of 1974.

OFFICE OF COMPREHENSIVE EMPLOYMENT AND TRAINING CETA PROGRAMS

Under the Comprehensive Employment and Training Act, the Secretary of Labor makes block grants to state and local units of government serving as prime sponsors under the act. Prime sponsors identify employment and training needs in their areas and plan and operate the job training and services needed to meet those needs. The goal of CETA is to increase the earned income of the entire spectrum of economically disadvantaged unemployed and underemployed persons.

Senior Community Service Employment Program. This program makes subsidized, part-time job opportunities in community service activities available to low-income persons aged 55 and above. Grants are made to national-level public and private nonprofit agencies and to units of state government.

Apprenticeship and Training. The **Bureau of Apprenticeship and Training** works closely with employers, labor unions, community planning groups, vocational schools, and others concerned with apprenticeship. The bureau formulates and promotes the furtherance of labor standards necessary to safeguard the welfare of apprentices and cooperates with states in promoting such standards and bringing employers and labor together for the formulation of apprenticeship programs. Programs must meet standards established by the bureau or a recognized State Apprenticeship Council to be registered.

Regional offices of the Bureau of Apprenticeship and Training conform to the Standard Federal Regions. For the correct name and address of a state apprenticeship agency or council, contact the state Employment Security Service.

Other Offices. The **Office of Strategic Planning and Policy Development**, the **Office of Financial Control and Management Systems**, and the **Office of Administration and Regional Management** provide the necessary planning, policy, financial, and administrative services for the Employment and Training Administration.

LABOR-MANAGEMENT SERVICES ADMINISTRATION

The **Assistant Secretary for Labor-Management Relations** has responsibility for the department's labor-management relations activities and serves as administrator for the administration.

Veterans' Reemployment. Veterans' reemployment rights are provided for in title 38, chapter 43, of the U.S. Code. The administration helps veterans, reservists, members of the national guards, and rejectees exercise their reemployment rights, pertaining to the job, seniority, status, and rate of pay they would have achieved had they not been away. General information is provided veterans and their preservice employers at the time the veteran is released from the armed forces, while technical assistance and more specific information is provided veterans and employers aimed at voluntary resolution of reemployment problems.

Pension and Welfare Plans. Administrators of private pension plans and welfare plans must file summaries of those plans with the administration, as well as certain reports. They must also meet strict fiduciary responsibility standards administered by the administration.

Labor Organizations. Under the Labor Management Reporting and Disclosure Act, all labor organizations must file with the administration copies of their constitutions and bylaws and annual financial reports. The act also prescribes rules for election of union officers, administration of trusteeships by labor organizations, rights of union members, and handling of union funds. Through technical assistance in all these areas, the administration seeks voluntary compliance with provisions of the act.

Labor-Management Relations Services. The administration offers a broad range of services to employers and unions.

Development, Research, and Evaluation. Administration functions in this area include review of collective bargaining performance and its contribution to meeting economic needs; development of policy for legislation and executive orders; study of the impact of private policies affecting collective bargaining; and coordination of labor/management relations research activities.

Regional offices of the Labor-Management Services Administration do not conform to the Standard Federal Regions and are listed below:

Region	Office Address	States Included
New York	1515 Broadway, New York, NY 10036	Ct., Mass., Me., N.H., N.J., N.Y., Puerto Rico, R.I., Vt., Virgin Islands
Philadelphia	3535 Market Street, Philadelphia, PA 19104	Del., Md., Pa., Va., W.Va.
Atlanta	1371 Peachtree Street NE, Atlanta, GA 30309	Ala., Fla., Ga., Ky., Miss., N.C., S.C., Tenn.
Chicago	230 South Dearborn Street, Chicago, IL 60604	Ill., Ind., Mich., Minn., Ohio, Wis.
Kansas City	911 Walnut Street, Kansas City, MO 64106	Ark., Colo., Iowa, Kans., La., Mo., Mont., Nebr., N.M., N.D., Okla., S.D., Texas, Utah, Wyo.
San Francisco	450 Golden Gate Avenue, San Francisco, CA 94102	Alaska, Ariz., Calif., Hawaii, Idaho, Oreg., Nev., Wash.

EMPLOYMENT STANDARDS ADMINISTRATION

The **Deputy Under Secretary for Employment Standards** has the responsibility for administering and directing employment standards programs dealing with minimum wage and overtime regulations; registration of farm labor contractors; determining prevailing wage rates to be paid on federal government contracts and subcontracts; nondiscrimination and affirmative action for minorities, women, veterans, and handicapped workers on government contracts and subcontracts; and workers' compensation programs for federal and certain private employers and employees. The regional offices of the administration conform to the Standard Federal Regions.

Wage and Hour Division. The administration of this division is responsible for a variety of programs designed to increase and protect low-wage incomes; safeguard the health and welfare of workers by discouraging excessively long hours of work; prevent curtailment of employment and earnings for students, trainees, and handicapped workers; minimize losses of income and job rights caused by indebtedness; and direct a program of farm labor contractor registration designed to protect the health, safety, and welfare of migrant labor.

The division also predetermines prevailing wage rates for federal construction, alteration and repair of public works subject to the Davis-Bacon and related acts, and a continuing program under the Service Contract Act. It also has enforcement responsibility in ensuring that prevailing wages and overtime standards are paid in accordance with the provisions of the Davis-Bacon and related acts, Service Contract, Public Contracts, Contract Work Hours, and Safety Standards acts.

Regional offices of the division conform to the Standard Federal Regions, with an additional office located at 1931 Ninth Avenue South, Birmingham, AL 35205.

Federal Contract Compliance Programs. The **Office of Federal Contract Compliance Programs** establishes policies and goals and provides leadership and coordination of the government's program to achieve nondiscrimination in employment by government contractors and subcontractors and in federally assisted construction programs. It administers programs to assure affirmative action by government contractors to employ and advance Vietnam-era veterans and handicapped workers.

Regional offices conform to the Standard Federal Regions.

Workers' Compensation Programs. The **Office of Workers' Compensation Programs** is responsible for the administration of the three basic federal workers' compensation laws: the Federal Employees' Compensation Act and related laws; the Longshoremen's and Harbor Workers' Compensation Act and its various extensions; and the "Black Lung" benefit payment provisions of the Federal Coal Mine Health and Safety Act of 1969 as amended.

District offices of this division do not conform to the Standard Federal Regions. They are listed below:

District Number	Address
1	JFK Federal Building, Boston, MA 02203
2	1515 Broadway, New York, NY 10036

District Number	Address
3	3535 Market Street, Philadelphia, PA 19104
4	31 Hopkins Plaza, Baltimore, MD 21201 (1)
5	3661 Virginia Beach Blvd. E., Norfolk, VA 23502 (1)
6	400 West Bay Street, Jacksonville, FL 32202 (1)
	311 West Monroe Street, Jacksonville, FL 32202 (2)
7	500 Camp Street, New Orleans, LA 70130 (1, 2)
8	2320 LaBranch Street, Houston, TX 77004 (1)
	601 Rosenberg Avenue, Galveston, TX 77553 (1)
9	1240 East Ninth Street, Cleveland, OH 44199 (2)
10	230South Dearborn Street, Chicago, IL 60604
11	1910 Federal Office Building, Kansas City, MO 64106 (2)
12	1961 Stout Street, Denver, CO 80294 (2)
13	450 Golden Gate Avenue, San Francisco, CA 94102
14	909 First Avenue, Seattle, WA 98104
15	300 Ala Moana Boulevard, Honolulu, HI 96850
16	Griffin Square Building, Dallas, TX 75201
17	1371 Peachtree Street NE, Atlanta, GA 30367
18	P.O. Box 3327, Long Beach, CA 90731 (1)
25	666 Eleventh Street NW, Washington, DC 20236 (2)
40	1717 K Street NW, Washington, DC 20211 (3)
50	P.O. Box 28608, Washington, DC 20005 (2)

(1) – Administers Longshoremen's and Harbor Workers' Compensation Act only.

(2) – Administers Federal Employees' Compensation Act only.

(3) – Administers District of Columbia Compensation Act only.

OCCUPATIONAL SAFETY AND HEALTH ADMINISTRATION

The **Assistant Secretary for Occupational Safety and Health** has responsibility for occupational safety and health activities. The administration, established by the Occupational Safety and Health Act of 1970, develops and promulgates occupational safety and health standards; develops and issues regulations; conducts investigations and inspections to determine the status of compliance with safety and health standards and regulations; and issues citations and proposes penalties for noncompliance with safety and health standards and regulations.

Regional offices conform to the Standard Federal Regions, except that the Boston office is at 16-18 North Street, One Dock Square Building, Boston, MA 02109.

MINE SAFETY AND HEALTH ADMINISTRATION

The **Assistant Secretary of Labor for Mine Safety and Health** has responsibility for safety and health in the nation's mines. The administration was established by the Federal Mine Safety and Health Amendments Act of 1977, which consolidated all provisions for mine safety under a single law, applicable to all types of mines—metal, nonmetal, and coal.

The administration develops and promulgates mandatory safety and health standards, ensures compliance with these standards, assesses civil penalties for violations, investigates accidents, cooperates with and provides assistance to the states in developing state mine safety and health programs, improves and expands training programs in cooperation with the states and the mining industry and, in coordination with the Department of Health and Human Services and Department of the Interior, contributes to the improvement and expansion of mine safety as well as health research and development.

The administration's headquarters staff is located at Arlington, Virginia, and has a field network of District, Subdistrict, and Field Offices Technology Centers, the Health and Safety Analysis Center, the Approval and Certification Center, and the Electrical Testing Laboratory.

For further information and location of field offices, contact the Mine Safety and Health Administration, Office of Information, 4015 Wilson Boulevard, Arlington, VA 22203, (703) 235-1452.

BUREAU OF LABOR STATISTICS

The **Bureau of Labor Statistics** is responsible for the Department of Labor's economic and statistical research activities, being the principal factfinding agency in the field of labor economics, especially with respect to the collection and analysis of data on labor requirements, labor force, employment, unemployment, hours of work, wages and employee compensation, prices, living conditions, labor/management relations, productivity and technological developments, occupational safety and health, structure and growth of the economy, urban conditions and related socioeconomic issues, and international aspects of certain of these subjects.

Information collected is issued in monthly press releases, special publications, and in the bureau's official publication, the *Monthly Labor Review*. Other major publications include: the *Consumer Price Index, Producer Prices and Price Indexes, Employment and Earnings, Current Wage Developments, Occupational Outlook Handbook*, and *Occupational Outlook Quarterly*. Regional offices issue additional reports and releases, usually presenting locality or regional detail.

Regional offices of the bureau do not conform to the Standard Federal Regions and are as follows:

Region	Address	States Included
Boston	Federal Building, Boston, MA 02203	Ct., Mass., Me., N.H., R.I., Vt.
New York	1515 Broadway, New York, NY 10036	N.J., N.Y., Puerto Rico, Virgin Islands, Canal Zone
Philadelphia	3535 Market Street, Philadelphia, PA 19104	D.C., Del., Md., Pa., Va., W.Va.

Region	Address	States Included
Atlanta	1371 Peachtree Street, Atlanta, GA 30309	Ala., Fla., Ga., Ky., Miss., N.C., S.C., Tenn.
Chicago	230 South Dearborn Street, Chicago, IL 60604	Ill., Ind., Mich., Minn., Ohio, Wis.
Kansas City	911 Walnut Street, Kansas City, MO 64106	Colo., Iowa, Kans., Mo., Mont., Nebr., N.D., S.D., Utah, Wyo.
Dallas	555 Griffin Square Building, Dallas, TX 75202	Ark., La., N.M., Okla., Texas
San Francisco	450 Golden Gate Avenue, San Francisco, CA 94102	Alaska, American Samoa, Ariz., Calif., Guam, Hawaii, Idaho, Nev., Oreg., Trust Territory of the Pacific Islands, Wash.

VETERANS EMPLOYMENT SERVICE

The **Veterans Employment Service** under the direction of the **Assistant Secretary for Veterans Employment** is responsible for assuring that the legal mandate and the policies of the Secretary of Labor and the United States Employment Service are carried out by the local public employment service offices. A field staff of regional and state directors for veterans employment and their assistants provides functional supervision to state employment services, helping assure that legal and policy requirements for veterans services are maintained effectively.

For the address of a state's veteran's employment service, contact the Department of Employment Security at the state capital or look in the telephone book under both federal and state government listings for veterans.

For further information concerning the Department of Labor, contact the Office of Information and Public Affairs, Department of Labor, 200 Constitution Avenue NW, Washington, DC 20210, (202) 523-7316.

EQUAL EMPLOYMENT OPPORTUNITY COMMISSION
2401 E Street NW
Washington, DC 20506
(202) 634-6930

Authorization. Created by title VII of the Civil Rights Act of 1964 (78 Stat. 253; 42 U.S.C. 2000e); Title VII, amended by the Equal Employment

Opportunity Act of 1972 (86 Stat. 103; 42 U.S.C. 2000e and the Pregnancy Discrimination Act of 1978 (92 Stat. 2076; 42 U.S.C. 2000e). Reorganization Plan No. 1 of 1978, effective May 6, 1978, transferred federal equal employment functions from the Civil Service Commission to the EEOC, effective January 1, 1979. On July 1, 1979, responsibility was transferred from the Department of Labor to the EEOC for enforcement of the Equal Pay Act of 1963 in private industry and state and local governments, as well as the Age Discrimination in Employment Act of 1967.

Purpose. Purposes are to end discrimination based on race, color, religion, sex, national origin, or age in hiring, promotion, firing, wages, testing, training, apprenticeship, and all other conditions of employment, and to promote voluntary action programs by employers, unions, and community organizations to make equal employment opportunity an actuality.

Activities. 1. Compliance Activities. The commission's 49 field offices receive written charges of discrimination against public and private employers, labor organizations, joint labor/management apprenticeship programs, and public and private employment agencies. Members of the commission may also initiate charges; field offices may initiate investigations to find violations of the Equal Pay and Age Discrimination in Employment Acts.

2. Complaints against the Federal Government. Federal employees or applicants who wish to file complaints with the commission rather than resolve their disputes within their agency, may do so if they are filed within two years of the alleged violation.

3. Other Activities. The commission participates in the development of the employment discrimination law through the issuance of guidelines, publication of significant commission decisions, and involvement in litigation brought under the Equal Pay and Age Discrimination in Employment Acts. The commission has direct liaison with governmental and private agencies and organizations concerned with fair employment practices laws.

For Further Information. Contact the Director, Office of Public Affairs, Equal Employment Opportunity Commission, 2401 E Street NW, Washington, DC 20506, (202) 634-6930.

FEDERAL LABOR RELATIONS AUTHORITY
500 C Street, SW
Washington, DC 20424
(202) 382-0711

Authorization. Created as an independent establishment by Reorganization Plan No. 2 of 1978 pursuant to Executive Order 12107 of December 28, 1978, to consolidate central policymaking functions in federal labor/management relations. Its duties are specified in Title VII of the Civil Service Reform Act of 1978 (92 Stat. 1191-1216; 5 U.S.C. 7101-7135), approved October 13, 1978.

Purpose. Oversees the federal service labor/management relations program. It administers the law that protects the right of employees of the federal government to organize, bargain collectively, and participate through labor organizations of their own choosing in decisions which affect them. The authority also ensures compliance with the statutory rights and obligations of federal employees and the labor organizations which represent them in their dealings with federal agencies.

Activities. The authority provides leadership in establishing policies and guidance relating to the federal service labor/management relations program. It determines the appropriateness of bargaining units; supervises or conducts representation elections; prescribes criteria and resolves issues relating to the granting of consultation rights to labor organization with respect to internal agency policies and government-wide rules and regulations; and resolves negotiability disputes, unfair labor practice complaints, and exceptions to arbitration awards.

The authority's general counsel investigates alleged unfair labor practices, files and prosecutes unfair labor practice complaints before the authority, and exercises such other powers as the authority may prescribe.

The Federal Service Impasses Panel provides assistance in resolving negotiation impasses between agencies and unions. The Foreign Service Labor Relations Board and the Foreign Service Impasse Disputes Panel administer provisions of chapter 2 of the Foreign Service Act of 1980 (94 Stat. 2071; 22 U.S.C. 3921), which establishes a statutory labor/management relations program for Foreign Service employees of the government.

For Further Information. Contact the Executive Director, Federal Labor Relations Authority, 500 C Street, SW, Washington, DC 20424, (202) 382-0711.

FEDERAL MEDIATION AND CONCILIATION SERVICE
2100 K Street NW
Washington, DC 20427
(202) 653-5290

Authorization. Created by the Labor-Management Relations Act, 1947 (61 Stat. 153; 29 U.S.C. 172)

Purpose. Promotes the development of sound and stable labor/management relations; prevents or minimizes work stoppages by assisting labor and management to settle their disputes through mediation; advocates collective bargaining, mediation, and voluntary arbitration as preferred processes for settling issues between employers and representatives of employees; develops the art, science, and practice of dispute resolution; and fosters constructive joint relationships of labor and management leaders to increase their mutual understanding and solution of common problems.

Activities. The service helps prevent disruptions in interstate commerce caused by labor/management disputes by providing mediators to assist disputing parties resolve their differences. It can intervene on its own or by invitation of either side in a dispute. Mediators have no law enforcement authority and must rely on persuasive techniques. It also helps provide qualified third-party neutrals as factfinders or arbitrators.

Mediators of the service assist representatives of labor and management in settling disputes about wages, hours, and other aspects of the employment relationship that arise in the course of negotiations. In this work, the mediator has a more basic function: encouraging and promoting better day-to-day relations between labor and management. On the joint request of employers and unions, it will help select arbitrators from a roster of private citizens who are qualified as neutrals to adjudicate matters in a dispute. The service has offices in

79 principal cities, with meeting facilities available for labor/management negotiations.

Regional Offices. Eastern Region—26 Federal Plaza, New York, NY 10278; Southern Region—1422 West Peachtree Street, NW, Atlanta, GA 30309; Central Region—175 West Jackson Boulevard, Chicago, IL 60604; Western Region—50 Francisco Street, San Francisco, CA 94133.

For Further Information. Contact Information Services, Federal Mediation and Conciliation Service, Washington, DC 20427, (202) 653-5290.

NATIONAL LABOR RELATIONS BOARD
1717 Pennsylvania Avenue, NW
Washington, DC 20570
(202) 655-4000

Authorization. Created by National Labor Relations Act of 1935 (Wagner Act), as amended by the acts of 1947 (Taft-Hartley Act) and 1959 (Landrum-Griffin Act).

Purpose. The National Labor Relations Board is responsible for administering the laws relating to labor relations and has the power to safeguard employees' rights to organize, determine through elections whether workers want unions to represent them at bargaining sessions, and prevent and remedy unfair labor practices.

Activities. 1. The board conducts secret-ballot elections among employees to determine whether they desire to be represented by a labor union; in addition, it conducts secret-ballot elections among employees who have been covered by a union-shop agreement to determine whether they wish to revoke the union's authority to make such agreements.

2. In the case of jurisdictional disputes, it decides which competing group of workers is entitled to perform the work.

3. In national emergency disputes, it conducts secret-ballot elections among the employees concerning employers' final settlement offers.

The board can act only when formally asked to do so. Individuals, employers, or unions may initiate cases by filing charges of unfair labor practices or petitions for employee representation elections with the board's field office which services the area where the case arises.

Field Offices. Field offices are located in the following cities (for address and telephone number of each, consult your local telephone directory): Albany, Albuquerque, Anchorage, Atlanta, Baltimore, Birmingham, Boston, Brooklyn (NY), Buffalo, Chicago, Cincinnati, Cleveland, Denver, Des Moines, Detroit, El Paso, Fort Worth, Grand Rapids, Hartford, Hato Rey (PR), Honolulu, Houston, Indianapolis, Jacksonville, Kansas City (KS), Little Rock, Las Vegas, Los Angeles, Memphis, Miami, Milwaukee, Minneapolis, Nashville, Newark, New Orleans, New York, Oakland, Peoria, Philadelphia, Phoenix, Pittsburgh, Portland (OR), St. Louis, San Antonio, San Diego, San Francisco, Seattle, Tampa, Tulsa, Washington (DC), Winston-Salem.

For Further Information. Contact the Information Branch, Office of the Executive Secretary, National Labor Relations Board, 1717 Pennsylvania Avenue, NW, Washington, DC 20570, (202) 632-4950.

NATIONAL MEDIATION BOARD
1425 K Street, NW
Washington, DC 20572
(202) 523-5920

and

NATIONAL RAILROAD ADJUSTMENT BOARD
10 West Jackson Boulevard
Chicago, IL 60604
(312) 886-7300

Authorization. The National Mediation Board was created on June 21, 1934, by act of Congress amending the Railway Labor Act (48 Stat. 1185, 45 U.S.C. 151-58, 160-62). The act was amended in April 1936 (49 Stat. 1189-91, 45 U.S.C. 1181-88); January 1951 (64 Stat. 1238, 45 U.S.C. 152); June 1966 (80 Stat. 208-9, 45 U.S.C. 153); and in April 1970 (84 Stat. 199-200, 45 U.S.C. 153).

Purpose. The National Mediation Board provides the railroad and airline industries with specific mechanisms for the adjustment of labor/management disputes; that is, the facilitation of agreements through collective bargaining, investigation of questions of representation, and the arbitration and establishment of procedures for emergency disputes. The board is assisted in its activities by the National Railroad Adjustment Board and other special boards of adjustment, which handle individual and group grievances arising under labor/management agreements.

Activities. Major responsibilities include: 1) the mediation of disputes over wages, hours, and working conditions which arise between rail and air carriers and organizations representing their employees, and 2) the investigation of representation disputes and certification of employee organizations as representatives of crafts or classes of carrier employees.

Disputes growing out of grievances or out of interpretation, or application of agreements concerning rates of pay, rules, or working conditions in the railroad industry are referable to the National Railroad Adjustment Board. In deadlocked cases, the National Mediation Board is authorized to appoint a referee to sit with the members of the division for the purpose of making an award.

In the airline industry, no national airline adjustment board has been established.

The board is charged with mediating disputes between carriers and labor organizations relating to initial contract negotiations or subsequent changes in rates of pay, rules, and working conditions. When the parties fail to reach accord in direct bargaining, either party may request the board's services, or the board may on its own motion invoke its services.

If a dispute arises among a carrier's employees as to whom is to be the representative of such employees, it is the board's duty to investigate such a dispute and determine by secret-ballot election whether or not and to whom a representation certification should be issued.

Additional duties of the board are the interpretation of agreements made under its mediatory auspices; the appointment of neutral referees when requested by the National Railroad Adjustment Board; appointment of neutrals to sit on System Boards and Special Boards of Adjustments; and the duty of notifying the President when parties have failed to reach agreement through the board's mediation efforts and when the dispute, in the board's judgment, threatens to interrupt interstate commerce to such a degree as to deprive any section of the country of essential transportation service.

For Further Information. Contact the Special Assistant to the Chairman, National Mediation Board, 1425 K Street, NW, Washington, DC 20572, (202) 523-5335.

OCCUPATIONAL SAFETY AND HEALTH REVIEW COMMISSION
1825 K Street, NW
Washington, DC 20006
(202) 634-7943

Authorization. Established by the Occupational Safety and Health Act of 1970 (84 Stat. 1590; 29 U.S.C. 651-678).

Purpose. The commission is a quasi-judicial agency concerned with providing safe and healthful working conditions for both the employer and employee. It adjudicates cases forwarded to it by the Department of Labor when disagreements arise over the results of safety and health inspections performed by the department.

Activities. The commission's functions are strictly adjudicatory; however, it is more a court system than a simple tribunal, for within the Review Commission there are two levels of adjudication.

The Occupational Safety and Health Act covers virtually every employer in the country. It is enforced by the Secretary of Labor and is an effort to reduce the incidence of personal injuries, illness, and deaths among working men and women which result from their employment. It requires each employer to furnish each of his employees employment and a place of employment which are free from recognized hazards that are causing or likely to cause death or serious physical harm and to comply with occupational safety and health standards promulgated under the act.

A case for adjudication by the commission arises when a citation is issued against an employer as a result of an inspection and it is contested within 15 working days thereafter. When a case is docketed it is assigned for hearing to a Review Commission judge, and the hearing will usually be held in or near the community where the alleged violation occurred. Once a case is decided, any person adversely affected may obtain a review of the decision in the United States Court of Appeals.

Offices of Review Commission Judges. 1365 Peachtree Street, NE, Atlanta, GA 30309; John W. McCormack Post Office and Courthouse, Boston, MA 02110; 55 East Monroe Street, Chicago, IL 60603; 1100 Commerce Street, Dallas, TX 75242; 1050 Seventeenth Street, Denver, CO 80265; 1515 Broadway, New York, NY 10036; 1114 Market Street, St. Louis, MO 63101.

For Further Information. Contact the Public Information Specialist, Occupational Safety and Health Review Commission, 1825 K Street, NW, Washington, DC 20006, (202) 634-7943.

VI

STATE AGENCIES CONCERNED WITH LABOR AND LABOR RELATIONS

STATE LABOR DEPARTMENTS

There is no organizational uniformity among the labor departments established in the 50 states and the District of Columbia. It should be pointed out that the Employment Security Agencies and the Occupational Information Coordinating Committees (which follow this listing of state labor departments) usually operate independently.

In general, state labor departments may be resonsible for all or some of the following functions: administration of apprenticeship programs; conducting conciliation and arbitration services; enforcement of child labor laws; industrial safety inspection and enforcement; planning and carrying out various labor relations programs; enforcement of minimum wage laws; compilation and publication of labor statistics; and administration of workmen's compensation programs.

For information about a state labor department, write or call the department, using the address or telephone number listed below.

Alabama, Department of Labor, 600 Administration Building, Montgomery 36130, (205) 832-6270

Alaska, Department of Labor, P.O. Box 1149, Juneau 99811, (907) 465-2700.

Arizona, Department of Labor, Industrial Commission, 1516 North Central, Phoenix 85007, (602) 255-4515.

Arkansas, Department of Labor, 1022 High Street, Little Rock 72202, (501) 371-1401.

California, Department of Industrial Relations, 455 Golden Gate Avenue, San Francisco 94102, (415) 557-3356.

Colorado, Department of Labor and Employment, 1313 Sherman Street, Denver 80203, (303) 866-5000.

Connecticut, Department of Labor, 200 Folly Brook Boulevard, Wethersfield 06109, (203) 566-4384.

Delaware, Department of Labor, 820 North French Street, Wilmington 19801, (302) 571-2710.

District of Columbia, Department of Employment Services, 500 C Street, NW, Washington 20001, (202) 727-6161.

Florida, Department of Labor and Employment Security, Berkeley Building, Tallahassee 32301, (904) 487-1837.

Georgia, Department of Labor, 254 Washington Street, SW, Atlanta 30334, (404) 656-4000.

Guam, Department of Labor, Government of Guam, P.O. Box 2950, Agana 96910, (671) 477-9821.

Hawaii, Department of Labor and Industrial Relations, 825 Mililani Street, Honolulu 96813, (808) 548-2211.

Idaho, Department of Labor and Industrial Service, 317 Main Street, Boise 83720, (208) 334-3950.

Illinois, Department of Labor, 100 North First Street, Springfield 62706, (217) 782-6206.

Indiana, Division of Labor, State Office Building, Indianapolis 46204, (317) 232-2663.

Iowa, Bureau of Labor, 307 East Seventh Street, Des Moines 50319, (515) 281-3606.

Kansas, Department of Human Resources, 401 Topeka Avenue, Topeka 66603, (913) 296-5000.

Kentucky, Department for Human Resources, 275 East Main Street, Frankfort 40601, (502) 564-2336.

Louisiana, Department of Labor, 1001 North Twenty-third Street, Baton Rouge 70802, (504) 342-3011.

Maine, Department of Labor, 20 Union Street, Augusta 04333, (207) 289-3788.

Maryland, Division of Labor and Industry, 1 South Calvert Street, Baltimore 21202, (301) 659-4180.

Massachusetts, Department of Labor and Industries, 100 Cambridge Street, Boston 02202, (617) 727-3454.

Michigan, Department of Labor, 309 North Washington Street, Lansing 48909, (517) 373-9435.

Minnesota, Department of Labor and Industry, 444 Lafayette Road, St. Paul 55101, (612) 296-6107.

Mississippi, Employment Security Commission, 1520 West Capital Street, Jackson 39205, (601) 354-8711.

Missouri, Department of Labor and Industrial Relations, 421 East Dunklin Street, Jefferson City 65104, (314) 751-4091.

Montana, Department of Labor and Industry, 35 South Last Chance Gulch, Helena 59620, (406) 449-2621.

Nebraska, Department of Labor, 550 South Sixteenth, Lincoln 68508, (402) 475-8451.

Nevada, Department of Labor, 505 East King Street, Carson City 89710, (702) 885-4850.

New Hampshire, Department of Labor, 1 Pillsbury Street, Concord 03301, (603) 271-3176.

New Jersey, Department of Labor, John Fitch Plaza, Trenton 08625, (609) 292-2323.

New Mexico, Labor and Industrial Commission, 509 Camino De Los Merquez, Santa Fe 87501, (505) 827-2756.

New York, Department of Labor, State Campus, Building 12, Albany 12240, (518) 457-5519.

North Carolina, Department of Labor, 4 East Edenton Street, Raleigh 27601, (919) 733-7166.

North Dakota, Department of Labor, State Capitol, Bismarck 58505, (701) 224-2660.

Ohio, Department of Industrial Relations, 2323 West Fifth Avenue, Columbus 43204, (614) 466-3271.

Oklahoma, Department of Labor, State Capitol, Oklahoma City 73105, (405) 521-2461.

Oregon, Bureau of Labor and Industries, 1400 SW Fifth Avenue, Portland 97201, (503) 229-5735.

Pennsylvania, Department of Labor and Industry, Labor and Industry Building, Harrisburg 17120, (717) 787-5279.

Puerto Rico, Department of Labor, Avenue Munoz Rivera #505, Rivera Martinez Building, Hato Rey 00918, (809) 754-2119.

Rhode Island, Department of Labor, 220 Elmwood Avenue, Providence 02907, (401) 277-2741.

South Carolina, Department of Labor, 3600 Forest Drive, Columbia 29204, (803) 758-2851.

South Dakota, Department of Labor, Capitol Building, Pierre 57501, (605) 773-3101.

Tennessee, Department of Labor, Union Building, Nashville 37219, (615) 741-2582.

Texas, Department of Labor and Standards, Thompson State Office Building, Austin 78711, (512) 475-3499.

Utah, Industrial Commission, 350 East 500 South Street, Salt Lake City 84111, (801) 533-5971.

Vermont, Department of Labor and Industry, State Office Building, Montpelier 05602, (802) 828-2286.

Virgin Islands, Department of Labor, P.O. Box 890, Christiansted, St. Croix 00820, (809) 773-1994.

Virginia, Department of Labor and Industry, 205 North Fourth Street, Richmond 23219, (804) 786-2376.

Washington, Department of Labor and Industries, General Administration Building, Olympia 98504, (206) 753-6341.

West Virginia, Department of Labor, 1900 Washington Street East, Charleston 25305, (304) 348-7890.

Wisconsin, Department of Industry, Labor and Human Relations, 201 East Washington Avenue, Madison 53702, (608) 266-3131.

Wyoming, Department of Labor and Statistics, Hathaway Building, Cheyenne 82001, (307) 777-7261.

STATE EMPLOYMENT SECURITY AGENCIES

Most state employment security agencies have two principal responsibilities: acting as a statewide employment agency and administering the state's unemployment compensation program.

The nation's 2,500 Job Service offices, also called the public employment service and located throughout the 50 states and District of Columbia, are run by the state employment security agencies under the direction of the U.S. Department of Labor's U.S. Employment Service. Providing help without charge, the Job Service centers offer testing and counseling services, help job-seekers find employment, and assist employers in locating qualified workers. All state employment security agencies develop detailed labor market data needed by employment and training specialists and guidance counselors who plan for local needs. The matter of equal job opportunity may also fall within the responsibility of the Job Service.

With millions of Americans out of work, the unemployment compensation sections of all state employment security agencies are assuming increasingly heavy administrative workloads and financial burdens. Working closely with the Job Service offices, every attempt is made, within the scope of job availability, to find employment for those who file unemployment benefit claims. Accordingly, the employment security agencies assume a heavy responsibility for the welfare of the nation's unemployed.

Alabama, Department of Industrial Relations, 649 Monroe Street, Montgomery 36130, (205) 832-6106.

Alaska, Employment Security Division, Fourth & Harris Streets, P.O. Box 3-7000, Juneau 99991, (907) 465-2712.

Arizona, Department of Economics Security, P.O. Box 6123, Phoenix 85005, (602) 255-4791.

Arkansas, Employment Security Commission, P.O. Box 2981, Capitol Mall, Little Rock 72203, (501) 371-2121.

California, Employment Development Department, 800 Capitol Mall, Sacramento 95814, (916) 445-8008.

Colorado, Division of Employment and Training, 251 East Twelfth Avenue, Denver 80203, (303) 839-5833.

Connecticut, Employment Security Division, 200 Folly Brook Boulevard, Wethersfield 06109, (203) 566-4280.

Delaware, Department of Labor, 801 West Street, Wilmington 19899, (302) 368-6707.

District of Columbia, District Unemployment Compensation Board, Sixth and Pennsylvania Avenue, NW, Washington 20001, (202) 724-3870.

Florida, Department of Commerce, Collins Building, Tallahassee 32304, (904) 488-7228.

Georgia, Employment Security Agency, 200 State Labor Building, Atlanta 30334, (404) 656-3000.

Guam, Department of Labor, Government of Guam, P.O. Box 2950, Agena 96910, (671) 477-9845.

Hawaii, Department of Labor and Industrial Relations, 825 Mililani Street, Honolulu 96813, (808) 548-2211.

Idaho, Department of Employment, 317 Main Street, P.O. Box 35, Boise 83707, (208) 334-2611.

Illinois, Bureau of Employment Security, 910 South Michigan Avenue, Chicago 60605, (312) 793-3183.

Indiana, Employment Security Division, 10 North Senate Avenue, Indianapolis 46204, (317) 232-7670.

Iowa, Iowa Department of Job Service, 1000 East Grand Avenue, Des Moines 50319, (515) 281-5387.

Kansas, Division of Employment, 401 Topeka Avenue, Topeka 66603, (913) 296-5000.

Kentucky, Department for Human Resources, Bureau for Manpower Services, 275 East Main Street, Frankfort 40621, (502) 564-5331.

Louisiana, Department of Employment Security, 1001 North Twenty-third Street, Baton Rouge 70804, (504) 342-3111.

Maine, Employment Security Commission, 20 Union Street, Augusta 04332, (207) 289-2411.

Maryland, Employment Security Administration, 1100 North Eutaw Street, Baltimore 21201, (301) 383-6452.

Massachusetts, Division of Employment Security, Charles F. Hurley ES Building, Boston 02114, (617) 727-6600.

Michigan, Michigan Employment Security Commission, 7310 Woodward Avenue, Detroit 48202, (313) 876-5500.

Minnesota, Department of Employment Security, 390 North Robert Street, St. Paul 55101, (612) 296-6791.

Mississippi, Employment Security Commission, 1520 West Capital Street, P.O. Box 1699, Jackson 39205, (601) 354-8711.

Missouri, Division of Employment Security, 421 East Dunklin Street, P.O. Box 59, Jefferson City 65101, (314) 751-3215.

Montana, Employment Security Division, Lockey & Roberts, P.O. Box 1728, Helena 59601, (406) 449-3662.

Nebraska, Division of Employment, 550 South Sixteenth Street, P.O. Box 94600, Lincoln 68509, (402) 455-8451.

Nevada, Employment Security Department, 500 East Third Street, Carson City 89713, (702) 885-4650.

New Hampshire, Department of Employment Security, 32 South Main Street, Concord 03301, (603) 224-3311.

New Jersey, Department of Labor and Industry, John Fitch Plaza, P.O. Box V, Trenton 08625, (609) 292-2323.

New Mexico, Employment Security Commission, 401 Broadway NE, P.O. Box 1928, Albuquerque 87103, (505) 842-3965.

New York, Department of Labor, State Campus, Building 112, Albany 12240, (518) 474-2121.

North Carolina, Employment Security Commission, 200 West Jones Street, P.O. Box 25903, Raleigh 27611, (919) 733-3098.

North Dakota, Employment Security Bureau, 1000 East Divide Avenue, P.O. Box 1537, Bismarck 58505, (701) 224-2825.

Ohio, Bureau of Employment Services, 145 South Front Street, P.O. Box 1618, Columbus 43216, (614) 466-4636.

Oklahoma, Employment Security Commission, Will Rogers Memorial Office Building, Oklahoma City 73105, (405) 521-3769.

Oregon, Employment Division, 875 Union Street NE, Salem 97311, (503) 378-8420.

Pennsylvania, Bureau of Employment Security, Seventh and Forster Streets, Harrisburg 17121, (717) 787-5279.

Puerto Rico, Bureau of Employment Security, Avenue Munoz Rivera #505, Rivera Martinez Building, Hato Rey 00918, (809) 754-5375.

Rhode Island, Department of Employment Security, 24 Mason Street, Providence 02903, (401) 277-3600.

South Carolina, Employment Security Commission, 1550 Gadsden Street, P.O. Box 995, Columbia 29202, (803) 758-2583.

South Dakota, Employment Security Department, 607 North Fourth Street, Aberdeen 57401, (605) 625-2340.

Tennessee, Department of Employment Security, 536 Cordell Hull Building, Nashville 37219, (615) 741-2131.

Texas, Employment Commission, 638 TEC BUILDING, Fifteenth and Congress Avenue, Austin 78778, (512) 397-4411.

Utah, Department of Employment Security, 174 Social Hall Avenue, P.O. Box 11249, Salt Lake City 84147, (801) 533-2400.

Vermont, Department of Employment Security, 5 Green Mountain Drive, Montpelier 05602, (802) 229-0311.

Virgin Islands, Employment Security Agency, 35 Norre Gade Street, P.O. Box 1092, Charlotte Amalie, St. Thomas 00801, (809) 774-7575.

Virginia, Employment Commission, 703 East Main Street, P.O. Box 1358, Richmond 23211, (804) 786-3004.

Washington, Employment Security Department, ES Building, 212 Maple Park, Olympia 98504, (206) 753-5243.

West Virginia, Department of Employment Security, 112 California Avenue, Charleston 25305, (304) 348-2630.

Wisconsin, Job Service Division, 201 East Washington Avenue, P.O. Box 7898, Madison 53701, (608) 266-3161.

Wyoming, Employment Security Commission, ESC Building, Center and Midwest Street, P.O. Box 2760, Casper 82601, (307) 234-4591.

STATE OCCUPATIONAL INFORMATION COORDINATING COMMITTEES

These information coordinating committees can help you find information about jobs in your state or area. The committee may provide the information directly or refer you to other sources. In many states, it can also tell you where you can go to use the state's career information system. To find out what career materials are available, write to the director of your state occupational information coordinating committee.

Alabama, Director, Alabama Occupational Information Coordinating Committee, 100 Commerce Street, Montgomery 36130, (205) 832-5737.

Alaska, Coordinator, Alaska Occupational Information Coordinating Committee, Pouch F, State Office Building, Juneau 99811, (907) 465-2980.

American Samoa, Executive Director, American Samoa SOICC, Governor's Office, Pago Pago 96799.

Arizona, Executive Director, Arizona State Occupational Information Coordinating Committee, 1535 West Jefferson, Phoenix 85007, (602) 255-3680.

Arkansas, Director, Arkansas State Occupational Information Coordinating Committee, P.O. Box 2981, Little Rock 72203, (501) 371-3551.

California, Executive Director, California Occupational Information Coordinating Committee, 1027 Tenth Street, Sacramento 95814, (916) 323-6544.

Colorado, Director, Office of Occupational Information, Colorado Occupational Information Coordinating Committee, 1313 Sherman Street, Denver 80203, (303) 866-3335.

Connecticut, Executive Director, Connecticut State Occupational Information Coordinating Committee, c/o Elm Hill School, 569 Maple Hill Avenue, Newington 06111 (203) 666-1441.

Delaware, Director, State Occupational Information Coordinating Committee of Delaware, Drummond Office Plaza, Building No. 3, Newark, 19711, (302) 368-6908.

District of Columbia, Executive Director, D.C. Occupational Information Coordinating Committee, 500 C Street, NW, Washington 20001, (202) 724-3965.

Florida, Director, Florida Occupational Information Coordinating Committee, 325 John Knox Road, Tallahassee 32303, (904) 386-6111.

Georgia, Executive Director, Georgia Occupational Information Coordinating Committee, 151 Ellis Street, NE, Atlanta 30303, (404) 656-3117.

Guam, Acting Executive Director, Guam Occupational Information Coordinating Committee, P.O. Box 2817, Agana 96910, (617) 477-8941.

Hawaii, Executive Director, Hawaii State Occupational Information Coordinating Committee, 1164 Bishop Street, Honolulu 96813, (808) 548-3496.

Idaho, Coordinator, Idaho Occupational Information Coordinating Committee, 650 West State Street, Boise 83720, (208) 334-3705.

Illinois, Executive Director, Illinois Occupational Information Coordinating Committee, 217 East Monroe, Springfield 62706, (217) 785-0789.

Indiana, Director, Indiana Occupational Information Coordinating Committee, 17 West Market Street, Indianapolis 46204, (317) 232-3625.

Iowa, Executive Director, Iowa State Occupational Information Coordinating Committee, 523 East Twelfth Street, Des Moines 50319, (515) 281-8076.

Kansas, Director, Kansas Occupational Information Coordinating Committee, 320 West Seventh, Topeka 66603, (913) 296-5286.

Kentucky, Coordinator, Kentucky Occupational Information Coordinating Committee, 275 East Main Street, Frankford 40621, (502) 564-4258.

Louisiana, Director, Louisiana State Occupational Information Coordinating Committee, P.O. Box 44094, Baton Rouge 70804, (504) 925-3593.

Maine, Executive Director, Maine State Occupational Information Coordinating Committee, State House Station 71, Augusta 04333, (207) 289-2331.

Maryland, Executive Director, Maryland Occupational Information Coordinating Committee, 1123 North Eutaw Street, Baltimore 21201, (301) 383-6350.

Massachusetts, Executive Director, Massachusetts Occupational Information Coordinating Committee, Charles F. Hurley Building, Government Center, Boston 02114, (617) 727-9740.

Michigan, Executive Coordinator, Michigan Occupational Information Coordinating Committee, 309 North Washington, Lansing 48909, (517) 373-0363.

Minnesota, SOICC Director, Department of Economic Security, 150 East Kellogg Boulevard, St. Paul 55101, (612) 296-2072.

Mississippi, SOICC Director, Vocational Technical Education, P.O. Box 771, Jackson 39205, (601) 354-6779.

Missouri, Director, Missouri Occupational Information Coordinating Committee, 630d East High Street, Jefferson City 65101, (314) 751-2624.

Montana, Program Manager, Montana State Occupational Information Coordinating Committee, P.O. Box 1728, Helena 59624, (406) 449-2741.

Nebraska, Executive Director, Nebraska Occupational Information Coordinating Committee, W. 300 Nebraska Hall, Lincoln 68588, (402) 472-2062.

Nevada, Director, Nevada Occupational Information Coordinating Committee, 505 East King Street, Carson City 89710, (702) 885-4577.

New Hampshire, SOICC Director, New Hampshire Occupational Information Coordinating Committee, c/o Department of Employment and Training, 155 Manchester Street, Concord 03301, (603) 271-3156.

New Jersey, Acting Staff Director, New Jersey Occupational Information Coordinating Committee, P.O. Box CN056, Trenton 08625, (609) 292-2626.

New Mexico, Director, New Mexico State Occupational Information Coordinating Committee, 130 South Capitol, Santa Fe 87501, (505) 827-3411.

New York, SOICC Director, New York Department of Labor, Labor Department Building #12, State Campus, Room 559A, Albany 12240, (518) 457-2930.

North Carolina, SOICC Director, North Carolina Department of Administration, 112 West Lane Street, Raleigh 27611, (919) 733-6700.

North Dakota, Director, North Dakota Occupational Information Coordinating Committee, 1424 West Century Avenue, Bismarck 58505, (701) 224-2733.

Northern Mariana Islands, Executive Director, Northern Mariana Islands Occupational Information Coordinating Committee, P.O. Box 149, Saipan 96950, Tel. 7136.

Ohio, Director, Ohio Occupational Information Coordinating Committee, 65 South Front Street, Columbus 43215, (614) 466-2095.

Oklahoma, Executive Director, Oklahoma Occupational Information Coordinating Committee, School of Occupational and Adult Education, 1515 West Sixth Street, Stillwater 74074, (405) 377-2000, ext. 311.

Oregon, Coordinator, Oregon Occupational Information Coordinating Committee, 875 Union Street, NE, Salem 97311, (503) 378-8146.

Pennsylvania, Director, Pennsylvania Occupational Information Coordinating Committee, Labor and Industry Building, Seventh and Forster Streets, Harrisburg 17120, (717) 787-3467.

Puerto Rico, Executive Director, Puerto Rico Occupational Information Coordinating committee, Cond. El Centro II, Munoz Rivera Avenue, Hato Rey 00918, (809) 753-7110.

Rhode Island, Executive Director, Rhode Island Occupational Information Coordinating Committee, 22 Hayes Street, Providence 02908, (401) 272-0830.

South Carolina, Director, South Carolina Occupational Information Coordinating Committee, 1550 Gadsden Street, Columbia 29202, (803) 758-3165.

South Dakota, Executive Director, South Dakota Occupational Coordinating Committee, 108 East Missouri, Pierre 57501, (605) 773-3935.

Tennessee, Director, Tennessee Occupational Information Coordinating Committee, Cordell Hull Building, Nashville 37219, (615) 741-6451.

Texas, Executive Director, Texas Occupational Information Coordinating Committee, Texas Employment Commission Building, Fifteenth and Congress, Austin 78778, (512) 397-4970.

Trust Territory of the Pacific, Director, Trust Territory of the Pacific Islands, Occupational Information Coordinating Committee, Office of Planning and Statistics, Saipan, Mariana Islands 96950.

Utah, Director, Utah Occupational Information Coordinating Committee, 139 East South Temple, Salt Lake City 84111, (801) 533-2028.

Vermont, Director, Vermont Occupational Information Coordinating Committee, P.O. Box 488, Montpelier 05602, (802) 229-0311.

Virgin Islands, Director, Virgin Islands Occupational Information Coordinating Committee, Department of Education, P.O. Box 630, Charlotte Amalie, St. Thomas 00801, (809) 774-0100.

Virginia, SOICC Director, Virginia Vocational and Adult Education, Department of Education, P.O. Box 6Q, Richmond 23216, (804) 225-2735.

Washington, SOICC Director, Washington Commission for Vocational Education, Building 17, Airdustrial Park, Mail Stop LS-10, Olympia 98504, (206) 754-1552.

West Virginia, Executive Director, West Virginia State Occupational Information Coordinating Committee, 1600½ Washington Street, East, Charleston 25311, (304) 348-0061.

Wisconsin, Director, Wisconsin Occupational Information Coordinating Committee, 1025 West Johnson, Madison 53706, (608) 263-1048.

Wyoming, Director, Wyoming Occupational Information Coordinating Committee, 2300 Capitol Avenue, Cheyenne 82002, (307) 777-7177.

VII

SOURCES OF LABOR INFORMATION
AND STATISTICS

The United States Department of Labor is the principal source of information about labor and the labor movement. Although the department's principal administrations issue a limited number of publications and reports, the Bureau of Labor Statistics is responsible for the bulk of the department's economic and statistical research activities.

As mentioned elsewhere in this almanac, the bureau is the government's principal factfinding agency in the field of labor economics, particularly with respect to collecting and analyzing data on labor requirements, labor force, employment, unemployment, hours of work, wages and employee compensation, prices, living conditions, labor/management relations, productivity and technological developments, occupational safety and health, structure and growth of the economy, urban conditions and related socioeconomic issues, and international aspects of certain of these subjects.

This section is divided into two parts: "Information Sources" and "Sources of Statistical Data." Although the U.S. Department of Labor collects, compiles, and disseminates most of this material, other important and pertinent reference material has been included also.

INFORMATION SOURCES

BIBLIOGRAPHIES AND BOOK LISTS

Books in Print, published annually by R. R. Bowker Company (1180 Avenue of the Americas, New York, NY 10036), may be consulted in many public libraries and bookstores. Although this compilation does not include every book published, publications of leading publishers will be found in these extensive listings which are arranged by author, subject, and title.

Commerce Clearing House, Inc. (4025 West Peterson Avenue, Chicago, IL 60646) publishes a number of specialized books on business, labor, pensions, ERISA, and Social Security. A catalog is available on request.

The *Monthly Labor Review* (see page 144) carries a list of new books on labor in each issue.

Public Affairs Information Service (11 West Fortieth Street, New York, NY 10018) publishes the PAIS *Bulletin* indexing the latest books, pamphlets, government publications, reports of public and private agencies, and periodical articles relating to economic and social conditions, public administration, and international relations, published in English throughout the world. Large public and university libraries are the best places to find this publication.

The United States Department of Labor issues a free monthly pamphlet, Publication No. 322, "Just Published," listing recent books related to the labor movement. *Publications of the Department of Labor, Subject Listing, January 1976 through December 1980*, was published in 1981 but due to budget restrictions, there are no plans for updating this. Copies of both publications are available on request from the Office of Information, U.S. Department of Labor, Washington, DC 20210.

(Note: Current periodicals and subscription services published by the Department of Labor's Bureau of Labor Statistics are listed under "Specialized Labor Periodicals and Subscription Services in this section.)

The Superintendent of Documents issues two helpful bibliographies: *Monthly Catalog of United States Government Publications* (available by subscription), and *Labor-Management Relations*, SB-064, (October 27, 1981) of the Subject Bibliography series which is free upon request. Both publications should be ordered from the Superintendent of Documents, U.S. Government Printing Office, Washington, DC 20402.

For those unfamiliar with government documents, a helpful guide is *Government Reference Books 80/81, A Biennial Guide to U.S. Government Publications*, compiled by Walter L. Newsome and published by Libraries Unlimited, P.O. Box 263, Littleton, CO 80160.

Government publications may be obtained by writing to the Superintendent of Documents, U.S. Government Printing Office, Washington, DC 20402. Many of the more popular publications are also available at the Government Bookstores located in Atlanta, Birmingham, Boston, Chicago, Cleveland, Columbus (Ohio), Dallas, Denver, Detroit, Houston, Jacksonville, Kansas City, Los Angeles, Milwaukee, New York City, Philadelphia, Pittsburgh, Pueblo, San Francisco, Seattle, and the District of Columbia. Addresses for each of these stores will be found in the telephone directory under United States Government, Printing Office-Retail Bookstore.

There are libraries throughout the country which the Library of Congress has designated "Depository Libraries" for government publications. Such libraries receive and keep the many government publications sent to them. Some libraries catalogue all their government publications; others catalogue only those which are shelved in the regular book collection and file the pamphlets in their vertical files. For the location of the nearest Depository Library, consult your public library reference librarian or write to the state library.

NEWSPAPER AND PERIODICAL INDEXES

Articles appearing in all important business and general circulation periodicals are indexed by author, subject, and title in the *Business Periodicals Index* and the *Readers' Guide to Periodical Literature*. Many public and almost all university libraries subscribe to these useful guides which are published frequently throughout the year and cumulated annually (H. W. Wilson Co., 950 University Avenue, Bronx, NY 10452).

The *New York Times Index*, published monthly and cumulated annually, is useful for finding information and dates about people and events, even though microfilm or regular copies of the newspaper are not available (229 West Forty-third Street, New York, NY 10036).

The *Public Affairs Information Service Bulletin* indexes periodicals, books, and government documents which bear on contemporary public issues and the making and evaluation of public policy (11 West Fortieth Street, New York, NY 10018).

Social Science Citation Index is an international multidisciplinary index to the literature of the social, behavioral, and related sciences (Institute of Scientific Information, 3501 Market Street, Philadelphia, PA 19104).

The *Wall Street Journal Index*, published annually, indexes news items and special articles which have appeared in this financial newspaper (22 Cortlandt Street, New York, NY 10007).

SPECIALIZED LABOR PERIODICALS AND SUBSCRIPTION SERVICES

Area Wage Survey Bulletins, $90, annually for series of 70 bulletins; individual area bulletins are available separately. Superintendent of Documents, U.S. Government Printing Office, Washington, DC 20402.

These bulletins cover office, professional, technical, maintenance, custodial, and material movement occupations in major metropolitan areas.

CPI Detailed Report, $28, monthly. Superintendent of Documents, U.S. Government Printing Office, Washington, DC 20402.

A comprehensive report on monthly consumer price indexes and rates of change. Includes data on commodity and service groups for 28 cities.

Note: Consumer Price Index data summary is available by mailgram within 24 hours of the CPI release. Provides unadjusted and seasonally adjusted U.S. City Average Data for All Urban Consumers (CPI-U) and for Urban Wage Earners and Clerical Workers (CPI-W). (NTISUP/158). $125 in contiguous United States. Available from National Technical Information Service, U.S. Department of Commerce, 5285 Port Royal Road, Springfield, VA 22151.

Current Wage Developments, $23, monthly. Superintendent of Documents, U.S. Government Printing Office, Washington, DC 20402.

Reports on specific wage and benefit changes from collective bargaining agreements. Includes data on strikes or lockouts, major agreements expiring, and statistics on compensation changes.

Employment and Earnings, $39, monthly (price includes annual supplement). Superintendent of Documents, U.S. Government Printing Office, Washington, DC 20402.

Gives current employment and earnings statistics for the nation as a whole, for individual states, and more than 200 areas. Included are household and establishment data, seasonally and not seasonally adjusted.

Industrial and Labor Relations Review, $14, quarterly. Cornell University, Ithaca, NY 14853.

Informed articles on industrial and labor relations.

Industrial Relations, A Journal of Economy and Society, $10, winter, spring, fall. Institute of Industrial Relations, University of California, Berkeley, CA 94720.

Articles on all aspects of the employment relationship.

Labor History, $18.50 (individuals), $23 (institutions), quarterly. Bobst Library, New York University, 70 Washington Square South, New York, NY 10012.

The Labor Law Journal, $50, monthly. Commerce Clearing House, 4025 West Peterson Avenue, Chicago, IL 60646.

" ... to promote sound thinking in labor law problems. To this end the *Journal* will contain a continuing survey of important legislative, administrative, and judicial developments, and signed articles on subjects pertaining to legal problems in the labor field."

Monthly Labor Review, $26. Superintendent of Documents, U.S. Government Printing Office, Washington, DC 20402.

The oldest and most authoritative government research journal in economics and social sciences. Regular features include articles on employment, wages, prices, and productivity.

Occupational Outlook Quarterly, $9. Superintendent of Documents, U.S. Government Printing Office, Washington, DC 20402.

Written in nontechnical language, it helps students and guidance counselors learn about new occupations, training opportunities, salary trends, and career counseling programs.

Personnel, $28.50, bimonthly. AMACOM-P, American Management Association, Saranac Lake, NY 12983.

Articles are concerned with "the management of people at work."

Personnel Administration, $30, monthly. American Society for Personnel Administration, 30 Park Drive, Berea, OH 44017.

" ... to further the professional aims of the society and the human resource management profession."

Personnel Journal, $34, monthly. A. C. Croft, Inc., 866 West Sixteenth Street, Costa Mesa, CA 92627.

"All aspects of personnel management and human resource development."

Producer Prices and Price Indexes, $34, monthly (price includes annual supplement). Superintendent of Documents, U.S. Government Printing Office, Washington, DC 20402.

Includes price movements of industrial commodities and farm products. Tables and charts give greater detail than are available in other published material.

U.S. Department of State Indexes of Living Costs Abroad, Quarters Allowances, and Hardship Differentials, Report 670, $6.50, quarterly. Superintendent of Documents, U.S. Government Printing Office, Washington, DC 20402.

Tabulations computed quarterly by the Allowances Staff of the Department of State for use in establishing allowances to compensate American civilian government employees for costs and hardships related to assignments abroad.

Three authoritative and very comprehensive subscription services cover many aspects of current labor law and labor relations, personnel management, wages and hours, unemployment insurance, arbitration, public employee bargaining, PSHA compliance, EEOC compliance,. and other subjects. Publishers of these services are: Bureau of National Affairs, 1231 Twenty-fifth Street, NW, Washington, DC 20037; Commerce Clearing House, 4025 West

Peterson Avenue, Chicago, IL 60646; and Prentice-Hall, Inc., Englewood Cliffs, NJ 07632. Catalogs are available from each publisher on request.

GENERAL LABOR PUBLICATIONS

Labor, every third week. Labor Co-operative Educational & Publishing Society, publisher, 400 First Street, NW, Washington, DC 20001.

Labor Beacon, monthly. Bill Dye, publisher, P.O. Box B, Michigan City, IN 46360.

Labor Herald, weekly. The Labor Herald, publisher, 6148 Reisterstown Road, Baltimore, MD 21215.

Labor Journal, quarterly. Labor Journal, publisher, P.O. Box 10021, Westport Station, Kansas City, MO 64111.

The Labor Journal, monthly. Kern County Labor Council, publisher, 200 West Jeffrey, Bakersfield, CA 93305.

Labor Leader, monthly. San Diego County Labor Council, publisher, 3945 Idaho Street, San Diego, CA 92104.

Labor News, quarterly. Amnesty International, USA, publisher, 304 West Fifty-eighth Street, New York, NY 10019.

Labor News, weekly. Labor News Company, publisher, 193 North Cherry Street, Galesburg, IL 61401.

Labor News, monthly. Belleville Trades and Labor Assembly, publisher, 606 Bornman, Belleville, IL 62221.

The Labor Paper, weekly. Peoria Labor News, publisher, 400 North Jefferson, Peoria, IL 61603.

Labor-Telegram, weekly. National Dynamics Corporation, publisher, P.O. Box 43, Altoona, PA 16603.

Labor Tribune, weekly. Edward Finkelstein, publisher, 505 South Ewing, St. Louis, MO 63103.

Labor World, biweekly. Labor World, Inc., publisher, 2002 London Road, Duluth, MN 55812.

Labor World, monthly. Chattanooga Labor Council, publisher, 3616 Conner Street, Chattanooga, TN 37411.

Labor World, monthly. Labor World Publishing Co., publisher, P.O. Box 5418, Spokane, WA 99205.

Labor Zionist Alliance Newsletter, quarterly. Labor Zionist Alliance, publisher, 575 Avenue of the Americas, New York, NY 10011.

It should be noted that many national and local unions issue publications on a regular basis. Examples are *The Federationist*, published by the AFL-CIO, but temporarily suspended for reasons of economy; *Labor Unity*, monthly publication of the Amalgamated Clothing and Textile Workers Union; *Solidarity*, published by the United Automobile Workers, and others.

ARCHIVAL AND LIBRARY FACILITIES

The *Department of Labor Library* is located in Room N2439, Frances Perkins Building, 200 Constitution Avenue, NW, Washington, DC. In addition, the department's Labor-Management Services Administration maintains two Public Documents rooms at 200 Constitution Avenue, NW. Reports filed under WPPDA* and ERISA* provisions are available for public viewing in Room N4677. LMRDA* reports may be seen in Room N5616. The Bureau of Labor Statistics has an Information Office in Room 1539, General Accounting Office Building, 441 G Street, NW, Washington, DC 20212. Questions regarding the Labor Department should be referred to the Office of Information and Public Affairs, Department of Labor, Room S1032, 200 Constitution Avenue, NW, Washington, DC 20210. Phone: (202) 523-7316.

The **International Ladies Garment Workers Union Archives** are located on the eighth floor of its building at 275 Seventh Avenue, New York, NY 10001. Phone: (212) 675-4771. The library contains nearly two million documents, letters, oral histories, and other materials which recount the union's turbulent history. The David Dubinsky collection contains more than 450,000 items relating to the years 1932-1966 when he was president. In the Heritage Exhibition are hundreds of artifacts ranging from documents to a sewing machine and a cutter's scissors.

The **Robert F. Wagner Labor Archives** are housed in the Bobst Library of New York University at 70 Washington Square South, New York, NY 10012. Phone: (212) 598-3709. The collection abounds in records, newspapers, and photographs about union activities in New York, correspondence, agreements, and other materials. It includes some 30,000 books, hundreds of copies of union journals, records of unions, letters of prominent union leaders, a file of union songs, oral histories from a variety of interviews with workers, and the Samuel Reiss photographs.

The **Arthur and Elizabeth Schlesinger Library on the History of Women in America** is a department of Radcliffe College and is located at 10 Garden Street, Cambridge, MA 02138. Phone: (617) 495-8647. This library contains a unique national repository of books, manuscripts, photographs, and other documents which chronicle the history of women in America from 1800 to the present. Over 300 manuscript collections are fully cataloged and provide source material on topics such as woman's rights and suffrage; social welfare and reform; pioneers in the professions; family history, women in politics, the labor movement, government service, and post-1920 feminism. In addition, the library contains a wide range of materials which make it the foremost resource for women's contributions to American life.

The **Martin P. Catherwood Library** and the **Labor Management Documentation Center** of Cornell University's New York State School of Industrial and Labor Relations are located at Ithaca, NY 14853. Phone: (607) 256-3183. This is the nation's largest academic collection on labor and industrial relations, whose primary purpose is to serve the instructional, research, and extension functions of the academic unit of which it is a part. The library has an international reputation for its holdings in the fields of collective bargaining,

---

*WPPDA—Welfare and Pension Plans Disclosure Act; ERISA—Employee Retirement Income Security Act of 1974; LMRDA—Labor Management Reporting and Disclosure Act.

labor history, labor law, labor union administration, labor economics, income security, human resources, and personnel administration. The library also has resources for studying the International Labor Organization and the World Federation of Trade Unions. The Documentation Center is the repository for the records of nine labor unions, six lobbying and educational groups, and several local labor unions and associations, as well as housing the intimate papers and oral history reminiscences of some 250 individuals prominent in the field of labor and industrial relations.

Other libraries or collections which specialize in labor history include the following:

The **Labadie Collection**, University of Michigan Library (one of the oldest special collections of radical/labor history in the United States).

The **Immigration History Research Center**, University of Minnesota (a collection of material on the immigrant labor experience).

Labor Records, State Historical Society of Wisconsin (resources on labor and working-class history).

Walter P. Reuther Library, Wayne State University (archives of labor and urban affairs).

Labor Archives of Texas, University of Texas at Arlington.

Urban Archives, Temple University.

Fred Lewis Pattee Library, Pennsylvania State University.

Labor History Resources Center, Ohio Historical Society.

Southern Labor Archives, Georgia State University (founded by the Southern Labor Historians Association).

Archives of Labor History, University of Maryland at College Park.

The **Catholic University** at Washington, DC (papers of Terrence Powderly and John Hayes).

Division of Research and Statistics, New York State Department of Labor, World Trade Center, New York City.

Approximately 50 colleges and universities have industrial relations library sections. For a thorough overview of archives, collections, and resources relating to the labor movement, see *Labor History*, Volume 23, No. 4 (Fall 1982), the entire issue of which was devoted to this subject.

SOURCES OF STATISTICAL DATA

MISCELLANEOUS PUBLICATIONS

The *Statistical Abstract of the United States*, published annually and sold by the Superintendent of Documents, U.S. Government Printing Office, Washington, DC 20402, will be found in most libraries. It contains a useful although selective group of statistical tables on labor. Titles of the tables pertaining to labor are: Employment Status; Labor Force Participation, Status; Labor Force Characteristics; Multiple Jobholders; Female Labor Force, Turnover Rates; Unemployment; Industry, Hours, Earnings; Output and Cost Indexes; Occupations; Earnings, Hourly and Weekly; Employee Compensation, Wage Rates; Labor Unions, Work Stoppages; Injury Rates.

General almanacs such as the *World Almanac* or *Information Please Almanac* contain a few labor statistics.

Many texts and other books on the labor movement contain original statistical tables which are usually listed in the table of contents.

Newspaper and periodical articles often include statistics which may be mentioned in the newspaper or periodical index.

DEPARTMENT OF LABOR PUBLICATIONS

Although the Bureau of Labor Statistics is the principal statistical gathering and publishing agency for the department, other administrations within the department periodically issue reports and statistics pertaining to their respective areas of responsibility. Because of budget reductions, no general bibliography or list of such publications is available presently. It is, therefore, necessary to contact each administration to ascertain what reports, statistics, or other information might be available on the subject for which data is required.

Two useful publications which might be overlooked are:

"Significant Provisions of State Unemployment Insurance Laws," issued by the Employment and Training Administration, Unemployment Insurance Service, which has usually been updated at the end of each year.

"State Workers' Compensation Laws," issued by the Employment Standards Administration, Office of Workers' Compensation Programs, Division of State Workers' Compensation Standards, which has also been updated each yearend.

The Women's Bureau has issued special reports and statistics from time to time, but apparently this bureau, in common with the rest of the department, has been forced to cut its publishing program.

BUREAU OF LABOR STATISTICS

It should be remembered that many of the important studies conducted by the bureau appeared initially in issues of the *Monthly Labor Review* and were reprinted later as separate publications. Most significant studies and publications issued by the bureau and other administrations within the Department of Labor are listed in the *Monthly Labor Review*.

The January, February, and March issues of the *Monthly Labor Review* have usually included articles on the following subjects:

1. State labor legislation enacted during the previous year.
2. Legislative revisions of unemployment insurance.
3. Scheduled wage increases and cost-of-living provisions for the coming year.
4. Industrial relations influenced by inflation and recession during the previous year.
5. Major enactments pertaining to workers' compensation during the previous year.

In October 1982 the bureau issued a useful bibliography: *BLS Publications on Productivity and Technology*, Report 671, free.

Four other important publications issued by the bureau were:

BLS Handbook of Methods, Volume 1, Bulletin 2134-1, $6.50.

Information about all major BLS programs except the Consumer Price Index; provides detailed descriptions of the bureau's major statistical series, and discusses the bureau's organization, staff, advisory councils, and data collection procedures.

Employment Projections for the 1980s, Bulletin 2030, 1979.

This presents the bureau's projections of the U.S. economy to the year 1990 and consists of reprints of four articles which appeared in the *Monthly Labor Review*.

Economic Projections to 1990, Bulletin 2121.

These projections are part of the ongoing program of the bureau for study of alternative patterns of economic growth. Topics include: new economic projections through 1990, an overview; the U.S. economy through 1990, an update; the outlook for industry output and employment through 1990; occupational employment growth through 1990; the 1995 labor force, a first look.

Handbook of Labor Statistics, Bulletin 2070, December 1980, and reissued, $15.

This presents comprehensive data which ends mostly with the month of December 1979 and which has not been updated because of budget restrictions, except for the statistical information which appears in the *Monthly Labor Review* and some of the data presented in the Bureau of Labor Statistics periodical publications which are listed in "Information Sources" in this section. Contents of the *Handbook* are listed below under Series of Labor Statistics.

Note: A recorded summary of principal Consumer Price Indexes, Producer Price Indexes, and Employment Situation numbers is available 24 hours a day by calling (202) 523-9658.

SERIES OF LABOR STATISTICS

Most of the following titles of statistical tables will be found in the *Handbook of Labor Statistics*, but other statistical sources have been included to give as complete a listing as possible. The key to the identifying numerals which follow each title will be found at the end of the listing on page 161.

LABOR FORCE, EMPLOYMENT, AND UNEMPLOYMENT

Labor Force and Employment Status

Employment status of the noninstitutional population by sex, 1947-1979 (1)
Employment status of the noninstitutional population, 16 years and over, selected years, 1950-1981 (2)

Total labor force and labor force participation rates by sex and age, 1947-1979 (1)

Civilian labor force by sex, race, and age, 1947-1979 (1)

Civilian labor force participation rates by sex, race, and age, 1947-1979 (1)

Civilian labor force participation rates by marital status, age, and sex, 1959-1979 (1)

Full- and part-time status of the civilian labor force by sex and age, 1963-1979 (1)

Experienced civilian labor force by occupation and sex, 1958-1979 (1)

Employment status of persons 16 to 19 years old and adults by race, 1954-1979 (1)

Employment status of persons 16 to 21 years old by race and major activity, 1963-1979 (1)

Employment status of persons 16 to 24 years old, 1947-1979 (1)

Employment status of the black and Hispanic-origin population by sex and age, 1975-1979 (1)

Employment status of persons of Mexican, Puerto Rican, and Cuban origin by sex and age, 1978-1979 (1)

Employment status by sex, age, race, and Hispanic origin, seasonally adjusted, 1980-1982 (2)

Employment status of the population in metropolitan and nonmetropolitan areas by sex, age, and race, 1978-1979 (1)

Employment status of the population in poverty and nonpoverty areas by race, 1978-1979 (1)

Employment status of male Vietnam-era veterans and nonveterans by age, race, and Hispanic origin, 1978-1979 (1)

Persons not in the labor force by sex, race, and age, 1947-1979 (1)

Job desire of persons 16 years and over not in the labor force and reasons for not seeking work by sex and race, 1970-1979 (1)

The Employment Situation (monthly) #365 (9)

State and Metropolitan Area Unemployment (monthly) #320 (9)

Real Earnings (monthly) #325 (9)

Earnings of Workers and Their Families (quarterly) #325 (9)

Employment in Perspective: Working Women (quarterly) #326 (9)

Employment in Perspective: Minority Workers (quarterly) #334 (9)

Employment

Employed persons by sex, race, and age, 1947-1979 (1)

Employment-population ratios by sex, age, and race, 1948-1979 (1)

Employed persons by occupation, race, and sex, 1972-1979 (1)

Employed persons by detailed occupation, 1974-1979 (1)

Employed persons by industry and occupation, 1976-1979 (1)

Employment by industry division and major manufacturing group, seasonally adjusted, 1980-1981 (2)

Nonagricultural workers on full-time schedules or on voluntary part time by selected characteristics, 1969-1979 (1)

Persons on part time for economic reasons by type of industry, sex, and age, 1957-1979 (1)

Nonagricultural workers on part time for economic reasons by usual full- or part-time status and selected characteristics, 1969-1979 (1)

Employed persons not at work by reason for not working, 1957-1979 (1)

Employed nonagricultural wage and salary workers not at work by reason for not working and pay status, 1967-1979 (1)
Selected employment indicators, seasonally adjusted, 1980-1982 (2)

Note: A recorded summary of principal Consumer Price Indexes, Producer Price Indexes, and Employment Situation numbers is available 24 hours a day by calling (202) 523-9658.

Unemployment

Major unemployment indicators, 1948-1979 (1)
Selected unemployment indicators, seasonally adjusted, 1980-1982 (2)
Unemployed persons 16 years and over and unemployment rates by sex and race, 1947-1979 (1)
Unemployed persons by sex and age, 1947-1979 (1)
Unemployed persons by race, sex, and age, 1954-1979 (1)
Unemployment rates by sex, race, and age, 1947-1979 (1)
Unemployment rates, by sex and age, seasonally adjusted, 1980-1982 (2)
Unemployment rates of black and Hispanic-origin workers by sex and age, 1975-1979 (1)
Unemployment rates by sex and marital status, 1955-1979 (1)
Unemployment rates and percent distribution of the unemployed by occupation, 1958-1979 (1)
Unemployment rates and percent distribution of the unemployed by sex, occupation, and age, 1972-1979 (1)
Unemployment rates and percent distribution of the unemployed by industry, 1948-1979 (1)
Unemployed persons, by reason for unemployment, seasonally adjusted, 1980-1982 (2)
Unemployed persons and percent distribution of the unemployed by duration, 1947-1979 (1)
Unemployed persons and unemployment rates by sex, age, race, and reason, 1969-1979 (1)
Long-term unemployment compared with total unemployment by sex, age, and race, 1969-1979 (1)
Long-term unemployment by industry and occupation, 1969-1979 (1)
Unemployed jobseekers by the job search methods used, sex, and age, 1972-1979 (1)
Unemployed jobseekers by the job search methods used, race, and sex, 1972-1979 (1)
Duration of unemployment, seasonally adjusted, 1980-1982 (2)
Unemployment insurance and employment service operations, 1981-1982 (2)

State and Area Data

Total labor force, employment, and unemployment levels in states, annual averages, 1975-1979 (1)
Unemployment rates for regions and states by sex and age, annual averages, 1975-1979 (1)

Unemployment rates for regions and states by race, annual averages, 1975-1979 (1)

Unemployment rates for Hispanic workers, selected states, annual averages, 1976-1979 (1)

SPECIAL LABOR FORCE DATA

Work Experience

Persons with work experience during the year by sex and extent of employment, 1950-1978 (1)

Extent of unemployment during the year by sex, 1957-1978 (1)

Persons with work experience during the year by industry and class of worker of longest job, 1955-1978 (1)

Percent of persons with work experience during the year who worked year round at full-time jobs by industry and class of worker of longest job, 1950-1978 (1)

Multiple Jobholders

Persons with two or more jobs by industry and class of worker of primary and secondary job, May, selected years, 1956-1979 (1)

Marital and Family Characteristics

Employment status of the population by marital status and sex, March, 1947-1979 (1)

Employment status of widowed, divorced, or separated persons by sex, March, 1970-1979 (1)

Labor force participation rates by marital status, sex, and age, March, 1947-1979 (1)

Labor force participation rates of widowed, divorced, or separated persons by sex and age, March, 1970-1979 (1)

Labor force and labor force participation rates of married women, spouse present, by presence and age of children, March, 1948-1979 (1)

Employment status of husbands by employment status of other family members, March, 1959-1979 (1)

Number of own children under 18 years of age by type of family and labor force status of mother, March, 1970-1979 (1)

Earnings, Work Schedules, and Absences from Work

Median usual weekly earnings of wage and salary workers by selected characteristics, May, selected years, 1967-1978 (1)

Median hourly earnings of wage and salary workers paid at hourly rates by selected characteristics, May, 1973-1978 (1)

Workweek of full-time nonfarm wage and salary workers by usual number of days and hours worked, May, 1973-1979 (1)

Number and percent of full-time nonfarm wage and salary workers by shift, sex, and race, May, 1973-1978 (1)

Percent of full-time wage and salary workers who worked long hours and received premium pay by occupation and industry, May, 1973-1979 (1)

Absence rates for full-time nonagricultural wage and salary workers by reasons for absence, May, 1973-1978 (1)

School Enrollment and Educational Attainment

Employment status of the population 14 to 24 years old by school enrollment, sex, and age, October, 1947-1978 (1)

Employment status of high school graduates not enrolled in college and of school dropouts 16 to 24 years old by selected characteristics, October, 1960-1978 (1)

Educational attainment of the civilian labor force by sex, race, and Hispanic-origin, March, selected years, 1959-1979 (1)

Median years of school completed by the civilian labor force by sex and age, March, selected years, 1959-1979 (1)

Median years of school completed by the employed by sex, occupation, and race, March, selected years, 1959-1979 (1)

Projections of the Labor Force

Civilian labor force by sex, age, and race; actual 1970 and 1977, projected 1985 and 1990 (1)

EMPLOYEES ON NONAGRICULTURAL PAYROLLS

Employment by Industry

Employees on nonagricultural payrolls by industry division, selected years, 1919-1979 (1)

Employment by industry, selected years, 1950-1981 (2)

Employees on manufacturing payrolls by major industry group, selected years, 1939-1979 (1)

Production or nonsupervisory workers on private nonagricultural payrolls by industry division, selected years, 1939-1979 (1)

Production workers on manufacturing payrolls by major industry group, selected years, 1929-1979 (1)

Nonproduction worker employment and ratios of nonproduction worker employment to total employment by major manufacturing industry group, 1939-1979 (1)

Women employees on nonagricultural payrolls by industry division, 1959-1979 (1)

Women employees on manufacturing payrolls by major industry group, 1959-1979 (1)

Employment by Region and State

Employees on nonagricultural payrolls by region and state, selected years, 1939-1979 (1)

Employees on manufacturing payrolls by region and state, selected years, 1939-1979 (1)

Employees on government payrolls by region and state, selected years, 1939-1979 (1)

Employment by state, 1981-1982 (2)

Labor Turnover

Labor turnover rates of employees on manufacturing payrolls, selected years, 1930-1979 (1)

Labor turnover rates of employees on manufacturing payrolls by major industry group, 1958-1979 (1)

Hours by Industry

Average weekly hours of production or nonsupervisory workers on private nonagricultural payrolls by industry division, selected years, 1932-1979 (1)

Average weekly hours of production workers on manufacturing payrolls by major industry group, selected years, 1947-1979 (1)

Average weekly overtime hours of production workers on manufacturing payrolls by major industry group, selected years, 1956-1979 (1)

Indexes of aggregate weekly hours of production or nonsupervisory workers on private nonagricultural payrolls by industry division, selected years, 1947-1979 (1)

Indexes of aggregate weekly hours of production workers on manufacturing payrolls by major industry group, selected years 1947-1979 (1)

Weekly hours, by industry division and major manufacturing group, seasonally adjusted, 1981-1982 (2)

Hours by State

Average weekly hours of production workers on manufacturing payrolls by state, selected years, 1947-1979 (1)

Earnings by Industry

Average hourly earnings of production or nonsupervisory workers on private nonagricultural payrolls by industry division, selected years, 1932-1979 (1)

Hourly earnings index for production or nonsupervisory workers on private nonagricultural payrolls by industry division, 1964-1979 (1)

Hourly earnings index, for production workers on private nonagricultural payrolls, by industry, 1981-1982 (2)

Average hourly earnings of production workers on manufacturing payrolls by major industry group, selected years, 1947-1979 (1)

Average hourly earnings, excluding overtime, of production workers on manufacturing payrolls by major industry group, selected years, 1941-1979 (1)

Hourly earnings, by industry division and major manufacturing group, 1980-1982 (2)

Average weekly earnings of production or nonsupervisory workers on private nonagricultural payrolls by industry division, selected years, 1922-1979 (1)

Average weekly earnings of production workers on manufacturing payrolls by major industry group, selected years, 1947-1979 (1)

Hours and earnings, by industry division, selected years, 1950-1981 (2)

Gross and spendable average weekly earnings of production or nonsupervisory workers on private nonagricultural payrolls by industry division, selected years, 1947-1979 (1)

Weekly earnings, by industry division and major manufacturing group, 1980-1982 (2)

Earnings by State

Average hourly earnings of production workers on manufacturing payrolls by state, 1948-1979 (1)

Average weekly earnings of production workers on manufacturing payrolls by state, 1948-1979 (1)

Employment and Earnings Periodical (5)

Area Wage Survey Bulletins (7)

Current Wage Developments (2)

OTHER EMPLOYMENT SURVEYS

Farm employment and wage rates, selected years, 1910-1979 (1)

Government employment and payrolls by level of government, selected years, 1940-1979 (1)

Employment in manufacturing industries by major occupational group, 1977 (1)

Employment in selected nonmanufacturing industries by major occupational group, 1978 (1)

PRODUCTIVITY DATA

Indexes of output per hour and related data, private business sector, selected years, 1947-1979 (1)

Indexes of output per hour, hourly compensation, and unit labor cost in the private business sector, and underlying data, selected years, 1947-1979 (1)

Indexes of output per employee hour, employee hours, and output, for selected industries, selected years, 1939-1978 (1)

Functional and summary indexes of output per employee year for the measured portion of the federal civilian government, fiscal years, 1968-1978 (1)

Annual indexes of productivity, hourly compensation, unit costs, and prices, selected years, 1950-1981 (2)

Annual changes in productivity, hourly compensation, unit costs, and prices, 1971-1981 (2)

Quarterly indexes of productivity, hourly compensation, unit costs, and prices, seasonally adjusted, 1979-1982 (2)

Percent change from preceding quarter and year in productivity, hourly compensation, unit costs, and prices, seasonally adjusted at annual rate, 1980-1982 (2)

Productivity and Costs; Business, Nonfarm Business, and Manufacturing Sectors (quarterly) #310 (9)

Productivity and costs: Nonfinancial Corporate Sector (quarterly) #310 (9)

COMPENSATION STUDIES

Occupational Pay and Benefits

Interarea pay comparisons—relative pay levels by occupational group and industry division, selected periods, 1961-1978 (1)

Percent increases in average straight-time hourly earnings, selected occupational groups in metropolitan areas, 1973-1978 (1)

Average earnings for selected plant occupations in metropolitan areas by sex, industry division, and region, 1967-1978 (1)

Average earnings for selected office occupations in metropolitan areas by sex, industry division and region, 1967-1978 (1)

Scheduled weekly hours (day shift) and percent of plant and office workers by weekly work schedule, all metropolitan areas, by industry division, 1959-1976 (1)

Paid vacations, all metropolitan areas, 1959-1976 (1)

Paid vacations, all metropolitan areas, by industry division, 1965-1976 (1)

Paid holidays, all metropolitan areas, by industry division, 1959-1976 (1)

Health, insurance, and pension plans, all metropolitan areas, by industry division, 1959-1976 (1)

Labor-management agreement coverage, all metropolitan areas, by industry division and region, 1960-1976 (1)

Indexes of union hourly wage rates in selected industries and trades, selected years, 1910-1978 (1)

Indexes of union hourly wage rates in selected building trades, selected years, 1910-1978 (1)

Indexes of union hourly wage rates in selected printing trades, selected years, 1910-1978 (1)

Average union rates for selected trades by city, 1978 (1)

Average annual salaries for selected professional, administrative, and technical occupations, 1961-1979 (1)

Average straight-time pay for selected occupations in 26 municipal governments, October 1977-September 1978 (1)

Indexes of average straight-time hourly earnings of men in production occupations in nonelectrical machinery manufacturing, selected metropolitan areas, selected years, 1945-1978 (1)

Wage and Compensation Data

Employment Cost Index, total compensation, by occupation and industry group, 1980-1982 (2)

Employment Cost Index, wages and salaries, by occupation and industry group, 1980-1982 (2)

Employment Cost Index, private nonfarm workers, by bargaining status, region, and area size, 1980-1982 (2)

Wage and compensation change, major collective bargaining settlements, 1977 to date (2)

Effective wage adjustments in collective bargaining units covering 1,000 workers or more, 1977 to date (2)

Employment Cost Index (quarterly) #316 (9)

Salary Trends

Indexes of salaries of federal employees in the United States covered by the General Schedule, selected years, 1939-1979 (1)

Indexes of annual maximum salary scales of firefighters and police in cities of 100,000 or more, selected years, 1924-1978 (1)

Indexes of average annual salaries of urban public classroom teachers by size of city and county, selected years, 1925-1978 (1)

Percent change in minimum and maximum annual salary scales of refuse collectors by city size and region, 1973-1978 (1)

General Wage and Benefit Changes

General wage changes in major collective bargaining units, 1954-1979 (1)

Percent changes in wages and benefits in collective bargaining settlements covering 5,000 workers or more, 1965-1979 (1)

Production workers in manufacturing affected by wage decisions, and median changes, 1959-1978 (1)

Production workers in manufacturing establishments where wage changes were effective, and median changes, 1959-1978 (1)

Major Collective Bargaining Settlements (quarterly) #317 (9)

Public Sector Collective Bargaining (quarterly) #392 (9)

Employee Compensation

Employee compensation, private nonagricultural economy, selected years, 1966-1977 (1)

Employee compensation, production and related workers, manufacturing industries, selected years, 1959-1977 (1)

PRICES AND LIVING CONDITIONS

Consumer Prices

Consumer Price Indexes, selected groups, and purchasing power of the consumer dollar, 1913-1979 (1)

Consumer Price Indexes, major groups, 1935-1979 (1)

The Consumer Price Indexes, commodity, service, and special groups, 1935-1979 (1)

Relative importance of major components of the Consumer Price Index, U.S. city average, at dates of major weight revisions (1)

Consumer Price Index—U.S. city average, and selected areas, 1981-1982 (2)

Consumer Price Index for All Urban Consumers, selected areas, all-items index, selected years, 1950-1979 (1)

Consumer Price Index for All Urban Consumers and revised CPI for Urban Wage Earners and Clerical Workers, U.S. city average—general summary and groups, subgroups, and selected items, 1981-1982 (2)

Consumer Price Index for Urban Wage Earners and Clerical Workers, annual averages and changes, 1967-1981 (2)

Consumer Price Index for All Urban Consumers: Cross classification of region and population size class by expenditure category and commodity and service group, 1982 (2)

CPI Detailed Report (3)

Consumer Price Index (monthly) #302 (9)

Producer Price Indexes (monthly) #304 (9)

Consumer Prices: Energy and Food (monthly) #306 (9)

Washington, D.C., Area: Consumer Price Index (bimonthly) #333 (9)

Washington, D.C., Area: Retail Food Price Index (bimonthly) #333 (9)

U.S. Export and Import Price Indexes (quarterly) #311 (9)

Consumer Expenditure Surveys (releases and announcements) #312 (9)

Department Store Inventory Price Indexes (semiannual) #303 (9)

Note: A recorded summary of principal Consumer Price Indexes, Producer Price Indexes, and Employment Situation numbers is available 24 hours a day by calling (202) 523-9658.

Producer Prices

Producer Price Indexes by stage of processing, selected years, 1947-1979 (1)

Producer Price Indexes, by stage of processing, 1981-1982 (2)

Producer Price Indexes by commodity group, selected years, 1926-1979 (1)

Producer Price Indexes, by commodity groupings, 1981-1982 (2)

Producer Price Indexes, for special commodity groupings, 1981-1982 (2)

Producer Price Indexes by durability of product, selected years, 1947-1979 (1)

Producer Price Indexes, by durability of product, 1981-1982 (2)

Industry sector price indexes for the output of selected industries, 1959-1979 (1)

Producer Price Indexes for the output of selected SIC industries, 1981-1982 (2)

Producer Prices and Price Indexes (6)

Note: A recorded summary of principal Consumer Price Indexes, Producer Price Indexes, and Employment Situation numbers is available 24 hours a day by calling (202) 523-9658.

Inport and Export Prices

U.S. import price indexes for selected categories of goods, 1967-1979 (1)
U.S. export price indexes for selected categories of goods, 1967-1979 (1)

Consumer Expenditures

Selected family characteristics, annual expenditures, and sources of income classified by family size, United States, 1972-1973 (1)
Selected family characteristics, annual expenditures, and sources of income classified by family income before taxes, United States, 1972-1973 (1)
Selected family characteristics, annual expenditures, and sources of income classified by age of family head, United States, 1972-1973 (1)
Selected family characteristics, annual expenditures, and sources of income classified by race of head, United States, 1972-1973 (1)
Selected family characteristics, annual expenditures, and sources of income classified by region, United States, 1972-1973 (1)

Family Budgets

Annual costs of a lower budget for a four-person family, autumn 1979 (1)
Annual costs of an intermediate budget for a four-person family, autumn 1979 (1)
Annual costs of a higher budget for a four-person family, autumn 1979 (1)
Indexes of comparative costs based on a lower budget for a four-person family, autumn 1979 (1)
Indexes of comparative costs based on an intermediate budget for a four-person family, autumn 1979 (1)
Indexes of comparative costs based on a higher budget for a four-person family, autumn 1979 (1)
Annual costs of a lower budget for a retired couple, autumn 1978 (1)
Annual costs of an intermediate budget for a retired couple, autumn 1978 (1)
Annual costs of a higher budget for a retired couple, autumn 1978 (1)
Indexes of comparative costs based on a lower budget for a retired couple, autumn 1978 (1)
Indexes of comparative costs based on an intermediate budget for a retired couple, autumn 1978 (1)
Indexes of comparative costs based on a higher budget for a retired couple, autumn 1978 (1)

UNIONS AND INDUSTRIAL RELATIONS

Union Membership

Distribution of national and international unions by industry and affiliation, selected years, 1956-1978 (1)

Membership of national and international unions by geographic area and affiliation, selected years, 1956-1978 (1)

Membership of national and international labor unions, selected years, 1933-1978 (1)

Union membership as a proportion of the labor force, 1930-1978 (1)

Distribution of national unions and employee associations by state, selected years, 1970-1978 (1)

Work Stoppages

Work stoppages in the United States, 1930-1979 (1)

Work stoppages by size of stoppage, 1969-1978 (1)

Duration of work stoppages ending in 1969-1978 (1)

Work stoppages by major issues, 1969-1978 (1)

Work stoppages by industry group, 1969-1978 (1)

Work stoppages by state, 1969-1978 (1)

Work stoppages involving 1,000 workers or more, 1947 to date (2)

Labor Relations

Intake and disposition of cases by the National Labor Relations Board, selected fiscal years, 1936-1979 (1)

Investigation findings under selected federal laws, selected fiscal years, 1939-1979 (1)

OCCUPATIONAL INJURIES AND ILLNESSES

Occupational injury and illness incidence rates by industry, United States, 1973-1978 (1)

Occupational injury and illness incidence rates by detailed industry, United States, 1977 and 1978 (1)

FOREIGN LABOR STATISTICS

Population and labor force, selected countries and selected years, 1947-1979 (1)

Labor force and unemployment in selected industrial countries, 1960-1979 (1)

Indexes of output per hour, hourly compensation, and unit labor costs in manufacturing, selected countries, 1960-1978 (1)

Average weekly hours of production workers in manufacturing, selected countries and selected years, 1955-1979 (1)

Estimated compensation per hour worked of production workers in manufacturing, selected countries and selected years, 1960-1979 (1)

U.S. Department of State Indexes of Living Costs Abroad (8)

Indexes of average hourly earnings of production workers in manufacturing, selected countries, 1960-1978 (1)

Indexes of average real hourly earnings of production workers in manufacturing, selected countries, 1960-1978 (1)

Indexes of consumer prices, selected countries and selected years, 1960-1979 (1)

Indexes of wholesale or producer prices, selected countries and selected years, 1960-1979 (1)

Work stoppages and time lost due to industrial disputes, selected countries, 1955-1979 (1)

GENERAL ECONOMIC DATA

National Income Accounts

Gross national product, selected years, 1929-1979 (1)

Gross national product in constant dollars, selected years, 1929-1979 (1)

National income by type of income, selected years, 1929-1979 (1)

Social Insurance

Old-age, survivors, and disability insurance benefits by type of beneficiary, 1970-1979 (1)

KEY TO LISTING

1. *Handbook of Labor Statistics*, Bulletin 2070, Bureau of Labor Statistics, December 1980.

2. *Monthly Labor Review*, Bureau of Labor Statistics.

3. *CPI Detailed Report*, monthly, Bureau of Labor Statistics.

4. *Current Wage Developments*, monthly, Bureau of Labor Statistics.

5. *Employment and Earnings*, monthly, Bureau of Labor Statistics.

6. *Producer Prices and Price Indexes*, monthly, Bureau of Labor Statistics.

7. *Area Wage Survey Bulletins*, annual series, Bureau of Labor Statistics.

8. *U.S. Department of State Indexes of Living Costs Abroad and Quarters Allowances*, quarterly, Superintendent of Documents, U.S. Government Printing Office.

9. "Mailing List for News Releases and Announcements," Bureau of Labor Statistics. Request releases from the Bureau of Labor Statistics, Washington, DC 20212.

   Note: Information about each of the above publications is given in the first part of this section.

VIII

GLOSSARY OF
LABOR TERMS

AAA American Arbitration Association. *See* Arbitration.

Administrative judge Once called a trial examiner, this employee of the National Labor Relations Board acts as a judge in preliminary investigations of charges involving unfair labor practices.

Advisory arbitration *See* Arbitration.

Affirmative action Company equal-employment plans and practices which seek to change the effects of discrimination by positive action. Such plans set forth goals for hiring and promoting women and minority groups as well as how such goals will be achieved.

AFL-CIO American Federation of Labor-Congress of Industrial Organizations, a federation created in 1955 of craft and industrial unions.

Agency shop A work place where nonunion employees are not required to join the union but must pay dues to the bargaining agent selected by the unionized employees.

American Arbitration Association *See* Arbitration.

American Federation of Labor A federation of craft unions formed in 1886.

Annual improvement factor A yearly wage increase given workers as their share of increased productivity.

Apprenticeship A period of service during which a worker is trained in a skilled trade under the instruction of a company or a master. *See* Bureau of Apprenticeship under "Employment and Training Administration," section V.

Arbitration A procedure under which two parties submit their differences to a third party, or arbitrator, agreeing to be bound by his decision which is known as the award. In advisory arbitration, the decision is not binding. The American Arbitration Association, a nonprofit group, founded in 1926, offers the services of some 21,000 skilled arbitrators.

Authorization card A union may ask employees to indicate on authorization cards their preference for an election as to whether or not they want a union, or their authorization to have the union represent them in collective bargaining.

Automation The term refers to one or more machines which can control themselves or "the application of feedback principles, whereby a mechanical system automatically observes and regulates its own performance, thus eliminating the need for human control."

Award   *See* Arbitration.

Back-loaded   A long-term contract in which there is a greater wage increase during the latter part of the agreement.

Back pay   Unpaid wages due an employee which were withheld illegally.

Back-to-work movement   Return of strikers to work before the strike is settled by their union.

Bargaining agent   A union which represents workers, both union and nonunion.

Bargaining unit   A group of workers who band together to bargain collectively with their employer or employers.

Bill of Rights   Guarantees in the Landrum-Griffin Act which says union members have the right to meet and discuss union matters and to have a fair trial in disciplinary hearings.

Blacklist   Lists of workers considered undesirable for employment, compiled by and exchanged among employers. The Federal Fair Labor Standards Act of 1938 outlawed this practice.

BLS   Bureau of Labor Statistics, a division of the U.S. Department of Labor.

Blue-collar workers   Manual wage earners whose duties require them to wear work clothes or protective clothing.

Boycott   Action taken by a labor union against what has been decided to be an unfair employer: a primary boycott being refusal of union members to do business with their employer, and a secondary boycott existing when a union influences or persuades others to join in the action.

Brotherhood   Many workers who organized the first unions used the work in the name of their societies to imply a certain fraternal bond.

Bumping   The right of a worker who is laid off for lack of work to take the place of another worker who has less seniority.

Business agent   The union officer responsible for helping enforce provisions of a contract, handling grievances, and running the union's affairs.

Call-in pay   Wages guaranteed an employee who reports for work even though he may not be kept busy during the period for which he was called into the shop.

Certification   Designation of a union as the exclusive bargaining agent for all employees by the National Labor Relations Board or a state labor agency.

CETA   Comprehensive Employment Training Act. *See* section IV on principal federal labor laws.

Checkoff   Authorization by employees to deduct their union dues from their paychecks and give the money over to the union.

Child labor   The employment of girls and boys who are too young to work for hire, or who are employed at jobs unsafe or unsuitable for children their age, or at occupations which are harmful to their welfare (as defined by the U.S. Department of Labor).

Civil Service A system for selecting employees for government service and later promoting them on the basis of merit for the work they do, and not for whom they know.

Closed shop A place of work where only members of a union may be hired; outlawed by the Taft-Hartley Act.

Closed union A union which limits its membership through high dues or restrictive rules in order to protect job opportunities.

Coalition bargaining The bargaining together by several unions representing different types of workers, all of whom are employed by the same employer.

Code of ethics Codes of conduct adopted by the AFL-CIO Ethical Practices Committee in an attempt to deal with the unethical practices of several affiliated unions.

COLA A cost-of-living adjustment which relates wage increases to the cost-of-living during the period covered by a union contract.

Collective bargaining The negotiations which take place between labor and management before an agreement is reached on wages, hours of work, and other matters relating to employment, as well as the administration and interpretation of the contract after it has been signed. Company-wide collective bargaining covers all employees of a company; plant-wide collective bargaining covers employees in only one plant; industry-wide or multiemployer collective bargaining covers a majority of union members in an industry; area-wide collective bargaining covers negotiations conducted between representatives of labor and management for two or more industries.

Collective negotiations Collective bargaining between a governmental body and public sector employees.

Collusion Secret and deceitful agreements or acts entered into between a union representative and an employer to defraud the union members covered by a collective bargaining agreement.

Common situs picketing Picketing by striking employees which is restricted to their own entrance to a building where there are other employers and employees not involved in the strike, who can use other entrances.

Company union An organization of employees sponsored by the employer, a practice doomed in 1935 when the National Labor Relations Act guaranteed employees the right to organize and bargain collectively.

Conciliation The act of a conciliator from the outside who brings parties together and presides over their meetings as they discuss their dispute, but who makes no recommendations. *See also* Arbitration; Mediation.

Congress of Industrial Organizations A federation of industrial unions organized in 1938 by John L. Lewis.

Conspiracy Doctrine A principle which holds that some acts considered legal when performed by an individual are illegal when carried out by a group.

Consumer price index The statistical measurement of the price changes in some 400 commodities and services, the prices being combined to make an index number.

Contract The collective bargaining agreement arrived at after negotiating between an employer and the employees.

Cooling-off period A period of time during a labor dispute when there can be neither a lockout nor a strike; an 80-day period may be invoked under the Taft-Hartley Act.

Craft union A labor union which represents only workers who perform the same type of work.

Craftsman An artisan, mechanic, or one engaged in a particular craft.

Depression A period during which there is high unemployment and low production.

Disability insurance Insurance which compensates an individual for loss of income because of an injury or illness not suffered while working.

Discouraged worker An unemployed individual who does not seek a job because he thinks there are no job opportunities for one with his qualifications.

Discrimination in hiring The illegal act of making an unfair distinction in hiring on the basis of race, religion, sex, or other reasons.

Economic strike A strike caused by disagreement over pay, hours, or other problems.

EEO Equal employment opportunity. *See* section IV on principal federal labor laws.

EEOC Equal Employment Opportunity Commission. *See* section V on federal government agencies.

Emergency dispute A dispute between labor and management which may imperil public health or safety.

Employee welfare funds Money used on behalf of union members for disabilities, health insurance, hospitalization, and retirement. Funds may be contributed by employees only, or employees and employers, usually on the basis of a percentage of earnings or some productivity measurement.

Employer associations Associations of employers which work to solve problems associated with unions and collective bargaining.

Employment agencies A private or publicly operated organization whose purpose is to bring together employers who have positions to be filled with applicants seeking employment.

End run The action of a union agent engaged in collective bargaining who moves from one management level to another, hoping to secure better terms for the agreement.

Escalator clause *See* COLA.

Escape clause A period specified in a union contract during which members may resign from the union.

Exempt employee One not covered by the provisions of the Fair Labor Standards Act. *See* section IV on principal federal labor laws.

Factfinding board A panel appointed by a government official to investigate a labor dispute, report on its findings, and make recommendations for its settlement.

Fair share The contribution which a nonunion employee must make to the union to help pay for its expenses as the collective bargaining agent.

Featherbedding Work rules which require the employment of more workers than are actually needed for the job.

Federal labor union An AFL-CIO charted local union which does not come within the jurisdiction of any national or international union.

Field examiner A National Labor Relations Board employee who makes preliminary investigations of unfair labor relations charges and also conducts certification elections.

Flexitime A schedule arrangement whereby workers may vary their times of arriving at and leaving work without affecting the number of hours they must work each week.

Free rider A nonunion employee who enjoys the benefits of the union contract but does not pay his share of the union's expenses.

Fringe benefit Benefits an employer may give his workers in addition to wages. These include such items as paid holidays, vacations, pensions, bonuses, profit sharing, stock purchase plans, accident and health insurance, tuition for evening courses, discounts on purchases of company products, free uniforms, etc.

Front-loaded A long-term contract in which there is a greater wage increase during the first part of the agreement period.

Full crew rule A union stipulation of the minimum number of workers required for a certain railroad operation.

General strike A widespread work stoppage conducted by many unions in a city, state or throughout a country.

Golden parachute An employment contract granted a top corporate executive which promises payment equal to several years' salaries if his company is purchased by or merged into another company.

Good faith bargaining Bargaining at which each party makes a sincere effort to reach agreement on a new contract.

Grandfather clause A clause in a labor contract which provides that employees on the payroll before an agreed-upon date will not be affected by certain terms of a new contract.

Graveyard shift A work shift which starts late in the evening.

Grievance A complaint raised by an employee or a union that the provisions of a labor contract or a traditional work practice are not being observed.

Grievance procedure Those provisions of a collective bargaining agreement which cover handling of grievances.

Guaranteed annual wage An agreement wherein an employer promises to pay his workers all or part of their regular wages even if the plant closes.

Hard-core unemployed Those who can and are willing to work but are unable to obtain employment even during periods when labor is in short supply.

Hidden unemployed Workers who believe it is futile for them to seek employment and who are not included in the unemployment figures.

Hiring hall An employment office operated by unions and managements, sometimes with state assistance or supervision.

Hot cargo Merchandise made and shipped from a plant at which there is a labor dispute.

Illegal strike A work stoppage conducted by union members, violating a no-strike clause; or a stoppage not authorized by union officials or a vote of the union members.

ILO International Labor Organization, founded after World War I and connected with the League of Nations.

Impasse A deadlock or standstill in labor negotiations.

Improper practice An unfair labor practice.

Incentive wage plan Piecework in which the work is done by the piece or unit and paid for by the unit rather than by the hour.

Increments A series of regular additions to an employee's wage or salary.

Independent union A union that is not affiliated with the AFL-CIO.

Industrial union A union of skilled and unskilled workers.

Industry-wide bargaining Negotiations conducted by several employers with one or more unions which represent all or most of the workers in an industry.

Inflation A period when prices climb because the supply of goods is not large enough to satisfy the public's purchasing power or demand, and as prices rise money loses its value.

Initiation fee The initial payment a new union member must make when joining a union.

Injunction A court order prohibiting one or more persons from doing a specified act, if the rights of another person or persons are threatened.

Job action A refusal to work in order to enforce compliance with certain demands.

Job enrichment or enlargement The assignment of additional duties to an employee.

Journeyman A skilled tradesman or an artisan who has completed an organized and recognized apprenticeship program.

Jurisdiction The area or territory within which union authority may be exercised.

Jurisdictional dispute A dispute in which two unions disagree over which one should do a specific job or which one should act as the bargaining agent for a certain plant or company.

Jurisdictional strike A strike resulting from a jurisdictional dispute.

Kickback The action of a union official or employer (supervisor) which forces a worker to pay him part of his wages in order to obtain and/or hold his job.

Labor Day A national holiday observed on the first Monday in September in honor of all working men and women.

Labor force The number of men and women in the United States who are employed, as determined by the Bureau of Labor Statistics of the U.S. Department of Labor.

Layoff A temporary or permanent release of employees from work because their services are no longer needed.

Local union A union which represents workers in a single plant or locality but is affiliated with a national or international union.

Lockout The action of an employer in closing his company or shop to keep employees from working during a strike or labor dispute, or to forestall a strike.

Maintenance-of-membership-clause A clause in a collective bargaining agreement which stipulates that union members must maintain their membership in the union until the expiration of the contract as a condition of their employment.

Maintenance of standards clause A clause prohibiting an employer from varying or changing any employment requirements or rules, even though not written into the contract, unless negotiated by the union and the employer.

Management prerogatives Certain prerogatives or privileges of management which an employer believes are not proper subjects for negotiation.

Master agreement A collective bargaining agreement which has been negotiated between several employers and one or more unions or between a union and one employer which has several plants or branches.

Mediation The action of a mediator, or third party, to help disagreeing parties settle their dispute by encouraging them to work out their differences, and possibly by making proposals for a settlement, but with no authority to compel that an agreement be reached.

Merit system The civil service practice of hiring and promoting on the basis of merit or capability.

Migrant labor Laborers who travel from place to place harvesting crops which must be picked as they ripen.

Minimum wage The lowest wage which may be paid in accordance with state or federal law. Minimum wage rates are set by Congress for employees engaged in interstate commerce, local and state government employees, most domestic workers, and some employees of chain stores.

Moonlighting Working at more than one job.

National emergency strike A work stoppage which is so widespread or critical that it threatens the health or safety of the entire nation.

National union The central organization of a labor union which has many "locals" or branches.

Negotiation The means by which management and labor confer and bargain with each other in order to settle the issues and draw up the terms of the labor contract.

New Deal The program of reform legislation President Franklin D. Roosevelt proposed when he accepted the Democratic Party nomination for president.

NLRB National Labor Relations Board. *See* section V on federal government agencies.

No-raiding agreement An agreement among unions not to entice members to resign from one union in order to sign up with another.

Open shop A company which employs either union or nonunion workers.

OSHA Occupational Safety and Health Act of 1970. *See* section IV on principal federal labor laws.

Outlaw strike A work stoppage or strike conducted by union members without proper authorization.

Paper union A union which has no members.

Parity Equality between pay scales of different groups of employees.

Past practice Certain customs which have become accepted work practices.

Pattern bargaining Collective bargaining in which a settlement previously arrived at by one or more other companies is adopted.

Permanent arbitrator or umpire An arbitrator who serves for a certain period or for the duration of a union contract.

Picket A person posted by a union at a work place at which there is a dispute or strike.

Piecework *See* Incentive wage plan.

Portable pension plan An employee pension plan which may be transferred from one employer to another.

Portal-to-portal pay Compensation received for the time spent at the workplace from the moment an employee enters the company gate until he leaves the gate at the end of his workday.

Poverty index The minimum income required to provide a family with an adequate diet, as determined by the Social Security Administration.

Preferential hiring A promise on the part of an employer to give preference in hiring to members of a union.

Premium pay An amount of money paid above a regular wage scale as an inducement or reward.

Production worker Manual wage earner. *See* Blue-collar worker.

Productivity A measurement of workers' ability to produce.

Professional An employee who has specialized knowledge and may have had academic preparation.

Profit sharing Sharing profits with employees, frequently in accordance with a formula which is usually based on length of service and salary.

Quickie strike An unplanned strike or walkout caused by some job problem or grievance, but not authorized by the union.

Raiding The attempt of a union to sign up workers who belong to another union.

Real wages What can be purchased with one's wages at a given time compared to some past period.

Regional bargaining Bargaining between a union and a number of employers located in a region.

Reopening clause A clause in a union contract which provides for reconsideration under certain stated conditions of wages and other matters during the life of the contract.

Retroactive pay Additional wages paid for work previously performed at a lower rate of pay.

Right-to-work laws Laws which make it illegal to require a worker to belong to a union in order to obtain or hold a job.

Robot An automatic device which can perform functions usually delegated to human beings, or which operates with what almost appears to be human intelligence.

Runaway shop A company or business which is unionized and moves its operation to another location in order to be rid of the union.

Scab A worker who replaces a union employee during a strike, refuses to strike, or returns to work before a strike has ended.

Seasonal unemployment Unemployment caused by lack of work due to seasonal needs for labor.

Seniority An individual's place on a list of employees who are ranked according to length of service.

Severance pay An allowance based on term of service which is given an employee when he resigns, is laid off, or dismissed.

Sheltered workshop A place of work for handicapped people.

Shop committee Employees who are elected by union members or appointed by union officials to represent the union in bargaining a matter with the employer.

Shop steward A union member elected as the union representative of a department or shop to deal with the management on behalf of the union.

Sit-down strike A strike in which the workers remain in the plant and force it to shut down.

Slowdown A reduced rate of production by workers who wish to gain certain benefits from their employer.

Speedup An increased rate of production demanded of workers without additional pay for their effort.

Stretch-out A requirement that workers do extra work or operate additional machines with no increase in pay.

Strike A work stoppage conducted by workers to obtain concessions from their employer.

Strike benefits Payments made by a union to its members during a strike.

Strikebreaker Someone who is not a regular employee of a company but who accepts a job with that company when the regular workers are on strike.

Strike fund Money obtained by a union from assessments on the members and held for use during a strike to pay expenses and strike benefits to the membership.

Strike notice By law a union must notify the employer of its intention to strike if there is a union contract in force, and under certain conditions a union must notify certain government agencies of its intent or else lose the rights granted to the union by the law.

Structural unemployment Unemployment caused by changes in the economy or other causes.

Sunshine bargaining Collective bargaining sessions open to the public.

Supplemental unemployment benefits Payments collected by laid-off workers in addition to state unemployment insurance benefits.

Sweatshop A business where employees are forced to work for low wages, long hours, and under conditions below accepted standards.

Sweetheart contract An agreement between a union and an employer which is favorable to the employer and arranged without participation by the union members.

Swing shift The work shift between the day and night shifts, usually the 4:00 p.m. to midnight shift.

Sympathy strike A strike in which the employees have no grievance against their own employer but are attempting to support another group of workers who are on strike.

Take-home pay The amount of money a worker receives after all deductions have been made from his earnings.

Technological unemployment Unemployment caused by the use of robots, automation, or other labor-saving machines.

Temporary restraining order A court order restraining an individual or group from performing a certain act during a limited period prior to a hearing set for the matter.

Trial examiner A person appointed to hold hearings, investigate, report on the facts, and sometimes make recommendations to an administrative agency.

Trusteeship Supervisory control by a national or international union over a local union.

Turnover The number of employees hired within a period to replace those who left; also the ratio of this number to the number of the average work force.

Underemployed Having less than full-time or adequate employment.

Unemployment The condition or state of being unemployed; a term referring to the number of workers out of work.

Unemployment insurance Insurance provided by the state which pays an income to a worker who is temporarily out of work, with the length of payment and amount varying from state to state.

Unfair labor practice An act of an employer or union which violates federal or state labor laws.

Uniformed services Municipal employees who traditionally work in uniform.

Union label A union trademark or insignia (which may have been registered with the U.S. Copyright Office) placed on each article, or on labels attached to their products, to indicate the goods were manufactured by union members.

Union organizer A union employee whose responsibility is to recruit new members to the union.

Union shop A shop where the employer is free to hire union or nonunion workers, but all new employees must join the union within a certain time limit, usually 30 days, and continue to pay dues to the union for the duration of the union contract.

Walkout A strike.

Welfare fund A fund established by a union and supported by member contributions to provide health and death benefits, as well as pensions in some instances.

Whipsaw strike A strike conducted against one employer of a group instead of all employers.

White-collar worker One who is not a manual or blue-collar worker, but usually a clerical, sales, professional, supervisory, or technical worker.

Wildcat strike A strike initiated by the workers without the authorization of their union.

Workmen's compensation insurance State-administered insurance paid to employees injured on the job or in the course of work, the amount and length of payments varying from state to state.

Work-to-rule A means of bringing pressure against an employer by performing only the job duties specifically set forth in the rules or regulations.

Yellow-dog contract A written or oral agreement made between an employee and an employer, providing that the employee will not join a union or, if a member, will resign; such contracts now being unenforceable in a court of law.

Zipper clause A provision in a labor contract which prohibits any further negotiations during the life of the contract.

United States Government (cont'd) ...
Internal Revenue Service, 119
Interstate Commerce Commission, 98
Joint Commission on the Economic
Report, 99
Manpower Administration, 105
National Industrial Recovery Board, 22
National Labor Board, 101
National Labor Relations Board, 24, 27,
35, 100, 101, 103, 104, 128, 164,
167, 170
National Mediation Board, 22, 102, 103,
129-30
National Recovery Administration, 101
Occupational Safety and Health Review
Commission, 130
Office of Economic Opportunity, 97
Pension Benefit Guaranty Corporation, 98
President's Committee on Employment of
the Handicapped, Executive orders, 105,
106
Railroad Labor Board, 102
Railroad Retirement Board, 22
Social Security Administration, 103
Standard Federal Administrative Regions,
109-10
Superintendent of Documents, U.S.
Government Printing Office, 142
Supreme Court, 18, 20, 21, 22, 23, 24,
25, 26, 27, 33, 34, 96, 98, 101, 102,
104
Wage Stabilization Board, 24
War Labor Board, 24, 97
United States Steel Corporation, 17, 23, 33
United States v. *Derby Lumber Company*, 24
United States v. *John L. Lewis*, 25
United Steelworkers of America, 24, 29, 31,
65, 93
United Steelworkers of America v. *Weber*,
35
United Tailoresses Society of New York, 12
United Telegraph Workers, 18, 65
United Textile Workers of America, 17, 27,
65
United Transportation Union, 65
United Transportation Union v. *Long Island
Railroad*, 34
United Union of Roofers, Waterproofers and
Allied Workers, 66
University of Maryland, Archives of Labor
History, 147
University of Michigan Library, Labadie Col-
lection, 147
University of Minnesota, Immigration History
Research Center, 147
University of Texas, Labor Archives of Texas,
147
University Professors, American Association
of, 39
Upholsterers' International Union of North
America, 15, 66
Upshaw, Gene, 57, 91
Urban Archives, Temple University, 147

Usery, W. J., Jr., 115
Utah Public Employees Association, 66
Utah (State)
Department of Employment Security, 136
Industrial Commission, 133
Occupational Information Coordinating
Committee, 140
Utah State AFL-CIO, 66
Utility Workers of New England, Brother-
hood of, 43
Utility Workers Union of America, 66
Utrata, Michael J., 45

Van Beck, Dorothy, 57
Van Buren, Martin, 13
Vance, Leonard, 113
Vanderveken, J., 49
Van Note, Jeff, 57
Variety Artists, American Guild of, 40
Vatalano, Ralph, 61, 91
Vaughn, Jacqueline, 40
Veech, Barbara, 57, 91
Vega, Vince, 51
Velasco, Peter G., 64, 91
Veneman, Wayne E., 113
Vermont (State)
Department of Employment Security, 136
Department of Labor and Industry, 133
Occupational Information Coordinating
Committee, 140
Vermont State Employees Association, Inc., 66
Vermont State Labor Council, 66
Vetsch, Ronald, 59
Viala, Fernie J., 53
Viela, Joseph, 46
Virgin Islands
Department of Labor, 133
Employment Security Agency, 136
Occupational Information Coordinating
Committee, 140
Virginia (State)
Department of Labor and Industry, 133
Employment Commission, 136
Occupational Information Coordinating
Committee, 140
Virginia State AFL-CIO, 66
Vogel, F. R., 38
Voie, Robert F., 52
Volkers, Paul, 44
Vrataric, Nicholas C., 65, 91

Wage and compensation data statistics, 157
Wage-price-rent freeze (1971), 30
Wagner, Robert F., 94, 101
Wagner, Robert F., Labor Archives, 146
Wagner Act (National Labor Relations Act
of 1935), 23, 101, 104
Wagner-Peyser Act of 1933, 22, 105
Wakshull, Samuel, 40
Walker, Al, 58